COUNSELOR'S GUIDE TO THE BRAIN AND ITS DISORDERS

COUNSELOR'S GUIDE TO THE BRAIN AND ITS DISORDERS

Knowing the Difference Between Disease and Sin

EDWARD T. WELCH

ZondervanPublishingHouse
Academic and Professional Books
Grand Rapids, Michigan

A Division of HarperCollinsPublishers

Counselor's Guide to the Brain and Its Disorders
Copyright © 1991 by Edward T. Welch

Requests for information should be addressed to:
Zondervan Publishing House
Academic and Professional Books
1415 Lake Drive S.E.
Grand Rapids, Michigan 49506

Library of Congress Cataloging-in-Publication Data

Welch, Edward T., 1953–
    Counselor's guide to the brain and its disorders / Edward T. Welch.
        p.   cm.
    Includes bibliographical references and index.
    ISBN 0-310-52941-7
        1. Pastoral counseling. 2. Brain—Diseases—Diagnosis. 3. Brain—Diseases—
    Religious aspects—Christianity. 4. Sin—Psychological aspects. 5. Psychiatry and
    religion. 6. Neuropsychology. I. Title.
    BV4012.2.W422   1991   91-674
    253.5'2—dc20   CIP

All Scripture quotations, unless otherwise noted, are taken from the
HOLY BIBLE: NEW INTERNATIONAL VERSION (North American Edition).
Copyright © 1973, 1978, 1984, by the International Bible Society.
Used by permission of Zondervan Bible Publishers.

Cover design by Fred Robinson, Zimmerman, Lauren & Richardson, Inc.
Edited by Susan Lutz

Printed in the United States of America

91 92 93 94 95 96 / CH / 10 9 8 7 6 5 4 3 2 1

To my parents
W. Edward and Anne H. Welch

Contents

Part 3:
Misdiagnosis: Counseling Problems with Medically Treatable Causes

Preface

The study of the brain and its disorders can challenge the neurosurgeon and intrigue the schoolchild. Filled with microscopic wonders, the brain remains the mysterious "seat of the soul." The study also offers much that is relevant for Christian counselors. Without it, counselors who are faced with unusual behavior are apt to misinterpret brain dysfunction and think only in terms of spiritual causes. All is not well, however, in the brain sciences.

Although there is much that is relevant for Christian counselors in the brain sciences, there is also much that is quite vexing. The new biological psychiatry (the voice of the brain sciences) is claiming more and more of the human experience as part of its domain, and it is quickly usurping moral and ethical territory that was once seen as belonging to the church. This is happening because brain researchers and psychiatrists are often preaching a new religion—but in scientific garb. Brain research is consistently embedded in a medical model that severely challenges the Christian view of persons and behavior. Basically, this medical model says that we are no longer moral beings who live before God; there is no place for faith, personal responsibility, or sin. Instead, it states, we are ultimately molecular, not spiritual. Biology, not Scripture, has the real answers to deep problems in living, and our guides are psychiatrists, the new secular priests.

This medical religion has already had a profound effect on the Christian church. Its terminology and technology have mystified an unprepared church that sees no alternative but to succumb to its perceived marvels. As a result, we underestimate the spiritual capacity of those who have alleged biological problems, and we excuse behavior that is sinful. But, perhaps even more tragic, Scripture is subtly questioned and there is a gradual erosion of biblical authority.

So this book must be written for those in the theological trenches. If we are to understand the brain and its disorders accurately, we must first have a well-established biblical view of the person and, especially, of personal responsibility during brain injury. My goal, however, is to provide more than a biblical foundation. I hope to offer a structure that is able to include and meaningfully interpret advances in medical science. Also, I want to show that a biblical approach is simply the best—more useful and reflective of the facts than any secular model. Then we can have renewed confidence in the teaching of Scripture.

With this foundation established, we will be free to move on to some medical information that should have immediate relevance for counselors. I will take a handful of common diseases that affect the brain and show how they affect our spirits but do not break them. A secret here—only known by Christians—is that even in the midst of brain and body disease, our spirits, by faith, can be vibrant and strong. This can give Christians hope where it is otherwise absent.

From there I will examine two other important areas. One is the realm of psychiatric diseases—schizophrenia, depression, anxiety, panic attacks, and manic-depression. This area is in dire need of biblical reinterpretation. For too long, Christians have been unable to respond to the claims of secular psychiatry. I hope that the model presented here will organize and give you a new perspective on these unusual symptoms.

The second critical area is misdiagnosis—mistaking sin for sickness and vice versa. That is, do counselees (and friends and family) have a spiritual problem, a medical problem, or both? Faced with this question, counselors have a tendency to err in one of two directions. They succumb to the pressures of the medical model and mistake sin for sickness, or they "throw out the baby with the bath water" and deny any possible medical component. The answer lies at neither extreme.

What we need are clear guidelines that will help practitioners distinguish between moral and physical problems. To this end, I will provide examples of misdiagnosis, review commonly misdiagnosed symptoms, and offer some nontechnical guidelines.

The terrain, as you see, is fairly broad and occasionally intimidating. I will be trying to bridge the sometimes incompatible and obscure worlds of medicine and theology. But don't be alarmed. Although you will probably need to stretch your vocabulary a bit (theologians and physicians share a certain penchant for specialized terminology), the concepts are fairly basic. You will not need to become an amateur physician or mini-theologian. Instead, you should finish this book realizing that a more precise understanding of Scripture and a few commonsense rules are all you need to be an informed and helpful counselor.

Although I try to cover a lot of territory in this book, I realize that I am being selective. There are many problems that are not included—candida, postviral fatigue syndrome, silent ischemia, AIDS, details of nutritional deficiencies, and some rare diseases that might affect intellect and mood. But a comprehensive manual is not my goal. Rather, since I am interested in laypersons, counselors, pastors, and physicians who want to be stretched in theology as well as medicine, I have simply tried to highlight the most common problems. I have included diseases that I encounter in my own counseling—diseases that are probably present in most counseling practices and average-sized churches. Diseases with a very low rate of occurrence or diseases that I see very infrequently are omitted or relegated to a passing reference in a table.

For the same reasons, I am not offering highly technical detail on either theological issues or specific diseases. This means that some people with a great deal of knowledge about a disease or an area of theology may be uncomfortable or take issue with the way I "round off" some of the data. I apologize for this, but in a book of this kind I see no alternative.

There is one other goal in this book that may not be quite as apparent. Along with the apologetic, theoretical, and applied emphases, there is also a devotional goal. I hope to edify you, to build up your faith. This may sound unusual, considering the technical nature of this book and the emphasis on diseases. But the technical material offers a very interesting overview of God's cellular creations. And as the diseases make us more aware of our physical frailty, they can encourage us to focus on a time when there will be no more sickness. They can lead us into hope as we anticipate the consummation of human existence at Jesus' return.

Edward Welch
Dana Point, California

Acknowledgments

I have tried to cite many of the ideas that contributed to this book, but the bibliography and footnotes are not the sum of my debt to others. My interest in and approach to the brain have been shaped by Dr. Thomas Schenckenberg of the Salt Lake City V.A. Medical Center. He would disagree with some of my perspectives and he is not responsible for any inaccuracies, but his influence has been notable. My views on biblical counseling have developed under the guidance of Dr. John F. Bettler, director of The Christian Counseling and Educational Foundation. Dr. Bettler also contributed, along with Dr. Paul Tripp and the entire CCEF staff, by providing me with the time and encouragement to complete this manuscript. David Powlison of CCEF and Raju Abraham, F.R.C.S., made helpful comments on part 1.

It was my privilege to work with Susan Lutz, a neighbor and friend, as Zondervan's editor. Her insightful comments and attention to detail were educational and certainly strengthened the manuscript. Many thanks to Mike Smith, imprint editor at Zondervan, who took a risk by supporting this project.

My wife, Sharon, deserves kudos for her constant personal and professional encouragement. Also, her interaction with me about both the biblical and medical material and her comments on style were indispensable. Her parents, Jack and Dorothy Cavanaugh, provided idyllic accommodations during the completion of this project. And my daughters, Lindsay and Lisa, provided just the right amount of distraction.

References and Style

The structure of the text adapts the recommendations of the *Publication Manual of the American Psychological Association* (3d ed.). When ideas are cited, the author and date will follow in parentheses with more complete citation in the bibliography. When a work is quoted, the author and date will be followed by the page number of the citation. For reading convenience, most quotes and case studies are blocked and indented.

All Scripture quotations, unless otherwise noted, are taken from the HOLY BIBLE: NEW INTERNATIONAL VERSION (North American Edition), copyright © 1973, 1978, 1984, by the International Bible Society.

1

Worlds in Collision: The Clash Between the Bible and the Brain Sciences

Men have an all but incurable propensity to prejudge all the great questions which interest them by stamping their prejudices upon their language.
—Sir James Fitzjames Stephan (1873)

There are many battles being fought today—disputes over territory, political ideology, tribal superiority. Yet without question, those that leave the most death and destruction in their wake are neither territorial nor political. Rather, they are religious—battles of belief. And their target is the most valuable of spoils—the human heart. It is here that we first encounter the new brain sciences: not in the laboratory, but on the battlefield.

What does a religious battle have to do with CT scans, neurons, psychiatric medications, and brain tumors? A great deal, in that much of the new brain research comes to us clothed in antibiblical garments.[1] Although once dependent on a biblical view of mind and body, the brain sciences (especially psychiatry) have renounced their biblical heritage and now stand as a rival. Their strategy, sometimes called the medical or disease model, has been to strip us of our spiritual natures and reduce us to physical matter alone—something that can be touched or measured. "The idea of an immaterial mind controlling the body," wrote the psychologist Donald O. Hebb, "has no place in science." From this perspective, true, lasting change comes through medicines, surgeries, and other medical techniques (e.g., Wender & Klein, 1981). The statement "behind every crooked thought there is a crooked molecule" sums up its position. Everything, including the spiritual, is understood only by way of biology.

> The materialist philosophers of the seventeenth and eighteenth centuries . . . foreshadowed the central gospel of modern neuroscience: that mental states come down to bodily events, and that there is only one substance in the universe—matter. . . . What our Victorian grandparents used to call "character" is contained in an intricate matrix of speech centers, motor pathways, and minute electrical circuits.(Hooper & Teresi, 1986, p. 7)

On the other side is a biblical worldview, which offers a broader perspective that includes both a material body and immaterial spirit.

At first glance, one might think that the multi-orbed biblical model would be more readily accepted than the medical model. After all, it acknowledges that the medical model contains kernels of truth, even as it asserts that there is more to humanity than its molecules. Yet history has shown that, when faced with the technical-sounding proclamations of science and medicine, Christians don't appreciate or understand the breadth of a biblical view of human life. They tend to be easy prey for the medical model. Taken by surprise by the "discoveries" of science, they are unprepared to interpret these developments biblically. As such, they are easily persuaded that the Scripture is very limited or even wrong in its statements about the body and the spirit.

The cholera epidemics of the 1800s (Rosenberg, 1962) provide a useful historical example of a church theologically unprepared to understand medical developments. During the first two epidemics in 1832 and 1849, the church was the epidemics' authoritative interpreter and adviser. There was no battle between theology and medicine. Unfortunately, from this prestigious position, the church's formulations were simplistic and incomplete. It usually explained the cholera outbreaks solely as evidence of divine retribution against sin, especially sin in the *other* group, the lower social classes.

While it is true that disease can be a result of divine discipline and can indicate a need for soul-searching and repentance, it is also true that it can be unrelated to personal sin. In fact, to say that sickness is *always* a result of personal sin is actually an old heresy that goes back to Job and his counselors. Instead of emphasizing this one dimension of biblical teaching, the nineteenth-century church could have, at least, taught that sin and sickness are not necessarily related. The church could also have stressed that the Bible encourages precise observation of our world (i.e., scientific investigation) as well as efforts to prevent and heal physical disease (medical treatment).

This incomplete or inaccurate use of Scripture eventually took its toll. The demise of the church's authority came during the 1866 cholera epidemic, when answers were perceived as having come more from public health initiatives than from prayer and fasting. As a result, the realm of Scripture's legitimate rule narrowed, and the domain of science increased.

> God was still in heaven, as most Americans would be quick to affirm. Yet the fact of his existence had ceased to be a central and meaningful reality in their lives. The warnings of the perceptive divines in 1832 were proving justified; material preoccupations and empirical habits of thought had not so much defeated as displaced the spiritual concerns of earlier generations. America seemed well on the way toward becoming a land of "practical atheists." (Rosenberg, 1962, p. 213)

What can we learn from this experience, especially as we struggle with AIDS or with diseases that affect behavior? First, we must continue to search the Scriptures and update our understanding of persons, sin, disease, and personal responsibility during the course of physical (including brain) disease. Furthermore, we must be humble and willing to be taught in this process because our theological work is never quite finished. Second, we must be alert to medical advances, especially those in psychiatry and the brain sciences, and be prepared to interpret this data through a biblical lens. Too often we envision a huge chasm between our Christian beliefs and issues in medicine. At first glance they seem to address separate domains. But Scripture addresses all areas of life, and medical sciences, especially when they discuss human behavior, cannot help but take some kind of religious stance.

Today we stand at the crossroads again, and this time the adversary is much more formidable. The medical or disease model of the 1800s is now accompanied by unprecedented prestige and assisted by an arsenal of technological and pharmacological marvels. For example, although we may at first be uncomfortable with the idea that fear, worry, drug abuse, or anger may be biologically based, when biological theories are allegedly supported by CT scans, MRIs, and a baffling array of medical procedures, we are more likely to agree without questions or reservations, even though we know the Bible adds a moral dimension to these experiences. Counselors who see schizophrenic symptoms abate after a trial of medication begin to wonder, "Will the biological revolution eventually find a treatment for adultery, stealing, lying, insolence, and coveting? Isn't modern man physical *and* spiritual? If so, where does the spiritual fit in?"

These and other questions challenge us to develop a biblical model of persons that can cogently address developments in modern medicine and psychiatry. Counselors without a clear biblical view may begin to second-guess the sufficiency of their biblical foundations, or they may adopt an approach that is part secular, part sacred. That is, they include a dash of the medical model and a sprinkle of biblical material. Either way, the results are the same—ultimately both faith and Scripture are compromised. What we need is a clear biblical perspective that is robust enough to include and explain recent developments in biological psychiatry, and that is the task of this book. To fail in developing such a holistic perspective is to risk another step toward "practical atheism."

Vocabulary

As part of this process of biblical reclamation, it is important to agree on the parameters of relevant words. Vocabulary is more powerful than we suspect. Words have various shades of meaning, and a speaker or writer may use them to form secret allegiances with certain philosophical positions. We would see this if an evangelical Christian were to talk with a Mormon. There would be striking similarities in language; for example, both a Mormon and an evangelical Christian would agree that Jesus Christ is the Son of God. However, further discussion and clarification of terms would demonstrate that although the words used by both speakers are identical, the meanings ascribed to them are dramatically different.

In the same way, there can be much overlap between words rooted in the Bible and words proceeding out of a medical model, but their meanings are not interchangeable. Since the medical model and Scripture are based in different and sometimes opposing beliefs, the associated vocabulary reflects those differences. Words such as *moral, functional, organic, mind,* and *psychological* need clearly demarcated boundaries. Otherwise, clear discussion is impossible.

Biblical Vocabulary

The distinguishing feature of biblical vocabulary is really quite simple: all words have a God-ward referent. The Bible presupposes that it is impossible to study human beings in isolation. All our actions, thoughts, relationships, work, and recreation—our entire lives—are lived before God.

> We may say without fear of contradiction that the most striking thing in the biblical portrayal of man lies in this, that it never asks attention for man in himself, but demands our fullest attention for *man in his relation with God.* (Berkouwer, 1971, p.195, italics added)

Sin. A word that makes obvious reference to our relationship with God is *sin.* The reference is so clear, in fact, that secular medicine and its medical model will only use it in quotes. They neither use the word nor want it. Thus, having it all to ourselves, you would think that its meaning would be clear to Christians. However, in the Christian church itself its meaning is uncertain (or ignored). To some, *sin* represents an outdated theology and an encumbrance to personal fulfillment. To others it is deemed archaic and of little practical consequence because it seems to ignore individual differences, personal freedom, and human motivations. In actuality, however, it is central to a biblical understanding of people. Our stand on the issue of sin will send ripples through all our theology and counseling.

Most Christians can agree that sin is disobedience or a violation of the Ten Commandments. But this view of sin is often limited to include only observable violations—overt behaviors that are changed by decisions of the will (and usually apply to people other than ourselves). But the truth about sin is far more sobering: it is a deceitful, covert, and ever-present inclination of the heart. As John Owen said, "Sin is never less quiet than when it seems most quiet, and its waters are, for the most part, deep when they are still" (1958, p. 11). For example, a favorite strategy of sin is to take objects that in themselves are good—things that are admired and enjoyed—and gradually transform them into objects of idolatrous worship. The list is endless: love, money, power, beauty, comfort, rest, and so on. These objects, all fine in themselves, can become ruling idols and lusts. Sin can furtively transform good things into foreign gods that enslave.

As a potentially powerful master, sin is undaunted by those things we consider powerful, such as logic, intelligence, money, or even human love. Nothing human can break its hold on life. For true change to occur, it must be preceded by something much more dynamic. It must be empowered by Christ, enabling us to respond to him in faith, repentance, and obedience. This truth is the heart and goal of all Christian counseling.

When viewed accurately from a biblical perspective, sin is not a death blow to "self-esteem." Rather, facing one's sin and taking responsibility for it becomes an opportunity to know more of the love of Christ. When we see our own unrighteousness in light of God's forgiving love in Christ, God's love is revealed in its greatness and we have cause for rejoicing, not sorrow. In Christ, sin no longer has any condemnatory power.

Sin is a pivotal doctrine of the Christian faith. It indicates that we are judged according to an outside standard—the Law of God—and are responsible when we inevitably fall short. It is part of our fabric and contaminates all our best motives. And it can be exposed by the Holy Spirit and forgiven through the blood of Christ. These are doctrinal basics.

Thus it is not surprising that this is where we find obvious and inevitable conflict with the medical model. At the heart of the medical model is a denial of human depravity. People are no longer considered evil. They are not responsible to anyone for their actions. Instead, their behavior—and their very nature—are placed into the ambiguous categories of *sick* and the ever-elusive *abnormal*.

Illnesses are things that happen to people, not something people are or do (e.g., Seigler & Osmond, 1974). Criminals are now said to have "diminished capacity" or "mental illness," and they must be "treated" rather than punished. There are no more perpetrators of evil, only victims. Only God's grace keeps our society from being fully consistent with its avowed belief in the current psychiatric position. Without this divine restraint, our culture would acknowledge no personal responsibility, no right and wrong—and there would only be chaos.

Moral. The word *moral* is an example of a term that has been caught between the biblical and secular medical perspectives. Therefore it has multiple meanings. From a medical perspective, "moral treatment" goes back at least to the 1790s when the French physician Philippe Pinel removed the chains from the poor and insane of Bicetre in 1793. This was paralleled by William Tuke, a Society of Friends merchant, when he opened the York Retreat in 1796. Their common goal was to revolutionize the cruel and verminous asylums and encourage self-control in the patient rather than use external restraint. Punishment was avoided, chains were never used, patients dressed in their best clothes and socialized, worked, and exercised. This humane treatment, which seemed to be very helpful, came to be known as moral treatment. From this perspective, moral is equivalent to fair, kind, or humane. If it had any spiritual connotations, they were quickly lost or secularized.

For the purposes of this text, *moral* will have a different meaning. It will be used as shorthand for our ongoing relationship to God. To say we are fundamentally moral means that, as persons created in his image, our lives stand in relationship to a Holy God. Our motives are ultimately related to him, we are wholly dependent on him, and all our intentions, character, and conduct fall within categories of right and wrong, righteousness and unrighteousness. As ambassadors of the King, we are responsible "for the things done while in the body, whether good or bad" (2 Cor. 5:10). The freedom we have in the gospel of Jesus Christ does not dissolve this responsibility or relationship; rather, it frees us from the condemnation that accompanies law-breaking and gives us liberating power to follow Christ.

Secular Vocabulary

Medical language comes with a veil of objectivity, "science," and technical precision. But the terms, especially psychiatric diagnoses, are more ambiguous than you might think. Certainly most medical professionals can agree on the meaning of *cancer* or *heart disease*, but words like *abnormal*, *functional*, and *schizophrenia* are much "fuzzier." They often come laden with covert assumptions, implications, and biases. And psychiatric diagnoses are often rooted in the shifting sands of cultural expectations rather than empirical facts.

The following comments will map out the larger fields of meaning for some common medical terms. Also, they will specify how these words will be used in the text.

The medical model. Having already referred to the medical model and established it as the opposition, I should clarify its different meanings. From a more technical perspective, the medical model is often associated with an approach called reductionism. Reductionism usually means that all behavior can be reduced to a biological or material foundation. Thus religion and faith can be reduced to sociology, sociology to psychology, psychology to biology, biology to chemistry, and chemistry to physics.

In practice, reductionism can be summarized by the following principles.

1. All psychiatric problems are diseases.
2. These diseases are caused principally by biological factors.
3. Treatment is by way of medicine and other therapies that treat the physical body.
4. Psychiatry is the "keeper of the keys." Nonmedical professionals are not qualified to treat these biological disorders.

Apart from the more obvious biblical problems, classic reductionism seems to sap life of its color. Beauty, truth, and love are reduced to molecules and crackling neurons in the human brain. Reductionism can reduce a book to atoms and ink to chemistry, but most people recognize that the symbols and written language are much more than physics or chemistry. In the same way, the laws of thermodynamics are inadequate to explain the love between husband and wife or parent and child.[2]

Another peculiarity of this brand of reductionism is that it appears to be more a political strategy than a method of discovering rock-hard truth. The hierarchical model of reductionism has the ring of a primitive territorial dispute: each "science" claims to be "better," or at least more scientific, than the one below it. The more foundational or ultimate, the more prestigious. Therefore psychiatry has spent much of the last century trying to gain the prestige of more traditional medical specialities (such as neurology), and the field of psychology has been desperately seeking to legitimize itself by taking on the scientific persona and language of medicine.

This rigid form of reductionism is certainly popular, but it is not the only perspective within the medical model spectrum. More philosophically astute brain scientists tend to avoid the subtle bigotry of the hierarchical, dominant/subordinate scheme. In its place, they envision something more enmeshed, complementary, and mutually enriching—more in tune with the American desire for equality. Within this more moderate position, reductionism might mean that the brain (biology) *explains* the spirit (religion). Or it might indicate that the brain *provides the basis for* the spirit, or the brain *predicts the action of* the spirit (Colby & Spar, 1983).

This democratic position is a step forward from the hierarchical approach, but at root it retains the same basic assumption. Standing in the Darwinian tradition, it maintains that personal responsibility is an unscientific idea that has no place in brain sciences. This version of the medical model would allow a moral "perspective," but only if it were clearly understood that this is not an ultimate or final way to understand behavior. Accordingly, Richard Restak in *Science Digest* (1983) poses the questions (and answer), " 'Is free will a fraud?' 'Do we make our own choices? Plot our own destinies?' 'Are we truly conscious?' New research indicates that the answer to all these questions may be no."

Another position within the medical model spectrum rests on a distinction between "normal" and "abnormal." In essence it states that when someone falls within the range of normal or "optimal," they are declared healthy and there is no significant, underlying biological problem. Values or behaviors outside that range are abnormal and must, under this rubric, represent a disorder with an underlying biological pathology. The treatment task is to restore the abnormal values to their normal ranges (e.g., Andreasen, 1984).

The problems with this approach are well-known, but unheeded. One obvious problem is that *abnormal* has nothing very certain about it (Murphy, 1972). It is an elastic, culture-laden idea, based in opinion and prejudice, that can be broadened to label everyone.[3] For example, until very recently homosexuality was considered by the psychiatric community to be abnormal—a mental illness. But now, without any new biological warrant, it is declared normal.

Despite psychiatry's best efforts, there is little agreement on what constitutes an abnormal mental disorder. Abnormal to one person is not the same as abnormal to another (Colby & Spar, 1983), and abnormal in one country is not abnormal to its neighbor (Payer, 1988). The psychiatric labels are so slippery that, as Jay Katz, a professor of psychiatry of Yale, indicated, "If you look at *DSM-III* [the official classification scheme for abnormalities or mental disorders] you can classify all of us under one rubric or another of mental disorder" (Slovenko, 1984). This is a brilliant marketing strategy to be sure, but not a good, reliable guideline.

Therefore, although the medical model claims to determine normal and abnormal objectively, there is nothing hard and fast about the distinctions it makes. Psychiatric diagnoses (declarations of abnormality) are notoriously unreliable and not universally valid. Yet this theoretical quicksand does not keep brain scientists from making dogmatic assertions.

The insidious part about the term *abnormal* is that, like other positions within the medical model, it sacrifices personal responsibility. It maintains that those with abnormal brains, because of diminished reasoning capacity, are not fully accountable for their actions. Instead, the culpable agents behind immoral behavior are genes, poverty, parental abuse, biochemical compulsions, and even junk food.[4]

To summarize, the medical model has a few variations, but there tends to be unanimity on at least two issues. First is the belief that biology provides the best explanation for behavior. Second is the position that abnormality is equivalent to diminished personal responsibility or the absence of it—an especially troublesome position in light of the potentially all-encompassing scope of *abnormal*. These theses are not mandatory in medicine, but they are the dominant positions in psychiatry and the brain sciences.

Psychological. Another term used within medicine with a broad range of meaning is *psychological*. It includes personality, behavior, thinking, emotions, perceptions, learning, motivation, intellectual prowess, or any personal discomfort that can respond to "talk therapy."

Within this spectrum of subheadings there are some terms that are incompatible with biblical categories, but others overlap fairly neatly with biblical data. Cognitive or mental events such as alertness, concentration, thinking, memory, emotions, sensations, and perceptions are all facets of the word *psychological* that have biblical counterparts. Yet, although they fit with biblical data, you might be surprised at the actual biblical category. These terms resist inclusion in the more obvious biblical category of *psuche*, or soul, from which *psychological* derives its name. Instead, all these terms are subsumed under the biblical category *body*. Implications from this fact will be developed in the next chapter. For now, remember that when the word *psychological* appears, it refers to *intellectual* functions such as those we have mentioned; synonyms for *psychological* here are *cognitive* and *intellect*.

Another use of *psychological*, especially in popular medical parlance, is "psychological problems." In the medical community these are usually the opposite of physical problems; that is, a person is assumed to have either physical *or* psychological problems. Physical problems are known diseases such as diabetes or heart disease. Psychological problems are difficulties in living that have no clear physical cause, such as "stress," not coping with the loss of a job, a difficult marriage, or family problems. In other words, physical problems are caused by the internal environment of the body, while psychological problems are caused by the external world.

This use of *psychological* is more at odds with biblical categories. Psychological problems defined this way have no biblical counterpart.

The closest the Scripture comes is to confront spiritual problems. And *spiritual* implies an entirely different realm of meaning, stressing that problems are related to sin (in oneself, others, or the world) and answers are found through faith.

Organic and functional. In medicine, the alleged distinction between physical and psychological problems is often referred to as organic or functional. Someone who poses the question "Is this an organic or functional disorder?" is asking whether or not an illness has demonstrable physical pathology.

Of the two terms, *organic* is the more straightforward. It refers to the physical and means the same as *disease*. It means that there are verifiable, structural changes in the body or brain. Strokes, multiple sclerosis, diabetes, and brain tumors are all organic disorders.

Like the related term *psychological*, *functional* is a bit less tidy. It is roughly the opposite of *organic*. Whereas organic indicates the presence of morbid (negative) changes in bodily structures, functional means that bodily structures are apparently intact—there is nothing apparently wrong physically. Organic problems have their origin in the body; functional problems have their origin in the mind or "psyche." This is not to say that functional problems are unrelated to physical changes. Psychological problems such as worry, grief, and depression are all accompanied by changes in the brain. Instead, functional means that these biological changes, if they could be measured, would not be significantly different from those of the rest of the population. They are not pathological or abnormal changes.

Although the terms *functional* and *organic* are used frequently, all is not well with the distinction, and we should be familiar with some of the ambiguity in the terms. First, a medical-model purist would say that all disagreeable problems are organic and that the organic/functional distinction is a myth. The body causes everything. In this view, the *real* underlying problem is physical and needs only somatic, medical treatment. This narrow view of *organic* ignores the presence of the the spiritual life—which the Bible clearly considers to be *the* cause of moral behavior.

A more widespread concern in the scientific community and elsewhere is that the categories of functional and organic are not large enough to handle the advances in brain research. Schizophrenia, depression, phobias, and other psychiatric diagnoses, originally considered to be functional, are now considered to have more in common with organic brain problems. In light of this, "functional" is developing a second-class status. More and more, it represents a temporary way station where diagnoses are waiting to have their biological causes uncovered so they can move into the "real" world of medicine. From a biblical perspective this is a somewhat complex issue that will be covered in chapter 8.

To summarize, the categories functional and organic are ambiguous and not universally recognized, but in the medical community they are still commonplace. In keeping with their popularity, I will use them throughout the book.

Mind and body. Two other terms that appear frequently in medically oriented literature are *mind* and *body.* These words are basically the same as functional and organic. Mind is similar to functional, body is similar to organic. The major difference is that whereas medical practitioners use functional and organic, philosophers use mind and body. Accordingly, they share the same ambiguities and biblical limitations.

Notes

1. I do not mean to imply that all medical doctors and brain scientists adhere to the medical model. In medicine, there are Christians and non-Christians who oppose a medical model, yet they are in the minority. The dominant religion in medicine today is the medical model.

2. C. S. Lewis (1949) has some interesting comments on this in a sermon called "Transpositions."

3. Thomas Szasz (1984, 1987), at his provocative best, suggests that psychiatry's predominant goal is power and influence, and the ambiguous nature of the word *abnormal* is perfectly suited to attaining this goal.

4. I am referring to the "Twinkie defense" of Dan White, who killed San Francisco mayor George Moscone and supervisor Harvey Milk in 1985. His attorneys argued that White's "diminished capacity" was a consequence of his biochemical reactions to junk food, including Hostess Twinkies.

Part I is the biblical and medical backbone for all that follows in this book. It may take a bit more work to assimilate than the other sections, but I hope you will find the effort worthwhile.

The biblical foundations discussed in chapter 2 address the thorny question of personal responsibility, especially when there are brain problems. The conclusion can briefly be summarized by 2 Corinthians 4:16: "Though outwardly we are wasting away, yet inwardly we are being renewed day by day." Our inner being remains alive, responsive, and responsible even though our fragile, clay-like brains and bodies may be cracked or broken. Working its way from the biblical principle of personal responsibility to the mind-body debate, the chapter offers a model designed to clarify the interaction between the mind (or spirit) and body. This model will then be applied in later parts of the book.

Chapter 3 is a brief tour of the brain. It is meant to be a friendly introduction that will later help you to understand some of the diseases that affect the brain. It is also intended to help you communicate with physicians, appreciate and understand the new brain research, and be awed by God's creative hand.

Chapter 4 will describe the many masks of brain dysfunction. This material will help you recognize brain problems in counselees and friends, allow you to begin to understand their world, and keep you from diagnosing sin when the problem is really brain sickness. Although you won't remember all the different behavioral consequences associated with brain problems, the review should alert you to a new way of understanding human thinking and behavior.

Chapter 5 is a brief review of popular medical diagnostic devices. It is intended to make you feel more at home with both the old techniques and the new, computerized approaches.

2

Biblical Foundations

Tell me, where is fancie bred:
In the heart or in the head.
　　　　　　　—Shakespeare, *Merchant of Venice*

W hen the medical model and the Bible square off, there are numerous theoretical arguments. The practical question, however, is basic and easily understood: *Are there times when I am not responsible for my behavior?* The Bible would clarify the question by asking, Are there times when I am not *morally* responsible for my behavior? Is there anything that can prohibit *spiritual* responsiveness? Are there any limits to my own personal culpability, such as when I am sick or have a "chemical imbalance"?[1] These are the practical issues at stake (Szasz, 1987).

When we take the issue of moral responsibility to the Bible, at first glance there seems to be little to discuss. The Scripture is clear. It plainly states that we are responsible for our sinful behavior: no exceptions, no excuses. Case closed. We are not necessarily responsible for broken arms, heart disease, or brain tumors, but we are responsible for sin in our hearts and our actions. Chemical imbalances, amnesia, ignorance, and a host of other problems may limit our ability to comprehend our world and communicate effectively, they may be potential *occasions* for sin, and they may *undermine our ability to resist temptation*, but they do not provide an excuse for sinful behavior or thinking.

> If a person sins and does what is forbidden in any of the LORD's commands, *even though he does not know it,* he is guilty and will be held responsible. (Lev. 5:17, italics added)

Now if you *unintentionally* fail to keep any of these commands the LORD gave Moses . . . and if this is done unintentionally without the community being aware of it, then the whole community is to offer a young bull for a burnt offering. (Num. 15:22, 24, italics added)

For we must all appear before the judgment seat of Christ, that each one may receive what is due him for the things done while in the body, whether good or bad. (2 Cor. 5:10)

This, however, is not the end of the discussion. Even though we are always accountable before God and responsible for sinful behavior, the Bible adds important qualifiers.

Scripture clarifies that, although we are always morally responsible, we are responsible *according to the purposes in our hearts.* For example, in ancient Israel, the penalty for murder was death. But if someone killed his neighbor "unintentionally, without malice aforethought" (Deut. 19:4), that person would be safe in a city of refuge. Indeed, God is concerned about overt and obvious violation of his law, but he is concerned about them *as* they are manifestations of the heart.

As another example, if you are living with an angry, demeaning father whose abusive speech gets the entire house in an uproar, you don't immediately say, "Dad must be rebuked for his sin." Instead, you try to understand the purposes of his heart. In so doing, you might recognize that he feels out of control, helpless, and without any impact in his world. How would you counsel him? Chances are you would look for ways to maximize his remaining abilities and remind him that he is a valuable presence in your home. Certainly the expression of his grief and confusion by way of abusive anger is sinful, but a wise child or caretaker will creatively respond to the purposes of the heart.

Would you call your father to repent? The rule of thumb is that if someone is able to be verbally or physically abusive, they are able to understand that their behavior is wrong. This does not mean that calling a brain-altered person to repentance is easy. You may have to seek counsel from those who have experienced similar problems in order to communicate effectively. Also, this does not mean that it is necessary to call a person to repentance with every obvious biblical infraction. For example, when my children are up late and tired, they tend to be impatient, slow to obey, and full of complaints. Their behavior is wrong. But their goal is not blatant rebelliousness—they are simply tired. Instead of disciplining them, my wife and I send them to bed. Then the next day we might remind them that God can help them when they are tired. Scripture doesn't stop here with its teaching on personal responsibility. It adds at least one more clarification. While it indicates that we are always morally responsible and specifically responsible according to the purposes of our hearts, the Bible also states that we are responsible according to our gifts, talents, abilities, knowledge, and understanding. When it says "Work," it doesn't say that everyone must produce two tents every day. No! It simply implores us to work, "unto the Lord," to the best of our abilities (e.g., Eph. 6:7).

Matthew 25:14–30 (also Luke 12:47–48) is an example of this principle. In these verses, the master treated each servant according to what was given him. The one who received five talents was responsible for five, no more or less. Likewise, the servant who received two was responsible for two, and the one who received one talent was accountable for his one. With greater gifts, there was increased responsibility.

This commonsense principle operates in most of our relationships. Although we never minimize or excuse sinful behavior, we treat people with one talent as if they have one talent, those with five as if they have five. We treat people according to their abilities. We approach an uneducated child differently from an educated and experienced adult, a mentally gifted child differently from one who is developmentally delayed. One child may get all "C's" on a report card and it will be time to celebrate and roast the fatted calf. Another child may also get all "C's" and it will be time to seriously consider curtailing outside activities.

This puts Christians in the unique position of upholding universal biblical standards while simultaneously being sympathetic to individual differences in abilities. As a general rule, however, we are proficient at upholding God's law, but poor at pinpointing different types of talents or lack of them. Sometimes we are unaware of who has five talents and who has one. For example, a fine Christian family had ongoing disciplinary problems with their daughter until they discovered that she could not understand requests that were either rapid or long. Although children younger than she were able to understand and respond, her world of language was relatively chaotic. As a result, what was previously considered to be sinful disobedience was "rediagnosed" as lack of ability (fewer talents) in one area. (Chapter 4 will elaborate on these brain-based individual differences.)

The Mind-and-Body Problem

Up to this point the medical model has challenged us to think through our theology of personal responsibility. This is certainly a critical counseling issue and one that is at the forefront of the differences between the medical and biblical perspectives. But there is a larger issue that is even more fundamental—namely, "Who are we? Of what do we consist?" More specifically, the question is, "What are mind and body, and how do they interact?"

The mind-and-body issue is an old one that may sound like a strictly academic question, but it is here at the level of anthropology—the study of the basic "ingredients" of persons—that the real issues and differences between medical philosophy and biblical worldview are revealed. Unfortunately, the common Christian view of the mind/body problem is unprepared to deal with the biological revolution in psychiatry. Without the theological foundations established, the Christian community is disorganized and susceptible to being taken "captive through hollow and deceptive philosophy" (Col. 2:8). Therefore the rest of this chapter will provide a biblical response to the question, "Who is the person?" It will not resolve all the inherent mysteries, but it will map out the basic biblical parameters with their counseling implications.

Scripture is not consumed by questions about mind and body, but it certainly has some clear and meaningful statements regarding them. From a biblical perspective, human beings are a unity of two parts: mind and body, spiritual and physical.[2] We are "composite beings—a natural organism tenanted by, or in a state of symbiosis with, a supernatural spirit" (Lewis, 1960, p. 126). We are "treasures in jars of clay" (2 Cor. 4:7) or spiritual beings clothed in an earthly tent (2 Cor. 5:1). This duality (Gundry, 1976)[3] or duplex (Adams, 1979) is introduced almost immediately in the Old Testament. God made man from two substances: dust and spirit (Gen. 2:7). This distinction is woven throughout the Old and New Testaments.

> If it were his [God's] intention and he withdrew his spirit and breath, all mankind would perish together and man would return to the dust.(Job 34:14–15)

> The dust returns to the ground it came from, and the spirit returns to God who gave it.(Eccl. 12:7)

Do not be afraid of those who kill the body but cannot kill the soul. Rather, be afraid of the One who can destroy both soul and body in hell. (Matt. 10:28)

Therefore we do not lose heart. Though outwardly we are wasting away, yet inwardly we are being renewed day by day. (2 Cor. 4:16)

For physical training is of some value, but godliness [spiritual training] has value for all things, holding promise for both the present life and the life to come. (1 Tim. 4:8)

Admittedly, this distinction is a bit awkward. It feels almost "unnatural" to consider ourselves as a duplex of tangible bodies and intangible spirits. Yet in many ways it should feel unnatural! Body and mind belong together.

> The spirit was once not a garrison, maintaining its post with difficulty in a hostile Nature [body], but was fully "at home" with its organism, like a king in his own country or a rider on his own horse—or better still, as the human part of a Centaur was "at home" with the equine part. (Lewis, 1960, p. 126)

It is only sin and death that make body and mind divisible. If there were no death or physical weakness, the distinctions between the two would be sufficiently blurred as to make them appear functionally indivisible. Since the Fall, however, even though they belong together, body and mind are capable of separation. Therefore, although Scripture emphasizes that the true person is the whole person—a unity of mind and body—in our fallen world, we must reckon with the twofold nature of persons and its counseling implications.

Definition of Mind

At the popular level, the word *mind* usually means intellect and thinking. To say that someone has a "good mind" is to say that he or she is smart or academically capable. From a more technical perspective, it usually refers to the "ego," or "self"—the self-conscious, rational, emotional, goal-oriented individual who can't be captured by an understanding of brain anatomy or physiology.[4]

The uniqueness of the biblical perspective. The biblical view acknowledges that we are self-conscious, rational, and goal-oriented individuals, but its view of mind is unique and should be clearly distinguished from secular views. As mentioned in chapter 1, the cardinal feature of the biblical view is its starting point—the person-before-God. It has no place for the notion that human beings can live apart from God's sustaining hand. Therefore, *mind* (from the Greek *dianoia*) is our intangible being that is *motivated by our relationship with God—for or against.* It is the center of *moral* initiative, moral judgment, and moral reasoning. It is the initiator of the *ethical* drama of life. For example, notice how the following verses use variations on the word *mind.* They consistently indicate that its Greek counterpart, *dianoia,* means *spiritual* understanding—or lack of it—not intelligence or morally neutral abilities.

> Do not conform any longer to the pattern of this world, but be transformed by the renewing of your *mind.* Then you will be able to test and approve what God's will is. (Rom. 12:2)

> I pray also that the eyes of your *heart* may be enlightened in order that you may know the hope to which he has called you. (Eph. 1:18)

> They are darkened in their *understanding* and separated from the life of God because of the ignorance that is in them due to the hardening of their hearts. (Eph. 4:18)

> Once you were alienated from God and were enemies in your *minds* because of your evil behavior. (Col. 1:21)

> This is the covenant I will make with the house of Israel after that time, declares the Lord. I will put my laws in their *minds* and write them on their hearts. (Heb. 8:10; cf. 10:16)

A change in vocabulary. Mind is not the only biblical word that refers to this immaterial center of moral initiative and moral judgment. In fact, since *mind* is easily confused with our modern understanding of intellect, other words may be less confusing and therefore worthy substitutes. The Bible has many words and phrases that overlap with *mind* (Greek: *phrenes, nous, dianoia*). Included are terms such as heart (*kardia*), spirit (*pneuma*), soul (*psuche;* Hebrew: *nephesh*), conscience (*suneidesis*), "inner self" (1 Peter 3:4), and "inner man" (Eph. 3:16). All these terms share one field of meaning: they all refer to the initiating, moral center of the person. For example, spirit and soul both refer to the person as volitional and morally responsible; but, at least in the apostle Paul's usage, spirit usually indicates the soul who is obedient.

Spirit would actually be a useful substitute for *mind* in that it avoids the secular implications of *mind* and is commonly understood as the nonphysical aspect of persons. However, along with *soul,* it has a tendency to be swept up in a dichotomy or trichotomy debate. That is, are we body and spirit, or are we body, soul, and spirit?

Perhaps the least confusing word would be *heart*. Even in its popular use, it means the most central, guiding aspect of the person. When people ask, "What do you really believe in your heart?" they are interested in understanding our deepest yearnings, our root motivations. The "heart of the matter" is the central idea and essence of a discussion. From a biblical perspective, the heart is called "the wellspring of life" that morally guides the entire person (Prov. 4:23). As such, *heart* will be the term of choice in this book.

> The heart in the Scripture is variously used; sometimes for the mind and understanding, sometimes for the will, sometimes for the affections, sometimes for the conscience, sometimes for the whole soul. Generally, it denotes the whole soul of man and all the faculties of it, not absolutely, but as they are all one principle of moral operations, as they concur in our doing good or evil. . . . the seat and subject of the law of sin is the heart of man. (Owen, 1958, p. 170)

Heart: Home to belief or reason? faith or intellect? In the same way that the biblical use of *mind* is distinct from our modern conception of intellect, the essence of the biblical word *heart* is not captured by the functions of intellect and emotions. *Although expressed by way of psychological processes (i.e., thinking, feeling), the heart possesses and operates according to a belief,* and its fundamental response is either faith or unbelief. This innate belief is different from intellectual understanding or emotional experience. It is not arrived at through reasoning or emotional experience, and it is not necessarily a belief that is held consciously. But it is the rudder that guides the ship, directing all our actions. The belief is this: in our hearts, *we know God* (Rom. 1:18–24). We know God the Creator through knowledge of the external world, and we know God the Holy One through subjective knowledge that is usually referred to as our conscience (Rom. 2:14).[5]

Faced with this belief, the instinctive reaction of our hearts is to suppress or deny it because it is an affront to our pride. We find the knowledge of God to be distressing because it means that we are dependent creatures rather than independent sovereigns. But whether or not we say we believe in God, the essence of the heart is its inescapable God-ward referent.

Thus the heart is not to be confused with the morally inert intellect so prized in Western culture. Memory, logic, and academic abilities are not, in themselves, moral functions. The *heart* is the moral helmsman that empowers, initiates, and directs the course of the intellect. It determines whether the intellect will be used for self-exaltation or in the service of God. Therefore the heart is never called "stupid" or "smart." The heart can be taught (e.g., 2 Tim. 3:16), but the substance of the teaching is the gospel of Christ that is apprehended by faith. Responsiveness then produces character, not intelligence. As the heart abides in Christ by faith, it can be honest and good (Luke 8:15), perfect (Ps. 101:2), single (Jer. 32:39), wise (Job 9:4), and meek (Matt. 11:29–30). Left to itself, it is full of unbelief and is called dull (Acts 28:27), hard (Mark 3:5), stony (Ezek. 11:19), deceitful and desperately wicked (Prov. 12:20). Its deepest need is not education. Rather, the heart must be made new by redemptive grace through a response of faith (Jer. 24:7; Ps. 51:10).

This distinction between heart and intellect (as we know it today) is admittedly awkward. Even though they are distinguishable, they are overlapping and interdependent. But if we press their unity too hard, there are obvious problems. For example, the smartest would possess the most spiritual acumen, and the child and mentally retarded would be morally inept. Scripture, however, emphasizes that the connection is more complex than that. In fact, it observes how the moral clarity of the heart is sometimes greatest in those who are intellectually the weakest. Children are often able to distinguish good from evil better than their parents, and they can have a mature and praiseworthy faith. Faith, not IQ, is the power behind true knowledge and understanding.

This is not to say that the intellect is unimportant. No, it is a very important quality. For example, if we had no ability to reason, think, and communicate, faith would be impossible. We would retain a sense of right and wrong because it is imbedded in our conscience/heart, but vibrant faith comes by hearing (Rom. 10:17). It is preceded by some kind of reasonable knowledge about the person of Christ. In 1 Corinthians 14:14–16, Paul indicates that understanding and intelligible speech are superior to the more private and nonrational phenomenon of speaking in tongues. He states that understandable speech—which uses rational processes—and not tongues edifies the entire church. Indeed, the intellect is very important. It serves the heart through receiving and processing information, and it is the heart's instrument for expressing itself.

The basic point of the distinction between heart and intellect is not to disparage the intellect or emotions, but to lay a theological foundation that will maintain personal responsibility for sinful behavior even when the intellect is marred. Our fundamental knowledge of God can be seared by sin but not erased by disease. A related point is that faith in Christ, while needing some intellectual processes, is not dependent on an average intellect. The gospel can be understood by two-year-olds—mental midgets by IQ standards.

The distinction does raise questions, however, especially with the most severe cases of brain injury. For example, what about people who are comatose? Are they responsible for their behavior? In a true coma, this question would be irrelevant because affected persons are not emitting behavior, so we have nothing to hold them accountable for. But can they be brought to faith or be spiritually encouraged during this time? It depends on the depth of the coma. To know Christ by faith, we must have some ability to process information from those around us. Unlike our knowledge of right and wrong, faith is not instinctive. The best rule is to encourage *everyone* to faith in Christ—neighbors, children, and the brain-injured. No doubt you have heard stories of people having been prepared to respond to Christ even while they were in a coma. Some, however, will not understand the message. In such cases our Christian ministry is probably limited to being physically present, caring for their physical needs, and believing that God is both a loving Father and a just Judge who holds people responsible according to their abilities.

One other very practical question concerns the insanity defense. Is it possible that some people can perform criminal acts under the influence of a disease? This is a complex biblical and legal issue, but the principles laid out so far at least suggest that many cases tried under the insanity defense have no biblical justification.

To summarize, the heart is the intangible aspect of persons that has a God-given, initiating, executive role. Subtly distinguishable from cognitive functions such as the intellect, the heart operates either by faith or by unbelief. By faith the state of the heart is manifested in the fruit of the Spirit: love, joy, peace, patience, kindness, goodness, faithfulness, gentleness, and self-control. By unbelief the heart is manifested by acts of the sinful or earthly nature: sexual immorality, impurity, lust, evil desires, and greed. Remediation or "treatment" is by teaching, rebuking, correcting, encouragement, training in righteousness (2 Tim. 3:16), purifying (James 4:8), self-control, and other spiritual disciplines.

Perhaps the heart's most exciting quality is that it can be renewed and thereby reflect the light of Christ even when the brain and other body organs are wasting away (2 Cor. 4:16). Without question, the heart needs the instrument of the intellect to have an intelligible faith, but even with severely damaged intellects there is an inherent moral sensitivity—we know God. In understanding this, Christians have an insight that is only hinted at in secular medicine. As the Russian neuropsychologist A. R. Luria indicated, "A man does not consist of memory alone. He has feeling, will, sensibility, *moral being*—matters to which neuropsychology cannot speak. And it is here . . . that you may find ways to touch him, and change him" (Sacks, 1985, p. 34, italics added).

Definition of the Body

The body component of the heart (mind) and body discussion is simply the material, physical body. It is the tangible aspect of the person, the stuff we can touch, the "outer man": brain, muscle, organs, bones, and nerve cells.

Historically denigrated, the body was, in Greek thought, as Philolaus said, a house of detention in which the soul is imprisoned to expiate its sin. Epictetus was ashamed to have a body and called himself a "poor soul shackled to a corpse." "Disdain the flesh," said Marcus Aurelius, "blood and bones and network, a twisted skein of nerves, veins, arteries" (Barclay, 1962, pp. 10–11).

The Bible, however, offers no support for these perspectives. No second-class citizen, the body is a "temple of the Holy Spirit" (1 Cor. 6:19) and is indispensable to the activity of the heart. Without the body we would have no access to the physical world and we simply would not be persons. Accordingly, Paul could not imagine a person without a corporeal nature (1 Cor. 15). The whole person consists of body and heart together; both are essential, and neither exists in isolation from the other.

The physical body is represented in the Bible by various Hebrew and Greek words.[6] In the Septuagint and Greek New Testament "body" is usually a translation of the Greek words *sōma* (body), *sarx* (flesh), and *melos* (members). Most often it is a translation of *sōma* (e.g., psychosomatic), in which case it consistently refers to the physical body.

The other words for "body" do not have the same technical consistency as *sōma* and are defined by the context. Most notable and prone to misinterpretation is the word translated "flesh" (*sarx*). "Flesh" may be used as a synonym for *sōma*, or body. In these cases, the flesh might be weak but it is never the human source of evil (e.g., John 6:53; Rom. 2:28; Gal. 4:13; Eph. 2:3). At other times, especially in the Pauline letters, it does *not* refer to the body. Rather, it is equivalent to the acts of the sinful nature and is contrasted with living by the Spirit (Rom. 8:4; Gal. 5:17). Perhaps the failure to distinguish between these two meanings of "flesh" lies behind the mistaken belief that the body is evil.

The unique contribution of the body to the whole person is that it is the *mediator* of action rather than the *initiator*. As mediator, it is not the source of sin.[7] Instead, it gives the heart access to the physical world, thus giving the heart a vehicle for concrete ministry and service in the material world. As mediator, the body can be

—Strong and healthy

—Physically ill and called weak (Greek: *asthenia*), fragile ("jars of clay"), decaying, and prone to hardships; or

—Weak (*asthenia*) in the sense that it has natural desires that must constantly be met

In any of these conditions, the body can influence the heart. When it is healthy, the heart can praise God for his gift of health, or it can respond in pride and forget God's provision. When the body is weak or physically ill, the heart can either declare that it is strong in the Lord (2 Cor. 12:10), or it can become embittered against God. When the body is weak in that it has natural desires (such as for food and rest), the heart can look to God for self-control; it can have good desires but an unresponsive body (Matt. 26:41), or it can indulge the passions of the body.

Therefore, even though it is not the initiator, the body is certainly not a bystander in the struggle called sanctification. Rather, it occupies a critical but precarious position. It is caught in the middle of a battle between the heart and sin. The spiritually revived heart desires self-control over bodily desires, but sin wants outright dominion of the person. To this end, sin strategically attacks the body's physical weaknesses (Rom. 6:12–13). Its most successful strategy is to prey on the ever-present, weak, but natural desires of the body, thereby exalting bodily passions so that they rule the entire person. For example, hunger, a normal and appropriate bodily desire, when dominated by sin through the heart, can become a ruling desire that takes the form of anorexia, bulimia, or gluttony. Also, our critical physical need for sleep and rest, when derailed by sin, can move us toward indolence and poverty. Drug abuse and sexual sin, both of which have bodily components, are other examples of the body's being dominated by sin.

Scripture counters by proclaiming that "sin shall not be your master, because you are not under law, but under grace" (Rom. 6:14). For believers, sin is a usurper with no rightful claim to our lives. So, with the assurance of "no condemnation" and the knowledge of God's power in us, we respond in faith when God's Word calls for self-control and discipline (1 Thess. 4:4). As Paul indicates, "I beat my body and make it my slave" (1 Cor. 9:27). This is not asceticism or physical self-denial; rather it is Paul's spiritual preparation to combat the tactics of Satan that prey on the natural weaknesses and desires of the body.

The body (brain) and the intellect. How is the body related to the intellect? Although our common conception of thinking, reasoning, memory, and other cognitive or intellectual processes refuse to be forced into the biblical category of *heart* because they lack a moral component, they fit neatly into the category *body.* Notice the similarity. Like the body, the cognitive functions can be weakened and "waste away," thus limiting the expression of the heart and the reality accessible to the heart. Consider, for example, the tragic weakening of the brain and intellectual processes in Alzheimer's disease. Affected persons can no longer reason effectively, remember, or plan. As their brains are affected, the victims' cognitive functions are similarly weakened.

The brain and emotions. A related question is, Where does this leave emotions? Emotions are surely an expression of the heart, but this does not exclude a physical origin for emotions as well. Emotions involve our entire being and cross the vague boundaries between heart and body. We "feel" emotions; they are bodily experiences. The language of the Old Testament even relates emotions to different body parts such as the "gut" and "spleen."

Emotions supply a fascinating case study for heart-body interdependence because they can be "initiated" by either the heart or the body. Despondency, for example, when rooted in the heart may have its cause in personal sin, being sinned against, or a sense of guilt. Yet this certainly does not exhaust the causes for despondency and depression. It is biblically possible that depression may be caused by bodily weakness. If so, it is not rooted in sinfulness (in ourselves or others). Rather, it is a result of living in a fallen world (and body) that groans until the day of final redemption.

Notice the prominent bodily symptoms of depression: lethargy, slowness of movement (even of the bowels), and slowness of intellect. These are certainly not moral issues. In fact, even feeling "blue"—an experience that violates no biblical commands—can be caused by physical problems. Counselors and counselees, however, can misinterpret these as being caused by the heart. Organic depression can *affect* the susceptible heart and move it toward despair, hopelessness, and an unbiblical view of oneself. But the physical features of depression are just that—physical—and they can be treated medically. In fact, even if depression is initially caused by the heart, the accompanying physical features, which may make the heart more prone to sin, may be treated medically.[8]

This is not to say that counselors are simply bystanders in the treatment of some types of depression. The unwarranted philosophy of many pastors and counselors is that depression that results from moral problems of the heart is treated "spiritually," whereas depression caused by bodily problems or "chemical imbalance" is treated medically. For various reasons, this is a troublesome perspective. Most important, it is an improper extension of the biblical view of heart and body.[9] Although body and heart can be examined somewhat independently, they constantly interact—and the heart leads the way.

Therefore, although medication and other physical treatments may alleviate the feeling of depression in some people, counseling depressed persons, formally or informally, is very important. Depressed persons are just like everyone else: they need practical, biblical teaching that will daily call them to faith in Christ (Heb. 3:12–13). But depressed persons need this even more! Depression provides an ideal opportunity for sin to gain ground and undermines one's ability to resist temptation. Sin is notorious for taking advantage of depression and transforming it into something that is self-consuming and guilt-provoking, characterized by despair, hopelessness, and often, anger. Satan knows that depression can be a test of faith that leads to greater spiritual maturity (James 1:2). In light of the high stakes in the battle, counselors must be diligent to "correct, rebuke and encourage—with great patience and careful instruction" (2 Tim. 4:2).

Like other emotions, all depressions are addressed by Scripture. That is not to say that Scripture guarantees that all depressions will

Table 2.1. Differences Between the Heart and Body

The Body	The Heart (Mind)
Broken leg	*Sin:* Sexual immorality, lust, evil
Atherosclerosis	desires, filthy language, malice,
Mental retardation	greed, anger, rage, murder, strife,
Feelings of depression	arrogance, boasting, disobedience
Hallucinations	to parents, unbelief, jealousy, gos-
Poor memory	sip, drunkenness, lying, idolatry,
Perceptual changes associated	pride
with	
psychosis	*Righteousness* (Fruit of the Spirit):
Health	Patience, love, joy, peace, gentle-
Difficulty planning and sequencing	ness, kindness, forgiveness, whole-
behaviors	some speech
Feelings of panic	
Comprehension difficulties	

disappear when biblical guidelines are followed. But Scripture does identify the resources to grow in obedient faith in the course of any difficulty. This being the case, counseling those with bodily problems is necessary. Counselors will not be made obsolete by advances in medicine.

Summary of the Duplex Nature

To summarize, the heart is the initiator of the moral life. It is affected by the body in that bodily problems, such as premenstrual syndrome (PMS), provide obstacles to personal holiness and sanctification, and they can be occasions for sin or undermine our resistance to temptation. But bodily problems are not powerful enough to make us sin, and they rarely keep us from living by faith.

The body, by contrast, is never attributed a purposeful, initiating, or executive function in Scripture. It is a mediator, serving the heart by providing it a mode of expression. The body is called weak and sick, not sinful. Its passions are to be controlled by the heart, not called to repentance. Remediation comes offering help, feeding, strengthening, healing, and removing stumbling blocks (1 Cor. 8). In the example of PMS, the physical features and "feelings" of depression are not sin. They are more accurately a consequence of living in bodies that are wasting away. Unfortunately, some counselors have difficulty distinguishing bodily weakness and sin. Table 2.1 illustrates some of the distinctions.

For pastors and counselors, the focus is the whole person: heart and body. Understanding the expressions of the heart as well as the idiosyncratic weaknesses and limitations of the body (brain, intellect, emotions) are all part of the process of biblical counseling.

Unity

To bring the whole person into clear focus, we must give some attention to the unity of the person. To this point I have emphasized our dual nature as human beings, but we are both a duplex and a unity. Neglect of this unity can be quite misleading and theoretically dangerous.

The unity of the person is typically described in analogies or metaphors; its mysterious nature defies more conventional, technical descriptions.[10] The most common metaphor to describe the unity of heart and body is the computer: the body is the hardware, the heart is the software, and both are necessary for operation. This metaphor has aspects of truth in that it illustrates the initiating action of the heart, but it does not capture the mystery and beauty of the unity of heart and body. More powerful, perhaps, are analogies from Scripture.

One that comes immediately to mind is the relationship between Christ and the church. Here is a delightful and intriguing picture of the unity between two distinct substances. Christ is obviously different from and separate from his church; but we are members of Christ's body (1 Cor. 12) and, by faith, are one with him (Rom. 6). We are in him and he is in us. What is his is ours. Anticipated by the created world, this relationship is beautifully illustrated by the vine and the branches (John 15). Jesus is the grapevine; we are the branches or shoots that are inseparable and indistinguishable from the vine.

In Ephesians 5:25–33, Paul uses an even more familiar picture.

> "For this reason a man will leave his father and mother and be united to his wife, and the two will become one flesh." This is a profound mystery—but I am talking about Christ and the church. (Vv. 31–32)

The analogy of marriage is especially useful as a means of making the unity of heart and body more familiar. Like the heart and the body, husband and wife are distinct. They are intended to come together for life and be separated only by death. They are of equal worth before God. They do not lose their individuality in unity; rather, they find it. They are managerially distinct; that is, they have different roles.

This managerial or functional distinction is especially intriguing. Although there has been much unbalanced exegesis and patently wrong behavior seeking shelter under the umbrella of leadership and submission, only exegetical chicanery suggests that *no* managerial distinction exists between husband and wife. The husband is called to loving leadership; the wife is called to submission. Fleshing out the precise nature of these differences is a tricky task that tends to be confounded by personal and cultural biases, yet Scripture is clear that there is *some* kind of role distinction between husband and wife. Similarly, heart and body have different roles: the heart has an executive, initiating role and the body a mediating one.[11]

Perhaps a less troublesome analogy that incorporates this managerial distinction is the Trinity. God is simultaneously three and one. The three persons, of equal moral and divine excellence, have separate offices or roles. The Father sends the Son. The Son is submissive to the Father, he is the *incarnation* [em-*bodi*-ment] of the Father, and does the Father's will rather than his own. The Spirit proceeds from the Father and mediates the presence of the Son.

These analogies suggest that although we may not fully understand the simultaneous unity and duality of the heart and body, we should be somewhat comfortable with it because the created world is filled with similar mysteries. Consider the implications:

Heart and body are both two and one. They are two: body cannot be reduced to heart, and heart cannot be reduced to body, but they are interdependent. They need each other. Human life cannot even be imagined without both the inner and the outer persons. Paul's discussion on the resurrection of the body is based on this reality. In the context of 1 Corinthians 15, the apostle cannot think of humans as one substance exclusive of the other; we are both body and soul. If there is death of the body, there must also be a resurrection of the body in order for humans to have eternal life.

Heart and body have the same value before God; neither is inferior to the other. The body is not inferior to the heart. The apparent subordination in Scripture is the temporal to the eternal, not material to spiritual (1 Tim. 4:8). This rules out any belief that the body is to be denied on the grounds that it is bad.

The equality of heart and body is evident in that both experience death and resurrection. The death and resurrection of the inner person, however, can take place now—at regeneration—while the death and resurrection of the body are still future. The inner person has already died with Christ; the outer person still awaits death and anticipates resurrection. As a result, Paul states that the outer person wastes away and anticipates renewal, while the inner person, in Christ, is presently being renewed day by day (2 Cor. 4:16).

There is a managerial distinction between heart and body. The heart is the initiator of action and is morally culpable in a unique way. The body is the mediator of the intents of the heart. It gives the heart access to the physical world while also prescribing certain cognitive and behavioral limits (e.g., we can't know everything; we can't fly). When this relationship is reversed—that is, when the body becomes "boss" (e.g., lack of sexual restraint or substance abuse)—chaos reigns.

> If your body makes all the decisions and gives all the orders, and if you obey, the physical can effectively destroy every other dimension of your personality. Your emotional life will be blunted and your spiritual life will be stifled and ultimately will become anemic. (Quoist, 1965, p.4)

With these analogies comes a word of caution. These mysteries, especially the Trinity, have a long history of theological controversy. In trying to explain them, theologians have been unsettled by their apparent contradictions (e.g., three and one) and have sought rationalistic answers. In so doing, they tend to examine some facts and ignore others. If we learn anything from these controversies, it is that human beings crave intellectually elegant answers rather than answers by faith.

The same thing has happened in the discussion of the mind and the body. To try to avoid this tendency, I leave you with a perspective that is intellectually unappealing but biblically sound. Persons are both two and one, unity and duplex. This is a brain teaser to be sure, but one that points us to the Creator God whose wisdom and knowledge are far greater than our own. It also points us to *our* Creator, who is the sustaining power that holds heart and body together. Apart from God's grace, the two are separated by death.

Building a Biblical Model

As a result of the two-and-one nature that constitutes human beings, there are at least four possible practical consequences. Since heart and body are united, what happens to one will necessarily influence the other. Therefore, (1) problems of the heart will affect the body, and (2) problems of the body will affect the heart. It is also true, however, that since heart and body are distinguishable, what happens to one will not *necessarily* influence the other. Therefore, (3) problems in the heart

Figure 2.2. The Heart Affecting the Body

The Body

Physical weakness and disease
Health

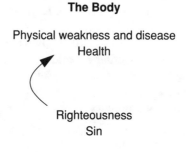

Righteousness
Sin

The Heart

will not affect the body, and (4) problems in the body will not affect the heart. From these four pieces we will construct a larger counseling model.

The Heart Affects the Body

The first counseling implication is well known. As a result of the constitutional unity of persons, what happens in the heart has bodily consequences. This is popularly called psychosomatics, a very active area of medical research (e.g., Ader, 1981; Cousins, 1983). The secular conception of this relationship is that stress (whatever stress is) alters the body's susceptibility to diseases. The theory is that when we are struggling to cope with problems in marriage, relationships, or work, the body gradually loses its ability to fight disease. With this we would all agree.

The Christian view has many things in common with the secular, but is distinctive in important ways. First, the biblical view is more specific in that health and life or disease and death are ultimately seen as a result of *moral choices*, not stress. Sin, unwise living (according to Proverbs), and guilt can lead to sickness; righteousness and the peace and joy of biblical living can lead to health (see Figure 2.2). Of course, these consequences do not always occur, but they are one possibility within the larger biblical model.

Honor your father and your mother, so that you may live long in the land the LORD your God is giving you. (Exod. 20:12)

If you pay attention to these laws and are careful to follow them, then the LORD your God will keep his covenant of love with you. . . . The LORD will keep you free from every disease. He will not inflict on you the horrible diseases you knew in Egypt, but he will inflict them on all who hate you. (Deut. 7:12, 15)

[Because of wickedness] the LORD afflicted Jehoram with an incurable disease of the bowels. In the course of time, at the end of the second year, his bowels came out because of the disease, and he died in great pain. (2 Chron. 21:18–19)

Because of your wrath there is no health in my body; my bones have no soundness because of my sin. My guilt has overwhelmed me like a burden too heavy to bear. My wounds fester and are loathsome because of my sinful folly. (Ps. 38:3–5; cf. Ps. 32)

Fear the LORD and shun evil. This will bring health to your body and nourishment to your bones. (Prov. 3:7b, 8)

The fear of the LORD adds length to life, but the years of the wicked are cut short. (Prov. 10:27)

For they [the father's words] are life to those who find them and health to a man's whole body. (Prov. 4:22)

Therefore confess your sins to each other and pray for each other so that you may be healed. (James 5:16)

A second aspect of the Christian view of psychosomatics is that it has an eternal perspective, not a temporal one. That is, although the heart-body connection is less than perfect on earth, from an eternal perspective there will always be physical consequences to the leanings of the heart. At the return of Christ, when eternity is ushered in, those who are declared righteous by his blood will have life, and those who refuse righteousness through Christ's sacrifice will experience death—a perfect psychosomatic connection. The psychosomatic relationship we see on earth is little more than a reminder of these eternal verities.

Meanwhile, until the return of Jesus, God is gracious. The psychosomatic connection is not an unbending rule. God does not treat us according to what our sins deserve, and he spares us from many diseases.

Figure 2.3. The Body Unaffected by the Heart

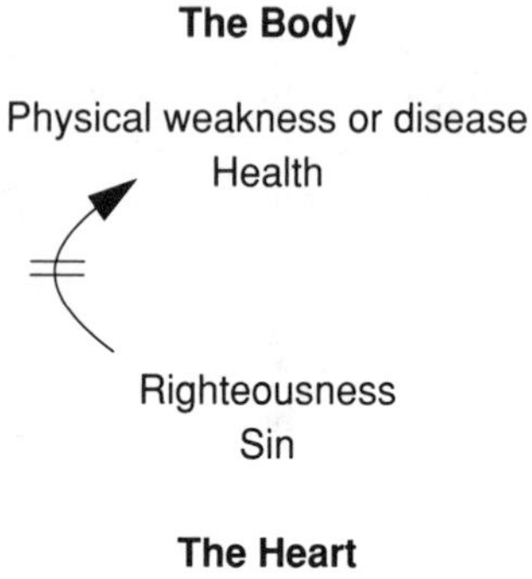

The Body

Physical weakness or disease
Health

Righteousness
Sin

The Heart

The Heart Does Not Affect the Body

Psychosomatics is well known because it emphasizes the obvious. We are one, and we all know it. Heart and body interrelate. But, as illustrated by Job's comforters, an idolatrous emphasis on this can lead to egregious misunderstandings with painful consequences. Because of the entrance of sin into the world, heart and body can appear almost isolated from each other, and the heart may appear to leave the body unaffected (Figure 2.3).

Sin does not lead to physical disability. Historically this is a neglected implication and has proved to be quite vexing. In Psalm 10, David cried out to God because of the prosperous ways of evil oppressors. It was as if he could not understand how evil persons could physically prosper in light of the physical curses that God pronounced on the disobedient. In Psalm 73, Asaph had more serious difficulties. He confessed incipient insanity as he was baffled by the apparent physical well-being of the ungodly. He asked, "How can the unrighteous prosper?" His shortsighted answer: "It's impossible! They shouldn't, they can't! The world is out of control!"

> I envied the arrogant when I saw the prosperity of the wicked. They have no struggles; their bodies are healthy and strong. They are free from the burdens common to man; they are not plagued by human ills. . . . Surely in vain have I kept my heart pure; in vain have I washed my hands in innocence. . . . When I tried to understand all this, it was oppressive to me. (vv. 3–5, 13, 16)

Asaph's mistake, as he came to realize, was his lack of faith. He saw only the temporal and not the eternal, his perspective rather than God's. Finally, he confesses, "I entered the sanctuary of God; then I understood their final destiny" (v. 17). So by faith he learned that God was just and sinners will indeed reap physical misery, though these consequences were not necessarily immediate. God's compassion and patience restrained his wrath and made it less predictable. God was enthroned, but the final expression of his righteousness would wait for the consummation.

This was actually better news than Asaph knew. If Asaph had turned its implications back on himself, he would have been full of joy. For if he had lived in a world where sin always led to immediate and commensurate physical disability, he would have been in trouble. More specifically, he would have been dead! Truly, we are more dependent on God's grace than we realize. God is not passive. He is actively restraining the consequences of sin in both the world and our bodies.

Righteousness does not lead to health. There is another side to this particular implication of disunity. Along with the one already mentioned (that is, evil in our hearts does not have immediate consequences in our bodies), the Bible also indicates that righteousness does not necessarily lead to health (2 Cor. 4:16). In fact, physical hardships are to be expected in the life of a growing Christian. Hebrews 12 states that in the same way that many Old Testament saints experienced physical suffering and death, and in the same way that Christ was seasoned by suffering, so we experience physical and emotional hardships. These are a form of loving discipline from our heavenly Father that are not necessarily consequences of personal sin.

Physical suffering can also be experienced through Satan's work. At times God allows Satan to test us, perhaps by way of physical disease. The book of Job points out that these physical buffetings are not the result of personal sin. Rather, they are testings that can be painful but faith-building experiences. Knowing this, we can avoid the ancient heresy that a big sickness means we committed a big sin. The book of Job should have put this heresy to rest once and for all. Unfortunately it has persisted. It was prevalent in New Testament times (John 9; Luke 13:1–5), and it is just as common today.[12]

A final explanation for how the righteous are affected by disease is the Edenic curse. Physical wasting away and death are consequences of the curse on all creation. Therefore, when people die, the message is not that they got what they deserved but that death is a time of tragedy and mourning, a reminder of the fact that all creation groans under the curse. It is also a reminder that one day the curse will be vanquished.

These possibilities—disease as a result of testing and discipline, satanic buffeting, or living under the Edenic curse—all permitted by the disunity of heart and body, raise an interesting question: How can we know the cause or causes of specific sicknesses? How do we know when sickness is a result of sin, discipline, Satan, or the Edenic curse? At times the Lord may give us insight into the causes of our own or another's sickness, but it can be dangerous to make these pronouncements without the confirmation of others. I believe that Scripture more often simplifies this problem by saying that we really don't have to know the exact cause of sickness. Certainly Job never knew the cause of his sickness. Instead, he was simply encouraged to grow in humble submission, repentance, and faith.

Likewise, when we are faced with physical disease, we should view it as an opportunity to take spiritual inventory and respond to Christ in repentance and faith (e.g., James 5:13–16). This is not because sickness is a result of specific sin, but because sickness is at least a time of spiritual battle and an ideal opportunity to put on the armor of God. Also, of course, it is a time to pray for healing and seek medical attention if appropriate.

To summarize, sickness and health are unpredictable. God is not "legalistic" in bringing immediate consequences of sin to bear on the body. For this we should be continually thankful.

The Body Does Not Affect the Inner Person

The third implication for counseling is that the body does not affect the heart. That is, the body or brain cannot affect the heart in such a way as to deprive it of moral responsibility or spiritual vitality (Figure 2.4). Instead, the apostle Paul suggests that physical weakness can actually *strengthen* us spiritually. He writes in 2 Corinthians 4:16, "Therefore we do not lose heart. Though outwardly we are wasting away, yet inwardly we are being renewed day by day."

What a delight to realize that sickness cannot rob us of faith and a dynamic knowledge of God. By God's grace we can have strong spirits even if we have decrepit bodies. Consider, for example, a seventy-two-year-old woman who was experiencing significant intellectual changes from Alzheimer's disease. Even though she was almost mute and could not remember many of the visitors (including her own children), she was

Figure 2.4. The Heart Unaffected by the Body

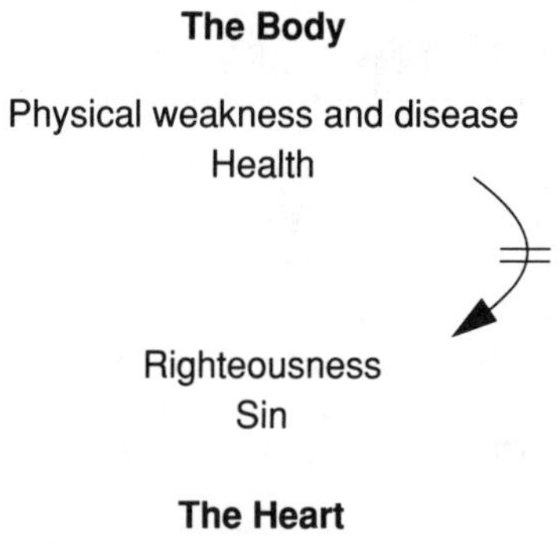

The Body

Physical weakness and disease
Health

Righteousness
Sin

The Heart

joyous and gracious, kind and patient with everyone. Her world was narrowing and she could comprehend little, but she would often remind people, "Jesus loves you." The body and intellect were declining quickly, but her spirit seemed to soar. By God's grace, her brain "weakness" did not take away her relationship with God.

Also, consider the following illustration from Oliver Sacks, M.D., a neurologist, who wrote without apparent religious intent. He describes a man with Korsakov's syndrome—a severe brain impairment that leaves its victims with no ongoing memory.

> One tended to speak of him, instinctively, as a spiritual casualty—a "lost soul": was it possible that he had really been "desouled" by a disease? "Do you think he *has* a soul?" I once asked the Sisters. They were outraged by my question, but could see why I asked it. "Watch Jimmie in chapel," they said, "and judge for yourself."
>
> I did, and I was moved, profoundly moved and impressed, because I saw here an intensity and steadiness of attention and concentration that I had never seen before in him or conceived him capable of. I watched him kneel and take the Sacrament on his tongue, and could not doubt the fullness and totality of Communion, the perfect alignment of his spirit with the spirit of the Mass. Fully, intensely, quietly, in the quietude of absolute concentration and attention, he entered and partook of the Holy Communion. He was wholly held, absorbed, by a feeling. There was no forgetting, no Korsakov's then, nor did it seem possible or imaginable that there should be; for he was no longer at the mercy of a faulty and fallible mechanism—that of meaningless sequences and memory traces—but was absorbed in an act, an act of his whole being, which carried feeling and meaning in an organic

continuity and unity, a continuity and unity so seamless it could not permit any break. (1985, pp. 37–38)[13]

We have all had diseases, illnesses, and physical suffering, but broken legs and high fevers neither separate us from God nor give us a moral reprieve from our responsibilities as image-bearers. Brain dysfunction is indeed a unique kind of physical disability, but the principle is the same. Brain dysfunction, at least if affected persons are alert and responsive, does not affect the moral capacity of the heart. Therefore those with brain impairment must be treated as image-bearers just like everyone else. To treat them differently would be disrespectful, prejudicial, and unbiblical. Their hearts remain receptive to God and spiritual encouragement.

The Body Affects (Limits) the Heart

There are, however, clear ways in which the body *does* affect the heart. This will be the focus of a large part of the remaining chapters. Physical weakness and disease can decrease our ability to express ourselves cogently, understand our world, or minister to others as we might desire. For example, an older woman, gifted in hospitality and service, will have limitations on her ministry if she is bedridden in a nursing home. Physical limitations put certain restrictions on the expression of her heart. This is not to say that ministry is impossible or that she is morally deficient. Without doubt, as long as she lives she can represent God in the world, but the scope of her ministry may have more specific and narrow parameters (Figure 2.5).

The brain, as part of the physical body, also affects the heart, but now the plot thickens. It is easy to see how physical problems in the body impose restrictions, and it is obvious that those restrictions neither extinguish ministry nor render us morally obtuse. However, what about brain disease—a physical weakness that seems to make a more direct assault on the heart? After all, the brain is where the person is. My body can be full of organ transplants or mechanical devices, yet "I" am still the same. But take away the brain and you take away the person. In what ways do physical problems in the brain affect the inner person? Do they make a person morally incompetent, or does brain damage only place limitations (albeit very complex at times) on the activity of the soul?

To answer these questions effectively, the term "brain damage" needs clarification. Brain damage is not a distinct category. Rather, it

Figure 2.5. The Body's Effect on the Heart

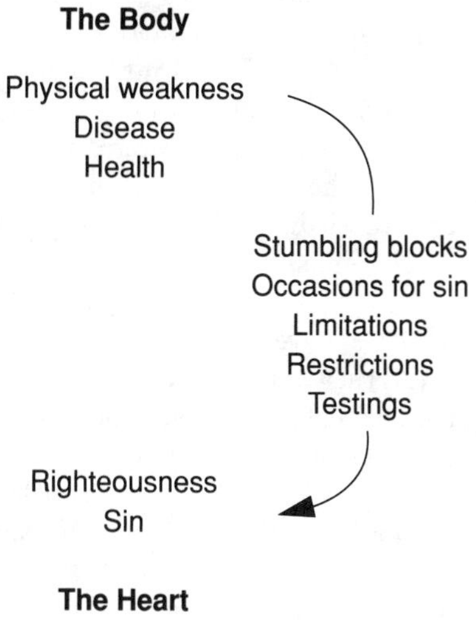

The Body

Physical weakness
Disease
Health

Stumbling blocks
Occasions for sin
Limitations
Restrictions
Testings

Righteousness
Sin

The Heart

represents a continuum of brain activity that actually includes everyone. None of us has a perfect brain. Like the distinction between normal and abnormal, the boundaries between normal brain function and brain damage are often arbitrary and determined by cultural convention rather than pathological evidence. Therefore these questions can be answered by starting with the familiar, such as ourselves, and then going to the more unfamiliar or ostensibly brain-injured.

Although I may want to deny it, I am organically impaired. I have a brain weakness that limits the expression of my heart. As a creature I have mental limitations. I can neither know nor do all things. As a fallen creature, with a body that is wasting away, I have even more limitations. There is a ceiling to my ability to remember, conceptualize, and comprehend. Accordingly, there are certain limitations on my teaching and counseling abilities, parenting skills, and abilities as a husband. My organic impairment, however, does not rob me of spiritual vigor or moral responsibility. I am able to know Christ, work, rear children, and be a husband to the best of my abilities, and I am without excuse for sin in my heart and behavior (but I am forgiven).

Others have brain limitations that are more noticeable. For example, some people cannot read, either from lack of education or from actual physical limitations (severe dyslexia). If the problem is physical, the affected persons may have to adjust the desires of their hearts. It is possible that certain forms of employment and ministry will be beyond their ability. But again, this will not lessen their moral responsibility or their impact on God's kingdom.

Children are perplexing creatures with well-known physical limits on their abilities. There are many things they cannot understand. They have a limited knowledge of the Bible, are unwise from inexperience, and are neurologically immature. In fact, their deficiencies are so severe that they need close supervision and are actually incapable of living independently; we have to tailor our counsel and teaching to their limitations. Yet they can still know God—quite clearly. Their moral keenness and spiritual vitality may put intellectually superior adults to shame. Jesus even tells us to imitate them in our faith.

People with alleged chemical imbalances (e.g., schizophrenia, mania, depression) are also on the brain-damage spectrum. It is likely that they have unique brain problems that make them more susceptible to fluctuating emotional experiences, hallucinations, or perceptual distortions (cf. chap. 8). During their fluctuating episodes of psychological changes, they might be unable to communicate or work as well as they once did, and their hearts might be unable to express themselves clearly. Also, affected persons can readily experience fear, hopelessness, or confusion. However, as even many secular physicians will say, their alleged imbalances are never an excuse for "bad" behavior. Furthermore, the Scriptures would add that they can still have faith and actually grow spiritually through their oftentimes painful experiences.

It would be a mistake to draw too radical a distinction between people with chemical imbalances and "normal" people. In counseling, if we know how to counsel ourselves, we know how to counsel someone with chemical imbalances. The major pitfalls occur when we (1) fail to understand these people's unique perceptions and emotions, (2) ignore that they may be more vulnerable to being tyrannized by sin, or (3) presume there *must* be a sinful root to their sometimes unusual or unpredictable behaviors.

The same principles and cautions apply to persons with more obvious brain damage (e.g., head injuries from car accidents, brain tumors). Severe brain damage often leaves its victims psychologically disorganized—that is, their world might seem like fragments of disconnected information. They might have difficulties with remembering, understanding, and concentrating to the point of being socially and vocationally inept. But if affected persons are aware of their surroundings and can respond to it, they are as morally responsible as anyone else, and it is likely that they would be able to respond in faith to the good news of Christ when it is shared creatively.

The major counseling dilemma in these cases is that we must enter a world that is foreign to our own—a world that is often very difficult to understand. It is difficult enough to understand ourselves, and even more difficult to understand our spouses or children. How much more difficult to understand the fragmented and unusual world of those with severe brain impairment! The purpose of the next chapter is to help us to understand these difficulties.

A Biblical Model

These four consequences, or pieces of the human puzzle, are naturally assembled into a larger biblical model (Figure 2.6). It consists of the heart and body standing in a relationship in which each component can—but does not have to—affect the other. The heart may either grow in grace or indulge the body, while the body may either grow strong or become weak.

Keep in mind that this pattern is part of the broader biblical teaching that deals with the question, How do our hearts deal with things that affect us?" The body is only one of many things that affects us. We are also affected by sexual abuse, Satan and the demonic world, poverty, spiritual "stumbling blocks" (Rom. 14:13), political oppression, divorce, and day-to-day marital problems. Like the body, all these issues are potentially treacherous, and counselors should understand their impact; but they need not keep our hearts from being focused on things above. In fact, some of these situations hold spiritual benefit in that they remind us that we are strong only in Christ and not in ourselves.

Consider how Satan has an impact on us (Eph. 6:10–18). Satan has a certain power that can provide occasions for sin and undermine our ability to resist temptation. In light of this threat, we are called to understand his influence and tactics and fight him with spiritual implements. But there is never a hint that Satan can render us morally helpless. Rather, in Christ we are guaranteed victory.

Another popular example would be the impact of having lived with an alcoholic parent. There is no question that people can be victimized or sinned against in alcoholic homes, and these injustices are not without

Figure 2.6. The Possible Interactions Between Body and Heart

The Body

Sickness, disease, weakness,
needs, desires, enslaving lusts, trials,
physical health and healing, stumbling blocks,
groanings, testings, limitations, psychosomatic
problems, cravings, occasions for sin,
consequences of sin

Righteousness	or	*Unrighteousness*

Righteousness
Self-control, endurance,
faith, hope, love,
"beating" the body and
making it a slave,
feeding and caring for the body
wisely, guarding the heart,
mortifying sin

Unrighteousness
Lust, sin that desires mastery,
pride, laziness, sensual indulgence,
sinful anger, unbelief,
disobedience,
ignorance, despair

The Heart

consequences. Relationships, enjoyment, and work can all be affected. As a result, counselors must understand those who have been victimized and their associated weakness. Also, counselors have the privilege of communicating that, although those weaknesses may be horrible encumbrances, they need never keep anyone from the knowledge of God and the fruit of the Spirit.

First Corinthians 6:12–20 further illustrates this dynamic truth. In this passage the apostle Paul mentions two popular mottoes of the day. The first, "Everything is permissible for me," was probably an expression of the freedom that Christians had from the Jewish ceremonial laws. For example, they were permitted to eat foods that were previously forbidden. But Paul was concerned about the interpretation of this expression. Permission, when viewed apart from faith, could become license not only to eat everything, but also to participate in sexual sin. "After all," the sinful logic went, "God is saying that we do not have to deny the body any more."

To preempt this thinking, Paul adds, "But not everything is

beneficial" and "I will not be mastered by anything." In terms of figure
2.6 we can say that Paul is warning that the unrighteous heart is prone to
lust, and when lust encounters the weaknesses of the body, it can exalt
bodily passions so that they master or rule the entire person.

In 1 Corinthians 9:24–27, Paul provides an example of how to deal
with the body.

> Do you not know that in a race all the runners run, but only one gets the
> prize? Run in such a way as to get the prize. Everyone who competes in the
> games goes into strict training. They do it to get a crown that will not last;
> but we do it to get a crown that will last forever. Therefore I do not run like
> a man running aimlessly; I do not fight like a man beating the air. No, I
> beat my body and make it my slave so that after I have preached to others, I
> myself will not be disqualified for the prize.

Aware of how sin can use the body to enslave, Paul's strategy is
twofold: to put to death (mortify) the deeds of the flesh and to hope or
aspire to eternal glory in Christ. As this becomes a pattern—that is,
when bodily passions are continually confronted by both mortification
and aspiration—the body is made fit for service and will not disqualify us
for the prize.

Notes

1. From a biblical perspective, these are actually part of the broader
question, "Can *anything* that impacts us—not just disease—remove, lessen, or
prohibit spiritual *vitality* or *responsiveness?*" "Anything that impacts us" can mean
the effects of culture, being sinned against by alcoholic parents, sexual assault,
Satan and demonization, poverty or wealth, personal failures, even physical
health—it is not just the impact of bodily disease. Likewise, personal responsibility is a subset of the larger category of spiritual vitality or spiritual responsiveness.
This includes the knowledge of God and his love for us through Christ, as well as
simple delight in Jesus, regardless of circumstances.

2. Perhaps I should say "at least" two parts. Some prefer body, soul, and
spirit.

3. Robert Gundry (1976), who has done some of the most thorough
biblical work on the study of the person, indicates that we are "ontological
dualities" within an "overarching unity." His book *Soma in Biblical Theology* is
technical but worthwhile reading.

4. Interestingly, while the body is obviously tangible, the "I" is physically
elusive. That is, at this point there is no clear physical or neuronal basis for the
initiating heart. For example, there have been brain operations in which surgeons
have had opportunities to stimulate the brain of alert patients electrically. This

electrical stimulation can elicit body movements, memories, emotions, and other cognitive activities, yet electrically stimulated activity is always distinguished from "me." Patients have said, after a surgeon's electrode prompted forgotten memories or sudden movements, "I didn't do that; you did. I didn't make that sound; you pulled it out of me" (Penfield, 1975). The person as one-who-makes-choices has not been physically captured.

5. This belief is not the same as saving faith in Christ.

6. Old Testament Hebrew words for "body" include *basar, gab, gev, geviyyah, guphah, geshem, nebelah.*

7. Romans 7:14–25 might be raised as evidence against this position, but John Murray provides this interpretation in his commentary on Romans: "We are not to suppose that 'the law of sin' springs from or has its seat in the physical. It would merely indicate . . . that the apostle brings to the forefront the concrete and overt ways in which the law of sin expresses itself and that our physical members cannot be divorced from the operation of the law of sin" (p. 267).

8. The only problem with psychoactive medication is that some psychiatrists have a tendency to prescribe the medical model along with medication.

9. Another problem is that there are no easy ways to differentiate between physical and nonphysical depression. This diagnostic ambiguity tends to permit psychiatrists to suggest that "when in doubt, it is physical and therefore under psychiatric purview"; they would delegate to pastors, counselors, and laypersons only matters involving minor bereavement.

10. Those who seek technical precision will be disappointed. As MacDonald Critchley (1979), the British neurologist, said, "We must admit that the divine banquet of the brain was, and still is, a feast with dishes that remain elusive in their blending, and with sauces whose ingredients are even now a secret (p. 267).

11. As with all analogies, it cannot be pressed too hard. Clearly, the husband is not the sole moral initiator, nor is the wife the vehicle of action (though some wives may feel that way). I am only saying that there is precedent in this metaphor for a managerial distinction.

12. James 5:14–16 may have contributed to the persistence of the position that sickness *must* imply an occasion of sin. This passage, however, makes it very clear that while sin *may* be the cause of sickness, it certainly is not always the case. James specifically says, *"If* he has sinned."

13. From Oliver Sacks, *The Man Who Mistook His Wife for a Hat* (New York: Summit, 1985). Copyright © 1970, 1981, 1983, 1984, 1985 by Oliver Sacks. Used by permission of Summit Books, a division of Simon & Schuster.

3
Biological Foundations

It is highly dishonourable for a reasonable soul
to live in so divinely built a mansion as the body she resides in
altogether unacquainted with the exquisite structure of it.

—Robert Boyle

This is the brain age. The nineteen-thirties and forties belonged to physics, the fifties and sixties to molecular biology, and the seventies, eighties, and nineties to the brain. Recent developments have been nothing short of astounding. Therefore it was no surprise when I heard a Christian brain scientist say, "Apart from the glory of redemption, there is nothing more exciting than studying the human brain and the relationship between the brain and behavior."

If the thought of neurophysiology or neuropsychology does not get your adrenalin pumping, I hope you will find that a brief summary of the practical findings in brain research will, at least, strengthen your general counseling ministry. You might even find it interesting.

The Brain

In approaching something as complex as the central nervous system (the brain and spinal cord), with its hundreds of associated technical terms, we should begin with the basic building blocks of the nervous system—the neurons—and proceed to a more panoramic view.

The Neuron

The brain consists largely of cells called *neurons* and *glial cells*. There are perhaps ten trillion of these microscopic cells in the brain. Although

59

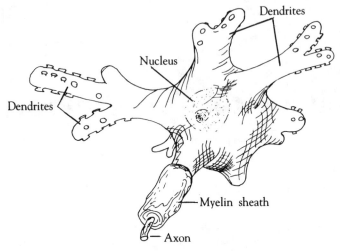

Figure 3.1. The Neuron

their size is difficult to comprehend, their organizational style, especially that of the neurons, is familiar. They interact as if they are part of a living, dynamic community: they are separate; they communicate; they come in many sizes and shapes; they live in clusters (called *nuclei* and *ganglia*); they adapt, learn, forget; and they need constant oxygen and nutrition.

Neurons, like other cells in the body, contain a nucleus, genetic material, a cell body, and membranes, yet they are unique in that they have extensions called *axons* and *dendrites* (Figure 3.1). These extensions are the means of communication within the brain—the "telephone wires" of the nervous system. The dendrites are heavily branched appendages that usually only receive information from other cells and carry that information back to the cell body. There can be dozens of dendrites on a cell body, accompanied by literally thousands of smaller branches and spines. The axons, by contrast, usually come only one per cell, smaller in diameter, and significantly less branched. They transmit information from the cell body to other cells rather than receive it.

Neurons share the brain with *glial cells* (Figure 3.2). Actually more numerous than neurons, these cells generally support the work of the neurons and occasionally act as microscopic garbage collectors: they repair nerve cells, maintain the proper chemical balance in the extracellular fluid, may help establish the blood-brain barrier,[1] and provide structural support by acting almost like "brain glue" (*glia* actually means "glue"). Glial cells include *astrocytes* (*astro*, "star"), which may be involved in transporting substances from blood vessels to neurons; *oligodendrocytes* (*oligo*, "few"; *dendro*, "tree"), which produce *myelin*—a fatty substance that surrounds and electrically insulates axons—and tiny *microglia*. Unlike neurons, glial cells are capable of cell division. Accordingly, brain tumors such as astrocytomas are abnormal proliferations of glial cells rather than neurons.

Nerve cell communication. The communication between neurons is electrochemical. This means that an electrical charge exists in neurons as a result of the relative concentrations, inside and outside the cell membranes, of electrically charged chemicals called ions. The electrical charge occurs as a result of at least two neuronal characteristics: (1) they retain certain negative ions because the negative ions are simply too large to fit through cell membranes, and (2) close to a million pumps, seen microscopically as small bumps on the cell membranes, make neurons selectively permeable to certain ions. The pumps retain potassium (K+) and exclude sodium (Na+). As a result, there are twenty times more K+ ions inside the cells than outside, and there are twenty times more Na+ outside the cells than inside. These characteristics and others combine to give nerve cells an electrical "resting potential" of -70 millivolts (mV).

When a "resting" nerve cell is stimulated by a neighboring cell (a process we will explain shortly), the membrane charge could become larger (further from zero) or smaller (closer to zero), depending on the type of stimulation. If the membrane voltage is lessened, or depolarized, to approximately -50 mV, an electrical charge called an action potential begins to race through the dendrite. The sodium-potassium pumps in the stimulated region that is temporarily shut down, Na+ rushes into the cell, and the membrane changes polarity to about +50 mV. This in turn starts a depolarization wave that affects neighboring pumps within the neuron until the domino-like wave proceeds from the dendrite through the cell body and on to the end of the axon. It then goes on to stimulate other neighboring cells. Meanwhile, after the wave passes through, the affected pumps immediately resume their work and the resting potential is restored.

This process, while appearing cumbersome, is actually quite

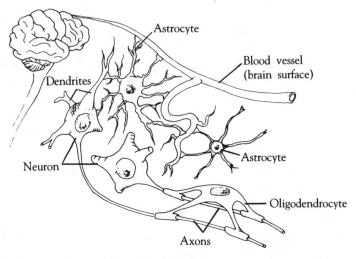

Figure 3.2. Glial Cells

efficient. Neurons can respond with new action potentials, or waves of depolarization, as frequently as 1000 times per second!

An unusual twist in the electrical activity of the brain is the way cells communicate their messages to each other. Neurons do not actually touch; rather, they are separated by small gaps called *synapses*[2] (Figure 3.3). When a wave of electrical activity comes to the end of an axon, it releases packages of chemicals called neurotransmitters. These neurotransmitters are made in the cell body, or they may be artificially added to the synaptic area by way of medication. For example, antidepressants and other psychoactive drugs have their effect by adding neurotransmitters to the synapses. When the neurotransmitters are released, they flow across the synapse, attach to the dendritic receptor molecules of the neighboring cell, and influence the electrochemical status of that cell. If the chemical message calls for depolarization, the neurotransmitters will initiate an action potential in the neuron's dendritic arm that will then proceed to the cell body and on to the axon. Meanwhile, the neurotransmitters are released from the dendrites and are either washed away or recycled and stored in the axon for future use.

With these neurotransmitters, the communication possibilities between neurons is even greater than their astronomical numbers suggest. With the abundance of cell dendrites, each of the more than 10 billion

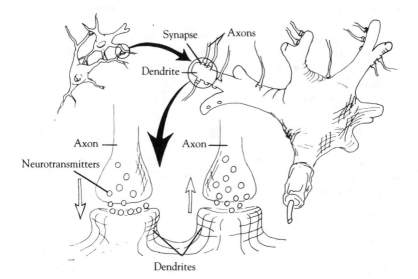

Figure 3.3. Neuronal Communication. When electrically stimulated, axon terminals release certain neurotransmitters that bind to a neighboring dendritic surface. After "communicating" their chemical message, neurotransmitters are released from their sites.

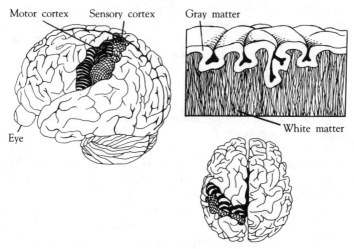

Figure 3.4. The Cortex

neurons may receive unique messages from up to 1000 neighboring neurons and send messages to another 1000. The complexity of communication is further multiplied by the number of different chemical combinations of neurotransmitters in the brain. It has been estimated that the brain may contain up to 200 different neurotransmitters,[3] each potentially carrying a distinct message. Considering that it took Cambridge neuroscientists more than three years to analyze the twenty-three neurons of a simple worm, we can be sure that we are far from understanding these interactions in the human brain. Indeed, the communication possibilities are unfathomable, and analogies to the most powerful computers are naive.

The Cortex

Let's turn from the microscopic to the macroscopic. If you envision a brain you are likely to imagine a rounded, wrinkled, pinkish-gray, gelatinous object. This exterior surface consists of a few millimeters of neuron-dense material called the *cortex* ("bark"), the brain's "thinking cap" (Figure 3.4). Although it is only the surface of the brain, the cortex is especially important for counselors because it is the site of most higher brain functions such as language, concentration, goal-oriented behavior, and other complex, cognitive activities. Anatomically it is prepared for complexity because it is dense with nerve cell bodies. In fact, there are so many of these darker-colored cell bodies that they actually make the cortex look gray compared with the rest of the brain—hence its popular name, "gray matter."

The cortex consists of two symmetrical hemispheres, left and right, which are "wired" contralaterally—that is, neural action in the right hemisphere will affect the left side of the body and vice versa. Therefore, if we have a stroke in the right hemisphere of the brain, the left side of the body will be affected. The hemispheres, however, are not isolated from each other. They are joined below the surface of the cortex by nerve bundles called *commissures*, also called the *corpus callosum* ("tough body")—(Figure 3.5).[4]

In normal brains the cortex is highly convoluted, or wrinkled. It has this irregular surface for a reason: it is the only way to get a lot of cortex into a little space. If the cortex could be removed and flattened, it would be a sheet measuring about two feet by three feet by two millimeters. We can see the difficulty of getting this into an area the size of a human skull. To make it fit, we would have to crumple the sheet into a ball. In the human brain, two-thirds of the cortex is "crumpled" under the surface fissures called *sulci*. The observable surface ridges, or *gyri*, between the fissures account for only a third of the total cortical area. Interestingly, the quantity and depth of these fissures, not the overall brain size, are the most obvious anatomical distinctions between the human and animal brain. In other words, humans have a larger cortex/brain ratio than animals.

There are a few cortical landmarks with which we should become familiar. First, the cortex has been mapped into four symmetrical areas called lobes, with a left and right side for each: the *frontal, parietal, occipital,* and *temporal* lobes (Figure 3.6). Although these divisions are fairly arbitrary and there are few clear boundaries on visual inspection, damage to any of the lobes has predictable and unique behavioral results. To put it simply for now, the frontal lobes mediate motor functioning (muscle movement), language production, and planning and organizing skills; the parietal lobes are particularly involved in tactile sensation; the occipital lobes are a visual area; and the temporal lobes mediate our senses of taste, smell, and hearing.

The frontal lobe includes two well-known areas: the motor strip, and a speech portion sometimes called Broca's area. The motor strip is the back section of the frontal lobe next to the central sulcus. At the risk of oversimplification, envision a somewhat distorted, upside-down man named HAL (H–Head, A–Arm, L–Leg) lying across the motor strip with his leg bent and tucked between the two hemispheres (Figure 3.7, after Goldberg, 1986). HAL is responsible for voluntary muscle movement. If there is some sort of neuronal dysfunction, such as a stroke, in the bottom part of the motor strip, the opposite side of the face will be paralyzed. If the dysfunction is largely at the top of the motor strip, there will probably be a noticeable limp in the opposite-side leg and the affected person will appear to be dragging the leg when walking. The reason HAL is distorted is that some areas of the body, such as the genitals, lips, and face, are more richly innervated and claim a disproportionate number of neurons on the motor strip.

The speech area is just in front of that section of the motor strip that controls the small muscles in the face. As we might guess, damage to this part usually affects a person's ability to articulate and produce language. But the problem is not a paralyzed vocal cord. Affected persons have a general disability in producing language—oral, written, or signed. They can understand language, but have difficulties expressing themselves.

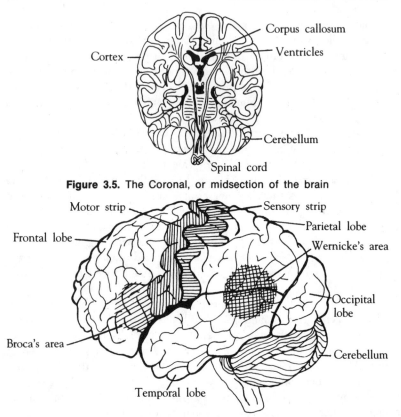

Figure 3.5. The Coronal, or midsection of the brain

Figure 3.6. The Four Lobes of the Brain

This portion is usually only in the left brain hemisphere, and it is often called Broca's area after the Parisian physician Paul Broca. He was one of the first to make the connection between aphasia, or language difficulties, and an anatomical lesion in this area.

The companion to Broca's area is called Wernicke's area. This part mediates the ability to *comprehend* language. It resides at the junction of the occipital, parietal, and temporal lobes.

One other portion that may be helpful to know is the primary tactile area. This area is the front section of the parietal lobe, next to the central sulcus and the motor strip. It roughly corresponds to HAL, but instead of being responsible for voluntary movement, it mediates the sense of touch.

Therefore stimulation in the primary sensory area causes some sort of tactile sensations.

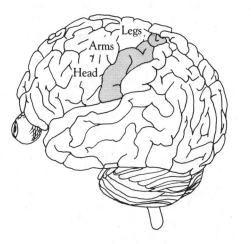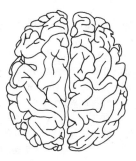

Figure 3.7. The Motor Strip

Subcortical Areas (Brain Stem and Basal Ganglia)

The subcortical area, the brain area under the cortex, is replete with so many labels that memorizing the entire Old Testament would probably be easier (and certainly more profitable) than mastering all the terms connected with it. Also, since the cortex is largely responsible for mediating the higher intellectual functions, the emphasis of this book is more cortical than subcortical. Yet there are certain subcortical landmarks that we need to know in order to understand topics discussed later in this book.

The *thalamus* (marriage bed) is a dense collection of cell bodies that acts as an integrating and relay center for sensory information to the cortex. It is certainly critical in normal brain function, but it is probably better known because it shares its name with a much smaller area called the hypothalamus. The *hypothalamus* ("under the thalamus") is the regulating center for the autonomic nervous system (ANS): it regulates temperature, appetite, thirst, water metabolism, blood sugar levels, growth, sleep, or just about every activity that is accomplished without voluntary control. The hypothalamic nuclei (bundles of neurons) work in concert with the neighboring pituitary gland, which will be discussed with the endocrine system.

The hypothalamus is also part of what has been called the *limbic system*. It was originally named by Broca in 1878, but in 1937 James Papez, a professor at Cornell, suggested that this ring-shaped area is the anatomical substrate for emotion. Although Papez was making little more than an semi-educated guess, he was actually prophetic. This area has since been associated with emotions and emotionally laden problems such as schizophrenia and addiction. There are several vaguely distinguishable structures in the limbic system, such as the *hippocampus* ("sea horse"), *mammillary body* (breast-like structure), *amygdala* ("almond"), *septum*, *fornix* (arch), and *cingulate gyrus*. Knowing this may simply leave you thankful that you didn't specialize in brain anatomy, but there is a great deal of research being done to study the limbic area.

Another subcortical area of interest, also surrounding the thalamus, is the *basal ganglia* (clusters of neurons). This area, in conjunction with the cortex and cerebellum, is largely responsible for controlling movement and muscle activity. We will learn more about the basal ganglia, especially the *substantia nigra*, later on in a discussion of Parkinson's disease—a disease characterized by a marked degeneration in this specific area.

The *cerebellum*, although not technically a subcortical structure, is located under the occipital area but is somewhat isolated from the rest of the brain. It mediates motor activity. Cerebellar dysfunction, often found in long-term alcoholics, can lead to awkwardness in posture as well as difficulties in walking and coordination (ataxia), weakness, and tremors. Recent evidence suggests that the cerebellum is also involed in emotions and memory (Hooper & Teresi, 1986), so it should soon be a focus of active investigation.

Around the base of the brain, specifically the medulla and pons, proceed twelve pairs of *cranial nerves*. These nerves are central to a neurological exam, and you are probably already familiar with some of them. Think of the cranial nerves as similar to those that come out of the spinal cord, but they come out of the base of the brain instead (Figure 3.8). Rather than innervating the body, the cranial nerves are concerned exclusively with sensation and fine muscle movements, especially in the head (Table 3.9).

In addition to the optic and auditory nerves, you may be acquainted

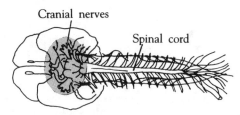

Cranial nerves

Spinal cord

Figure 3.8. Cranial Nerves and the Spinal Cord

with the trigeminal nerve.[5] A section of this nerve is numbed by a dentist before drilling. Facial tics are a result of trigeminal stimulation; and *tic douloureux*, or trigeminal neuralgia, a relatively common complaint, is pain in the area served by this nerve.

The ventricles and meninges. The *ventricles* are a series of fluid-filled cavities and canals that produce and contain cerebrospinal fluid (CSF). For centuries, these fluid compartments were considered to be the source of higher intellectual processes or "the seat of the soul." Today, although the ventricles are still important in normal brain functioning, the cortex is seen to be the anatomical focal point.

The brain has four small ventricles: the two lateral ventricles and the third and fourth ventricles. These small reservoirs filter the blood of white cells, corpuscles, and platelets to produce CSF. They are also involved in a system that nourishes and protects the fragile matter the brain is composed of. The ventricles' ductlike plumbing eventually surrounds the entire central nervous system, brain, and spinal cord in membranes called *meninges*.

The meninges actually consist of three layers that look like a tough skin around the central nervous system (CNS). The outermost layer adheres to the skull and is called the *dura mater*.[6] The innermost layer, not quite as tough as the dura mater, adheres to the glial cells of the brain and is called the *pia mater*. The middle membrane is called the *arachnoid layer*. Between the outer and middle meninges are tiny blood vessels, and between the inner and middle meninges is CSF. We are likely to hear more of this system in connection with problems such as meningitis (inflammation in the meninges), menigioma (tumor in the meningeal layers), and subdural hematoma (bleeding under the dura mater).

Table 3.9. Cranial Nerves and Their Functions

I	Olfactory	Smell
II	Optic	Vision
III	Oculomotor	Eye movement
IV	Trochlear	Eye movement
V	Trigeminal	Feeling in the face, chewing
VI	Abducens	Eye movement
VII	Facial	Taste, salivation, tears, facial movement
VIII	Auditory	Hearing, balance
IX	Glossopharyngeal	Taste, salivation, swallowing
X	Vagus	Swallowing, control of larynx, abdomen
XI	Accessory motor	Movement in head and shoulders
XII	Hypoglossal	Tongue movement

The Autonomic Nervous System

Also in the subcortical region is the initiating center of the autonomic nervous system (ANS). This unified system, as its name suggests, is responsible for most of the automatic functions in the body. It is controlled largely by commands from the hypothalamus, which provides oversight for two functionally and anatomically distinct divisions of the ANS: the *parasympathetic* nervous system (PNS) and the *sympathetic* nervous system (SNS).

The sympathetic division is probably the better known and is of greater interest to counselors. For example, it is especially sensitive to chemicals in psychoactive and street drugs, and it reacts when a person worries or is afraid. The SNS mobilizes the internal organs of the body for emergencies, preparing the body for "fight or flight." The heart races, the lungs expand, the eyes dilate, the mouth feels dry, and mental and metabolic activities are increased. The name itself can reveal much about this system. It is called "sympathetic" because of the old but somewhat accurate belief that it responded to suffering and changes in feelings. That is, when a person experienced intense emotion, the SNS would respond. The name "sympathetic" also applies because the nerves that leave the spinal cord in the same general area tend to respond in unison, or sympathetically. They affect many organs in concert.

Anatomically the SNS leaves the spinal cord in the thoracic (middle) and lumbar (lower) sections, and it sends very short axons to a chain of ganglia (nerve "communities") outside the spinal cord. From there they synapse with postganglionic nerves that affect target organs (Figure 3.10 and Table 3.11). The chemical neurotransmitter in these axons is occasionally acetylcholine, in which case the neurons are called *cholinergic*; otherwise the neurotransmitter is norepinephrine (noradrenaline) and the neurons are called *adrenergic*. You may recognize these terms because many psychoactive drugs and their side effects are called adrenergic, cholinergic, anticholinergic, and sympathomimetic. All these indicate that a drug affects the SNS in a particular way.

The parasympathetic nervous system (PNS) is constantly sparring with the sympathetic system. While the SNS mobilizes, the PNS wants to conserve energy, carry out daily "housekeeping," and maintain internal calm. It too can respond to emotions or drugs. PNS stimulation results in a slowed heartbeat, salivation (e.g., eating, drooling during sleep), decreased breathing rate, and an active digestion system. Since PNS responses generally cause less wear and tear on the body, relaxation techniques—intended to activate the PNS—are increasingly popular medical recommendations.

The parasympathetic system innervates target organs by way of axons that leave the spinal column both above and below those of the SNS—thus, "para" ("beside, alongside of") sympathetic. These axons proceed to ganglia that are next to the target organs, rather than next to the spinal cord; their predominant neurotransmitter, acetylcholine, makes it a *cholinergic* system. In chapter 7 we will consider anticholinergic drugs, which inhibit the parasympathetic system, giving the sympathetic system more opportunity to exert itself. Anticholinergic side effects include dry mouth, blurry vision, and constipation.

It is noteworthy that there has recently been renewed interest in using our understanding of the ANS to detect drug abuse. As Table 3.11 indicates, the pupils tend to be very sensitive to PNS or SNS stimulation. When the PNS is stimulated, the pupil will contract; when the SNS is stimulated, the pupils will dilate considerably. This point is useful because most psychoactive drugs, licit and illicit, will effect neurotransmitters in the ANS and thus have some effect on pupil size. Barbiturates, sedatives, and other drugs that have a calming effect will constrict the pupils. Amphetamines, cocaine, and other stimulant-type drugs will dilate the pupils. At present there are kits available that specify how to observe these changes.[7]

The Body
The brain is not the only organ in the body of interest to counselors. Although the brain is the organ that ultimately affects behavior, many

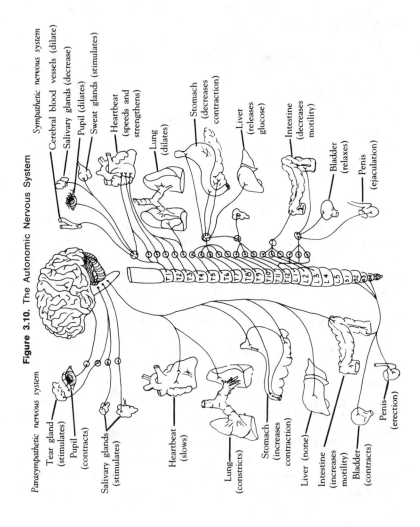

Figure 3.10. The Autonomic Nervous System

Parasympathetic nervous system

Tear gland (stimulates)
Pupil (contracts)
Salivary glands (stimulates)
Heartbeat (slows)
Lung (constricts)
Stomach (increases contraction)
Liver (none)
Intestine (increases motility)
Bladder (contracts)
Penis (erection)

Sympathetic nervous system

Cerebral blood vessels (dilate)
Salivary glands (decrease)
Pupil (dilates)
Sweat glands (stimulates)
Heartbeat (speeds and strengthens)
Lung (dilates)
Stomach (decreases contraction)
Liver (releases glucose)
Intestine (decreases motility)
Bladder (relaxes)
Penis (ejaculation)

Table 3.11. Functions of the Sympathetic
and Parasympathetic Nervous Systems

Organ	Effect of sympathetic stimulation (A)	Effect of parasympathetic stimulation (B)
Pupil	Dilated	Contracted
Sweat glands	Open	None
Tear glands	Constricted	Stimulated
Salivary glands	Constricted	Stimulated
Heart	Increased rate	Slowed rate
	Increased force of beat	Decreased atrial force
Lungs	Dilated	Constricted
Liver	Glucose released	None
Gastrointestinal tract	Inhibited	Motility and secretion stimulated
Kidney (bladder)	Decreased output	Contracted
Penis	Ejaculation	Erection
Basal metabolism	Increased	None
Mental activity	Increased	None
Adrenal cortex secretion	Increased	None

other organ systems in the body can influence the brain by changing the chemical composition of the blood. Let us look at a rudimentary review of some of the more common offenders.

The Endocrine Glands

The central nervous system (CNS) is one of two major control systems in the body, the other being the endocrine system (Table 3.12). This system, which is highly interdependent with the CNS and can equally affect psychological functioning, consists of a series of glands that, rather than communicating electrochemically, secrete hormones into the bloodstream. These glands are scattered throughout the body and include the thyroid, the adrenals, the pancreas, and the gonads, or sex glands (testes and ovaries). Of the endocrine system's ten glands, at least three are especially important to counselors.

The adrenal glands are located above the kidneys. The adrenal cortex secretes steroids such as aldosterone, cortisol, and corticosterone. The adrenal medulla secretes epinephrine (also called adrenaline) and norepinephrine (noradrenaline). You may recall that epinephrine and norepinephrine are active neurotransmitters in the sympathetic nervous system. Therefore stimulation of the adrenal medulla will more or less strengthen an SNS response. Its unique contribution is that while the sympathetic *neuronal* stimulation of target organs will have an immediate

Table 3.12. Endocrine Functions

Gland (location)	Hormone	Effect
Posterior pituitary (brain)	Antidiuretic	Controls rate of water excretion
	Oxytocin	Milk production
Anterior pituitary (brain)	Growth	Stimulates growth
	Thyroptropin	Stimulates thyroxin
	Corticotropin	Metabolism of glucose, protein, and fat
	Follicle-stimulating Luteinizing	Development of egg or sperm
	Luteotropic	Growth of gonads
Thyroid (neck)	Thyroxin	Metabolic rate (hyperthyroid [Graves' disease] and hypothyroidism [myxedema])
Parathyroid (neck)	Parathormone	Increases blood calcium
Pancreas (gut)	Insulin	Promotes glucose absorption (diabetes, hypoglycemia)
	Glucagon	Increases glucose production
Adrenal medulla (above kidneys)	Epinephrine Norepinephrine	Stimulates SNS (Cushing's disease)
Adrenal cortex (above kidneys)	Aldosterone Cortisol Corticosterone	Sodium retention, potassium loss, glycogen production in liver
Gonads	Androgen (m) Estrogen (f)	Sex characteristics and sexual arousal

effect (such as one's drawing in breath when surprised or frightened), the adrenal medulla release of hormones will have a less immediate but more prolonged response.

The pituitary gland, especially its anterior portion, is runner-up to the hypothalamus for the title "most influential." The pituitary is the only endocrine gland located in the central nervous system, and it is actually connected to the hypothalamus. It releases a host of hormones, but it is most influential in regulating the output of the adrenal cortex, the thyroid, and the gonads.

The thyroid is another endocrine gland that exerts a general influence on body metabolism through its hormone, thyroxin. It is not uncommon to find hyperthyroidism (toxic goiter, thyrotoxicosis, or Graves' disease) misdiagnosed as anxiety, or hypothyroidism as depression and psychosis.

The Lungs

Although the brain accounts for only 2 percent of overall body weight, it is oxygen-hungry and receives about 30 percent of the oxygen-rich blood leaving the heart. This means that the lungs must be working adequately for proper brain functioning. Any form of oxygen deprivation, or hypoxia, may have psychological consequences. Known culprits include asthma, pneumonia, emphysema, blood clots in the lungs, high altitudes, and general anesthesia. Furthermore, respiratory drugs, both prescription and over the counter, have also been known to mimic counseling or psychiatric problems (Hall et al., 1985).

The Heart

Heart problems are often unrecognized causes of psychological changes. Some of the known diseases that can affect intellect and emotions are heart failure, atrial tachycardia (fast heartbeat), and heart valve disease. *Heart failure* is a general term used when the heart fails to pump blood at a rate commensurate with the body's needs. *Congestive heart failure* is a type that is usually a consequence of the heart's being deficient at moving blood that is "heavy" with excess salt and water. These problems have been known to cause confusion, depression, and decreased memory and concentration, especially in older people.

Sudden episodes of rapid heartbeats (paroxysmal atrial tachycardia) and heart valve dysfunctions such as mitral valve prolapse and atrial or mitral valve stenosis have provoked anxiety and other emotional changes.

> After the death of her husband, a fifty-four-year-old woman became anxious and filled with a sense of guilt. At times, her heart would feel like it was beating rapidly and she would become particularly tense and fearful. With some prodding by family members, she agreed to see a psychiatrist. The psychiatrist noticed the woman's swollen ankles and heard her concern about heart palpitations. After some investigation, she was diagnosed as having mitral valve stenosis. She underwent corrective surgery and subsequently had no further attacks of anxiety, sense of guilt, or excessive fears. (Schulman, 1977)

A growing body of evidence suggests that some people who undergo major surgery, especially heart bypass surgery, experience surgically related intellectual or emotional changes. The actual cause of these changes is unclear.

The Kidneys and Liver

The kidneys and liver play key roles in detoxifying the body of ingested toxins such as alcohol and drugs and of chemicals found in the body such as hormones.[8] Chronic disease in these organs affects brain function and can have effects ranging from moodiness to coma or death. Common liver diseases include hepatitis, cirrhosis (especially from alcoholism), and liver cancer.

Notes

1. The blood brain barrier makes the brain selectively permeable to certain chemicals. Therefore it protects the brain from rapid changes in the chemicals of the blood that might accompany eating, stress, or drug intake.

2. *Synapse* was coined by a famous British brain scientist, Sir Charles Sherrington. It means "to clasp tightly." The name was given before electron microscopes indicated the presence of a small gap between neurons.

3. Some of the thirty or so known neurotransmitters are acetylcholine, dopamine, GABA, noradrenaline, histamine, and peptides.

4. Technically the corpus callosum is the largest of the nerve fiber collections that, as a whole, are referred to as the cerebral commissures (Bogen, 1985).

5. The trigeminal nerve has three branches. The ophthalmic affects sensation in the eye, tear glands, nose, and forehead; the maxillary affects the cheeks, upper teeth and gums, and lower eyelids; and the mandibular affects most of the lower jaw.

6. Anthony Smith (1984) indicates that "dura" accurately denotes toughness, and "mater" apparently goes back to the Arab belief that the meninges gave rise to all other membranes in the body—thus it was maternal.

7. For example, Veract, Inc., 338 South Glendora Avenue, West Covina, CA 91790.

8. The kidney is also involved in maintaining the proper concentrations of certain chemicals called *electrolytes*. These electrically charged ions are indispensable to normal body and brain functioning. They include sodium (hypo- and hypernatremia), potassium (hyper- and hypokalemia), calcium, and hydrogen, which determines pH levels (acidosis and alkalosis).

4

The Brain and Behavior

Having surveyed basic features of anatomy and physiology, we move on to a subject with more immediate and very important counseling implications. This is the field of neuropsychology. As the name suggests, it deals with the relationship between brain dysfunction and associated behavioral, intellectual, and emotional changes (see appendix A). There are several reasons why it is important to understand the brain-behavior relationship.

First, this knowledge will help us develop the neglected biblical category of *asthenia,* or "weakness." For most pastors and counselors, this category is nearly vacant. As a result, intellectual or emotional idiosyncrasies are ignored, people are misunderstood, and symptoms of brain impairment can be confused with sin. This section provides an explanation of asthenia and offers examples of asthenic disorders such as inattention, problems of ordering in sequence, and difficulty understanding language.

> People in the church never sit down [with people having chronic diseases, especially those that can affect the brain] and say, "What is it like?" People must be more willing to understand and accept those who are different. It seems like everyone must be a success—or conform. I think we have to be careful not to use worldly judgments (A patient).

Second, brain problems might initially emerge as changes in personality, intellect, or emotions and not as traditional medical symptoms such as nausea, vomiting, and other physical phenomena. As a result, affected persons may seek the help of pastors and counselors rather than physicians. Knowledgeable counselors are able to detect physical, potentially life-threatening problems and make referrals to appropriate physicians.

Third, brain injury and disease have predictable behavioral corre-lates. That is, if we know the degree of brain damage a person has suffered, we can estimate the social, familial, and vocational repercus-sions of the injury. For example, if someone experiences a coma for more than a week, there will be fairly predictable and persistent counseling problems. If we are aware of these problems, we can accurately and effectively counsel both the affected person and the family.

Very few families are warned about the cognitive changes that accompany brain damage. Most medical practice is concerned with physical functioning, so when patients are physically stable they are pronounced cured. Unfortunately, many families wrongly surmise that physical healing includes similar healing of cognitive functions, including the emotions and intellect. This is simply not the case. With severe brain injury there may be almost immediate physical well-being, but also persistent changes in personality and intellect that can have devastating consequences.

General Brain Dysfunction

We will review the behaviors associated with specific parts of the brain, but first we should consider some characteristic changes that accompany any and all diffuse brain dysfunction. These will be particularly applicable to moderate and severe dementia, head injuries from car accidents, and major strokes—brain injuries that affect the entire brain rather than one portion. As we study the symptoms, we should consider how they can be confused with sin and also provide fertile soil for sinful reactions.

There are several problems associated with diffuse brain disorders.

Poor Self-regulation and Self-control

The greatest handicap associated with moderate to severe brain injury is the difficulties with self-regulation or self-control.[1] Not to be confused with the fruit of the Spirit (Gal 5:22ff.), this kind of self-control is a decreased ability to control certain emotions, avoid distractions, think before acting, follow through on a complex plan or set of directions, or remain physically still. People may turn from elation to tears with no apparent provocation. They may begin a task, only to be immediately sidetracked by something irrelevant. There is a certain childish immaturity in their behavior that is not necessarily morally wrong; we expect it in children, but we are frustrated by it in adults, especially if they were able to "control themselves" prior to receiving the brain injury.

I recently witnessed an example of this lack of control. An elaborate surprise party was planned for a pastor's fortieth birthday and scheduled for a Sunday evening. After the morning service that very day, a church member who had a moderate brain injury due to a car accident told the pastor on the way out of church, "See you at your birthday party tonight, pastor." The brain-injured person knew it was a surprise, but it was as if he could not keep the information from coming out of his mouth. This is admittedly a mundane example. But multiply situations like this, and we understand why families can be left in pieces emotionally.

Impulsiveness is the key word. Emotionally it can look like childishness, moodiness, emotional lability (rapid emotional fluctuations), or depression. Cognitively and behaviorally, it can take the appearance of poor judgment, inattentiveness, or difficulty learning new behaviors, especially more complex ones (Bond, 1984; Lezak, 1978). When coupled with sin, impulsiveness can look like impatience, irritability, or anger.

> At age twenty-seven, a young man had a bad fall at work that resulted in fractured frontal bones and subsequent infections and abscesses. Seven years later he continued to experience the consequences. At one time a thoughtful, stable man interested in his family, now he was talkative, restless, and grossly uninhibited. His wife divorced him because of his general irresponsibility and preoccupation with pornography. He spent his settlement money in a matter of months. He seemed unconcerned about his difficulties. (Lishman, 1973)

Poor Concentration

Problems with self-regulation also impair attention, concentration, and the ability to track conversations. Brain-damaged people struggle with controlling what they emit and also have difficulties focusing on data that come to them. With less control over the mass of information they constantly encounter, life may be characterized by randomness and chaos. There is a continuous competition involving unrelated ideas, noises, conversations, and sights. It may be almost impossible for an affected person to concentrate on one task, because meaningless stimuli or ideas continually distract. In the middle of a serious conversation a brain-injured person may laugh at a joke—heard the day before—or may be repeatedly sidetracked by the noise of an air conditioner. Concentrating on a twenty-to-forty-minute sermon cannot even be imagined.

Lack of Self-awareness

Another bothersome result of brain damage is a general lack of self-awareness. Brain-impaired adults often seem unaware of their deficits. If they are aware, they seem to be unable to use the information in daily living (Lezak, 1986). While they may acknowledge certain problems, an awareness of these limitations does not inform their day-to-day decision making. For example, a young man may realize that he tends to lose his way to previously familiar places, but at the next opportunity he will get into the car with total assurance that he will be able to arrive independently at any destination he chooses—only to find that he is hopelessly lost and must call home long-distance-collect.

> A forty-five-year-old man was involved in a head-on automobile accident that resuted in total blindness and significant frontal lobe damage. Upon recovery, his only apparent problem was the blindness; otherwise, he was alert and physically healthy. Yet his awareness of his blindness fluctuated. Sometimes he would deny any visual problems; other times he admitted he was blind. However, although admitting blindness, he explicitly stated that with proper light or different circumstances he would be able to see perfectly. He could accept that his statements were incongruous, but he either would not or could not use such information to alter his conviction about blindness. (Stuss & Benson, 1986)

Poor Generalization

An unusual and frustrating learning problem related to poor self-awareness is the impaired ability to move from the specific to the general, from the concrete to the abstract. This may sound like a strictly academic issue, but it has a profound impact on all areas of life.

Suppose you are a counselor who is working with a brain-injured man because he is struggling with outbursts of anger at home. After the man understands the biblical roots of his anger, it is time for him to "put on" a new way of handling the frustrating situation. Perhaps, realizing that the process of change is laborious, you wisely offer to practice role-playing with the man during the counseling session. Afterward, both of you are persuaded that domestic change is sure to follow—after all, he grasped the concept in your office and he reports to being highly motivated to change. But to your surprise, at his next session the man reports that there was absolutely no change. He reports that frequently he was sinfully angry with his family. Now what?

A problem like this can have a variety of causes. One cause that is often overlooked is that the person may have trouble translating a behavior learned in a counseling office into the home: that is, taking a *specific* behavior learned in one context and *generalizing* it into other contexts. As counselors we may actually have to go to the home and walk through a biblical response—perhaps quite a few times—before the change enters the client's repertoire.

We are continually learning specifics that must be generalized. Specific information is assimilated into a larger category and used in novel situations. We take this ability for granted. If we learn how to make one bed, we can make any; if we learn social etiquette with a sibling, we can be socially appropriate with a stranger. But the brain-impaired may have trouble with this unconscious generalizing process that is a part of all learning. Their world may consist of pieces of datum that are difficult to abstract into an integrated and meaningful whole.[2]

Social Ineptitude

As a result of all these difficulties, brain injury is often equated with social ineptitude. Old friends quickly become impatient and may fade away. Divorce is commonplace. Spiritual growth and patience are usually found only in families that are able to sort out the brain weakness from the sinful behavior.

Specific Brain Areas

These "generic" problems associated with diffuse brain injuries can be sorted out into more specific cognitive changes associated with certain portions of the brain.

The Frontal Lobes

Occupying 30 to 40 percent of the surface of the brain, the frontal lobes are usually subdivided into four areas: the motor, premotor, and prefrontal cortices and Broca's area.

Opposite-side weakness. The motor area is fairly well understood (remember HAL?). It sends neurons without interruption to the spinal cord and thence to the muscles. Disruption in the motor strip produces weakness or paralysis in the opposite, or contralateral, side of the body. That is, disruption in the right motor strip will affect movement on the left side of the body and vice versa.

Poor coordination. The premotor area, directly in front of the motor strip, is more complex because of its greater communication with other parts of the brain. Whereas the motor area nerves go immediately to the spinal column without interruption (and thus have less input from neighboring cells), the premotor area communicates with many subcortical brain areas (e.g., basal ganglia, thalamus, brainstem reticular formation) before entering the spinal cord to affect body movements. As a result, disruption in this area tends to affect the integration and refinement of movement.

The consequences of Parkinson's disease illustrate a disruption of the premotor pathway. Affected persons are not paralyzed, but their movements are slow, tremulous, and uncoordinated.

Broca's aphasia. Broca's area mediates language function. In 1861, Paul Broca popularized the idea of a connection between an anatomical problem in this area and a disruption in language function. In a presentation to the Society of Anthropology in Paris, he introduced a patient whom he called "Tan." Tan was an old man who had suffered a stroke that affected the right side of his body (left brain hemisphere), and his vocabulary was so impaired that it was limited to one word: *tan*. Soon Tan died, and an autopsy revealed damage in the left frontal lobe. This association paved the way for an entirely new way to think about brain function. Prior to Broca's discovery, it was almost unthinkable to locate a "spiritual" function such as language in the brain.

Broca's area is typically either in the left or right hemisphere—not both—and its precise location is in front of the head and face area of the motor strip. In more than 90 percent of humans, Broca's area is located in the left hemisphere, where it is part of a package that includes preferences for hand, eye, and foot. That is, if you are right-handed you are likely to be right-footed, have a preference for your right eye, and have language mediated by your left hemisphere (remember contralateral circuitry). The relationship is not perfect, however. Ninety-six percent of right-handers and 70 percent of left-handers have language mediated by the left hemisphere. Of the other left-handers, half are right-hemisphere-dominant for language and half have language function in both hemispheres.[3]

Disruption in Broca's area produces Broca's aphasia, also called expressive, nonfluent, or motor aphasia. In simple terms, it means an impairment in the ability to understand written or spoken language. More specifically, it is characterized by (1) a difficulty or inability to communicate effectively—usually there are only a few, often stereotyped or repetitive verbal responses, (2) writing that is usually as impaired as speech, and (3) intact ability to comprehend.

The degree of aphasia may vary from mild or partial, in which the patient occasionally uses the wrong word, to severe, in which the patient is unable to utter a single syllable. When aphasia is severe, as it is after some strokes, then other brain functions are certainly affected. If the impaired area extends back to the parietal lobe, it may result in a global aphasia in which patients can neither speak nor understand.

Consider the following examples of fairly severe Broca's aphasia. Mrs. Smith, sixty-eight years old, had recently been admitted to a hospital with a diagnosis of a left hemisphere stroke (cerebral vascular accident).

"How are you doing Mrs. Smith?"

"And one, uh-uh, todaaay. Uh!"

"I wanted to come visit you and pray with you. It seems as if you are having a difficult time with your speech."

"Uh, one, yes yes." (Note the repetition of certain words.)

J. M. was a twenty-one-year-old soldier who was wounded nine months before the interview. He had a severe right-sided paralysis consistent with left hemisphere damage. As part of the examination he was asked to tell a story about a picture that shows a "cookie theft."

"What did you do before you went to Vietnam?"

"Forces."

"You were in the army?"

"Special forces." (Poor articulation.)

"What did you do?"

"Boom!"

"I don't understand."

"'Splosions."

(Further questioning by examiner.)

"Me . . . one guy."

"Were you alone when you were injured?"

"Recon . . . scout."

"What happened?"

"Mortar."

(On presentation of the "cookie theft" picture for description.)

"Cookie jar . . . fall over . . . chair . . . water . . . empty . . . ov . . . ov . . ."

"Overflow?"

"Yeah." (Goodglass & Kaplan, 1983, p. 76)

It is important to realize that if the dysfunction is limited to the left motor strip and Broca's area, the person, while verbally impaired, probably has relatively normal comprehension. So while we cannot dialogue easily, we can speak to and encourage the patient. In fact, the more feedback we can give the person, the better. Aphasics tend to be uncertain of themselves and are quite shaken by what happened. They are usually hungry for encouragement and commendation. And since their memory may be impaired, they need encouragement as often as possible—and then they need it repeated again.

The most fascinating area of the frontal lobes is the prefrontal cortex. This is the area that has achieved notoriety through the accounts of Phineas Gage and prefrontal lobotomies. Phineas Gage was a nineteenth-century construction worker who was injured in an explosion when a four-foot-by-one-inch round bar penetrated his prefrontal area. After a period of physical recovery, this congenial man with a fine work record was said to have the "animal passions of a man, yet the mind [maturity rather than intellect] of a child." He soon became a pivotal case study in the relationship between the prefrontal area and behavior.

Prefrontal lobotomies, developed in 1936 by the Portuguese neurologist Egaz Moniz, further advanced our understanding of the prefrontal area. These surgeries often left agitated patients more docile, and many patients subsequently demonstrated unusual personality changes.[4]

Several behaviors tend to be characteristic of people with prefrontal dysfunction, although many of them overlap with the symptoms of general brain dysfunction. This is a result of the size of the frontal lobe. If a person has damage to all the brain, the frontal lobe will probably contribute the most because of its prominence. Also, in some brain damage, such as from head injuries, the brutal impact seems to be focused on the frontal lobes.

Planning and goal-directed behavior. The ability to move toward a goal—to make choices—almost defines humanness. Yet this critical capacity is disrupted in prefrontal lobe dysfunction. The prefrontal area is vitally interconnected with virtually every other brain area and tends to have an executive, organizing function. Thus disruption affects the capacity to move toward a goal. Although frontal lobe patients can articulate goals and make plans, they have varying degrees of success in actually moving toward those goals.

The following conditions contribute to the weakening of goal-directed behavior:

Inflexibility and perseveration. I once saw a first grader's arithmetic test in which the first problem was "5 + 3." The boy answered correctly "8." The second problem was "3 + 4," but again the boy answered "8." For the remaining ten problems the boy continued to go with his lucky number 8. This is most likely an example of mental inflexibility or perseveration ("persevering" on the same response). It is not uncommon with children, but it can be a sign of brain problems in adults.

Consider the game "Simon says." The person who is "it" gives various commands to the participants that are to be obeyed only if they are preceded by the phrase "Simon says." If the leader gives a command that is not preceded by "Simon says" and a participant follows the command, that person is out of the game. The reason we all eventually lose in a fast-paced round of "Simon says" is because we perseverate. The leader of the game takes advantage of the fact that we all get into cognitive ruts. This is normal. The mental inflexibility and inability of brain-injured people to stop some behaviors is only quantitatively different than our own. This, however, is enough to make it very difficult for them to change. They often exasperate a family as they appear stuck, unteachable, rebellious, "passive-aggressive," and unwilling to learn from mistakes. Yet the real problem may lie at the level of "weakness" rather than sin. Their behavior may call for patience and concrete, creative teaching rather than rebuke.

A test that is often used to determine perseveration is called the Wisconsin Card Sorting Test. This test consists of a series of cards that can be sorted in three different ways: (1) according to the number of geometric objects they contain, (2) according to the color of the geometric objects, or (3) according to their shape (circle, triangle, square). The examiner asks the person taking the test to categorize the objects, and the person will sort in one of the three ways. After the person has a categorizing routine, the examiner will "change the rules" and indicate that the examinee is "incorrect" and must change the category. Non-impaired persons can do this almost immediately. Persons with frontal lobe damage, however, can virtually go on endlessly and never switch categories in spite of constant reiteration that the present strategy is "incorrect."

When we translate this into the real world of social relationships, the problem can obviously be very frustrating. Affected people often seem to emit behaviors that are permanently programmed into their repertoire.

Poor self-awareness. Cognitive inflexibility overlaps with a general lack of awareness that injured persons exhibit toward their deficiencies. Many brain-altered patients don't understand the extent to which they have changed! They might be unable to shift perspectives and see themselves as brain-injured, or if they are aware of the problems, they may be unable to anticipate how these problems could interfere with daily life. As a result, the people can be indifferent or apparently unconcerned, even in the face of paralysis or significant pain. They may even deny any problems outright.

Most of this disordered awareness is directly related to the brain changes, but some of it is related more to character or spiritual issues. Distinguishing between the two is not always easy. As a general rule, clear violation of biblical principles can always be addressed, but only when the brain-injured person can be confronted with (and understand) very concrete examples of sinful behavior. Behaviors that are bothersome but not necessarily sinful can also be addressed. Here again, it is best done with specific illustrations of the behavior and specific recommendations on what behavior would be more appropriate. In many of these situations, it might be easier for the family to implement some creative changes rather than expect significant behavioral changes by the brain-injured person.

Whatever the cause of indifference or denial, these symptoms are common in frontally impaired people, and they can make counseling and rehabilitation extremely difficult (Stuss & Benson, 1986). After all, if people don't think there is a problem, they have no reason to change.

Not surprisingly, indifference, lack of awareness, and denial are the most frequent complaints cited by families of brain-injured persons. *Problems with sequencing and ordering.* If I were to cut out the individual frames of a simple comic strip, rearrange their order, and ask you to assemble the strip correctly, you would probably perform the task effortlessly. For people with prefrontal problems, however, the task may be arduous or impossible. Their approach to the problem may be random without any particular strategy. Sometimes they will not change the order of the scenes at all and instead develop a very private explanation (one that makes sense to only themselves) as to why the present order is the correct one. Practically, this means that a person may articulate a certain goal but never get past an initial, small step toward its completion.

To confuse the issue, brain-injured persons may accomplish relatively simple tasks or tasks that were easily mastered before the brain damage, and onlookers then overestimate their organizational abilities. In the face of slightly more complex or unfamiliar jobs, sequencing problems become more apparent. The resulting ineptitude is then sometimes misinterpreted as laziness and leaves family, friends, or employers bewildered or angry.

A slight variation on this theme is the inadequate visual search and scanning strategies of persons with frontal lobe damage. For example, when asked to look at a picture and explain it, brain-damaged people will give an impression based on the first visual fixation. There will be no plan for viewing the entire scene, and many significant features will be ignored (impulsiveness). Creative researchers have compared the difference in eye movements of brain-injured and neurologically normal adults in this activity. The researchers found that compared with "normal" adults, the eye movements of frontal lobe patients were haphazard. Affected people just seem unable to generate specific plans to help them understand themselves or the world around them.

Decreased motor behavior. Recent studies suggest that prefrontal patients generate less behavior internally. They seem less active, without spontaneity or initiative, and are in constant need of direction and prodding.

The patient no longer carries out the necessary daily activities of life, such as getting out of bed in the morning, washing or dressing himself, or even urinating or defecating in the toilet. . . . The actual ability to carry out the various activities of daily living is not impaired. . . . *What is impaired is the ability to initiate spontaneously a desired or an automatic motor task.* (Hecaen & Albert, 1975, p. 139, italics added)

Affected people seem lazy, uncaring, and selfish, but the real problem may be more physical than moral. Usually, when given very specific directions, persons will respond. But this too can be most frustrating. It is almost like parents' hovering over children to get them to clean up their rooms. In situations such as these, it often seems easier to skirt around the brain-injured and take over their tasks. This, however, is rarely the best route. A better approach might be to give the brain-injured person smaller jobs that can be done daily.

Some brain researchers have commented how this decreased motor output looks like a *dissociation between knowing and doing* (Stuss & Benson, 1984), and indeed, their observations are corroborated by the experiences of many families. Patients may "recognize" their errors and understand the feedback of others, but they frequently do not modify their behavior accordingly (Luria, 1973; Konow & Pribram, 1970). To compound their lack of initiative, they seem to lack a self-critical capacity and seem indifferent to their mistakes.

Patience, imposing a predictable schedule, and specific, action-oriented rather than conceptual instruction are some of the ways to circumvent these problems. But even in the best of situations, these difficulties take their toll on families.

Inattention. Disturbances of attention are commonplace after prefrontal dysfunction. Indeed, difficulties attending to important parts of the environment may underlie many prefrontal problems. Though alert, affected persons may be unable to direct effort and concentrate on a specific task. Rather, important tasks are in constant competition with irrelevant stimuli. For example, instead of focusing on the meaning of a statement or question, brain-injured persons may be focusing on outside noises, a speaker's irrelevant body movements, "umms" and "uhs," or the color of the speaker's eyebrows. Thus, brain-injured people may go to the garage to do a specific task, but three hours later the task is untouched. The family is dumbfounded as to how the person spent all that time in the garage with nothing to show for it.

Common-sense assistance might include keeping statements and questions brief, asking them to do one thing at a time, keeping conversation areas relatively quiet and free from distractions such as other conversations or TV. Also, ask questions. Find out if they understand what they were supposed to do. If it is not too frustrating for them, have them repeat your comments along with a specific plan to carry them out. Some children have benefited from having pictures posted of the task they must accomplish and the steps that break down the task into smaller units. Children can then follow the illustrated step-by-step directions and accomplish an otherwise complex and previously undoable job (such as making a bed). Similar creative procedures can also be used with adults.

The "frontal lobe personality." A number of studies and case illustrations have indicated that for families and friends, one of most problematic long-term effects of frontal lobe injury is personality change. By this observers mean that frontal lobe injuries are followed by unusual changes in individual styles. Affected persons just seem different, not like themselves.

From a biblical perspective, "frontal lobe personality" is a bit ambiguous because what we call "personality" is really a combination of the physical and spiritual. The spiritual (heart) qualities of personality consist of moral conduct and character while the more "hard-wired" or physical aspects include intellectual strength and weakness. Furthermore, these dual aspects indicate that there must be two types of "treatment." Changes of the heart are more dependent on faith than normal brain functioning. This being so, pastors, counselors, and families can be hopeful of change, and they can be instruments of change as they proclaim Christ and encourage the brain-altered person in trust and obedience. Physical changes, by contrast, are best treated by new rehabilitation procedures, time, and patience. With this distinction in mind, some of the behaviors described below that are consistent with "acts of the sinful nature" are not necessarily as incorrigible as some might think (unless there is hardness of heart).

Two different personality patterns tend to emerge from the research literature. Both patterns can have a profound effect on spouses and families and are signals for more active pastoral and counseling care.

Apathetic and indifferent. Blumer and Benson (1975) refer to one group as pseudo-depressed. They appear depressed in that they are slow and without initiative or drive. These persons also demonstrate shallow emotional responses, lack of insight, behavior that is socially appropriate but automatic, placid compliance, and an inability to anticipate or plan ahead. Blumer and Benson describe a person who demonstrated automatic behavior and placid compliance to the point that, although he was able to perform sexually, he could do so only when his wife issued step-by-step instructions! *Puerile, euphoric, and indifferent.* This group can best be illustrated by the post-traumatic personality of Phineas Gage.

> The equilibrium or balance, so to speak, between his intellectual faculties and animal propensities seems to have been destroyed. He is fitful, irreverent, indulging at times in the grossest profanity, manifesting but little deference for his fellows, impatient of restraint and advice when it conflicts with his desires, at times pertinaciously obstinate, yet capricious and vacillating, devising many plans of operation, which are no sooner arranged than they are abandoned in turn for others appearing more feasible. (Blumer & Benson, 1975, p.153)

Those who demonstrate these symptoms are often polite and friendly, and on first acquaintance they seem fine. Closer inspection, however, usually reveals a host of difficulties, especially for the families. They may want to lie in bed all day, indulge in childish pranks, and if they are men, talk incessantly about women and sexual relationships. They are notorious for being easily influenced to do wrong, but not right. And they seem unconcerned about the problems they create. Certainly they can be a nightmare for families.

Parietal Lobes

The parietal lobes produce a motley array of symptoms: problems with comprehension, unusual tactile sensations, and a loose cluster of symptoms that result from problems integrating tactile, auditory, and visual data. Anatomical problems toward the front of the parietal lobe tend to affect touch and tactile sensations; lesions in the back, closer to the parietal-occipital-temporal lobe junction, tend to produce the more complex phenomena.[5]

Wernicke's (receptive, fluent) aphasia. In 1874 the German physician Carl Wernicke discovered an area in the parietal-temporal region that was critical to speech. Disruption in this area produced an aphasia that was in many ways the flip side of Broca's or expressive aphasia. As noted earlier, Broca's aphasia is characterized by normal comprehension of the written and spoken word but difficulties *producing* language. Wernicke's aphasia, however, is characterized by poor comprehension (reception) of written or spoken language but clear word production. These aphasics often produce words that are inappropriate, incorrect, made-up, disconnected, or meaningless—a veritable "word salad"—not unlike some of the writing in Lewis Carroll's *Alice in Wonderland:*

> 'Twas brillig, and the slithy toves
> Did gyre and gimble in the wabe;
> All mimsy were the borogroves,
> And the mome raths outgrabe. . . .

Furthermore, affected persons rarely perceive the nature of their own deficits.

An analogy might be helpful. In Broca's aphasia it is as if a competent secretary is typing on a broken machine. In Wernicke's aphasia, the machine is fine but the secretary incompetent (Ajax, 1973).

Consider the following transcript of a fifty-six-year-old man who had a left hemisphere stroke that left him with a right-sided paralysis. In this examination, performed nine months after the stroke, his physical problems were gone but his aphasia persisted. He was asked to describe a picture. There are no typographical errors in the transcript that follows.

Well this is . . . mother is away here working her work outo' here to get her better, but when she's looking, the two boys looking in the other part. One their small tile into her time here. She's working another time because she's getting too. So the two boys work together an' one is sneakin' around here, making his . . . work an' his further funnas his time he had. He an' the other fellow were running around the work here, while mother another time she was doing that without everything wrong here. It isn't right, because she's making a time here of work here, letting mother getting all wet here about something. The kids aren't right here because they just say one here and one here—that's all right, although the fellow here is breakin' between the two of them, they're coming around too. (Goodglass & Kaplan, 1983, pp. 81–82)

Curiously, those with left hemisphere disruption can sometimes comprehend emotional *intonation*, even though they do not understand the written and spoken word. As such, they can "fake it" in some conversations because they may be aided by emotional cues. Also, they may be a good judge of character because they tend to be more proficient at reading body language and recognizing sincerity. However, if the aphasia is severe, traditional counseling is nearly impossible. Affected people may understand your concern but not your language. In these most extreme cases, people remain responsible for wrong behavior (not eccentric or unusual behavior), but they are unlikely to hear and understand the gospel. Yet, since it is always difficult to know exactly what a person is able to understand, when in doubt encourage them—in the most simple of language—with the love of Jesus. When the injury is in the right hemisphere, difficulty with language comprehension may be spared. Affected persons may have adequate comprehension. However, they often have difficulty perceiving emotional expression in faces and language. Therefore, family members may have to rely on words themselves to convey meaning rather than tone of voice.

Disorders of body awareness. Perhaps the best known of the parietal disorders is unilateral (one-sided) neglect. Persons with unilateral neglect live as though half their bodies and visual space simply do not exist. Usually the neglected side will be the left, denoting a lesion in the right hemisphere of the brain; occasionally it will be the right. Affected persons will eat food on the right side of the plate, comb the right side of their hair and leave the left side unkempt, shave only the right side of their face, and put makeup on only one side of the face and lips! Other senses may also be affected. That is, there may be neglect of touch or sound that comes from the left side. Furthermore, although some persons may have an intellectual awareness of the neglect and try to give themselves reminders to pay attention to the neglected side (Sacks, 1987), the majority of people will either deny the problem (anosognosia) or appear indifferent to it (anosodiaphoria). This denial can even extend to more obvious deficits such as blindness and paralysis.

As a counselor, you need to realize that indifference or denial can have an organic component; it is related to deficiencies of spatial awareness and sensory integration. It should not be confused with an obstinate, self-willed denial. The denial, however, can become an occasion for sinful responses and can gradually progress to gross delusions and an unwillingness to hear counsel.

Other unusual symptoms that are part of distorted body awareness include a sense that part of the body is dead, lifeless—"not me." Also, some affected people may feel as if they have another appendage protruding from some strange place, such as above the shoulder.

. . . his paralysed left arm and leg "belonged to someone else."

. . . had erotic sensations aroused by his left side which he imagined belonged to a woman lying beside him.

. . . following his stroke he thought his paralysed leg belonged to the man in the next bed. (P. 235)

[After an above-the-knee amputation] the patient not only denied that he had ever been amputated but he insisted that he had an intact and useful left leg which he could see and feel. The most that he would concede was that the left leg was "a little shorter." (P. 236)

Some patients regarded the left arm as "strange, ugly, disfigured, artificial, enlarged, shapeless, thickened, shortened, or snake-like." (P. 236).

"I can't believe I have an arm. Have you taken it off? I had this terrible shock this morning when I touched my left hand; I thought it was the head of a reptile." (Critchley, 1966, p. 236)

"When I close my eyes, I'm not even sure where my right leg is; for some reason I used to think it was somewhere above my shoulder, even above my head." (Luria, 1972, p. 43)

Lost in space (and time). Spatial disorientation is also a common experience in parietal disorders. Space just makes no sense to those thus affected: *right, left, backward, forward, up,* and *down* are recognizable but meaningless words. These persons have difficulty reading maps, are unable to draw a map of very familiar areas, and sometime can find themselves spatially disoriented in previously familiar surroundings. For example, a fifty-six-year-old woman who experienced a mild stroke in her left parietal lobe was relatively unaffected with the notable exception that she was disoriented in her own house. After living in the same house for twenty years, she now needed directions to find the bathroom. She was constantly asking her husband where kitchen supplies were kept in the kitchen she had arranged.

Sense of time may also be chaotic. Affected persons may be unable to judge the passage of time, and they may be constantly confused as to time of day and year (Critchley, 1966).

This senselessness of space and time is very difficult to imagine, but it is easy to understand how it could be disruptive. Perceptions would consist of isolated fragments of reality that would be difficult to integrate. It would be like taking dozens of one-thousand-piece, brain-twisting puzzles, throwing them all together, and assembling them without any pictorial clues. It has been suggested that this confusion may even underlie the indifference and denial that so many exhibit. Perhaps affected people simply cannot connect the disparate data they perceive, and they cannot comprehend the nature of their disabilities.

Somatosensory disorders. The only anatomically defined area in the parietal lobe is the somatosensory strip. Disruption within the somatosensory strip, which mediates our sense of touch, can lead to a variety of tactile experiences. Tingling, numbness, pins and needles, and a sense that something is being held are fairly common. More unusual experiences include disorders of pain perception. Some people continue to feel pain but seem indifferent to it. They may smile when getting a shot or simply not react to something very painful. Another unusual problem, interesting but with no significant counseling implications, is poor tactile discrimination. Affected persons are unable to identify an object by touch. When they see the object they will know it immediately, but with eyes closed or in the dark, they can only offer (sometimes humorous) guesses.

Integration of tactile, auditory, and visual data. The largest portion of the parietal lobe is a complex integration area that has important counseling implications.

Apraxias. Apraxias are inabilities to carry out purposeful movements even though there is no apparent weakness or abnormalities in the limbs. Affected persons have the muscular capacity to perform specific tasks, but their fine motor control is deficient. Included are difficulties drawing, writing, and performing other familiar sequences of movements (constructional apraxias), difficulties dressing oneself (dressing apraxias), and difficulty coordinating intent and action (ideokinetic apraxias).

Ideokinetic apraxia is especially curious. For example, an affected person may be able to use a house key to unlock a door on his own without apparent difficulty, yet be completely unable to respond to another's verbal command to do that very thing. In a similar way, some people will at times be unable to feed themselves. When they think about performing a common task, they get confused. Usually ideokinetic apraxias are accompanied by some degree of aphasia.

Calculation problems, writing problems, and confusion between right and left. These three symptoms are included together because they often come as a package (called Gerstmann's syndrome). Problems with calculation are self-explanatory: affected persons simply have difficulties with previously familiar calculations. Yet there are different causes. For example, it may coincide with a selective inability to read or write numbers, or it may be a result of difficulties in spatially organizing the problem, in which case they may be able to do orally presented arithmetic. Difficulties writing can also have various causes and nuances. But they are usually accompanied by problems reading, speaking, or both.

Visual perception. When the brain dysfunction occurs closer to the occipital area (the primary visual area), a person can have unusual visual problems. One of these is called visual agnosia ("not knowing"). In visual agnosia a person has difficulty naming or recognizing familiar objects. For example, one man alternately claimed he was "blind," "couldn't see very well," and "things look sort of blurry." At one moment he would describe an object; at the next, he would say he couldn't see it, but he would follow the object if it moved. His family claimed he was becoming a pathological liar, but his real problem was a small stroke in the rear area of the parietal lobe.

Temporal Lobe

The temporal lobe is another complex area. It mediates hearing, tasting, and smelling as well as more subtle functions that are a result of its integrating activities.

Frontal lobe symptoms. The first set of symptoms should sound strangely familiar. They are replicas of some frontal lobe symptoms.

Like persons with frontal lobe impairment, those with temporal lobe dysfunction have difficulties with attention, concentration, and recognizing or attending to unusual or new features in their surroundings.

Categorizing and organizing various words and concepts are also a problem. For example, given a list of "chairs, table, car, bus, sofa, and train," most people could place these objects in two categories: furniture and transportation. A temporal lobe patient may be unable to see any organizational pattern. At first this may seem like a fairly innocuous problem, but upon reflection it is clear that this would make life very difficult. As mentioned in connection with the frontal and parietal lobes, the world would be a mass of data that were unrelated and chaotic. And it would demand all the spiritual resources available to the person to refrain from either withdrawal or lashing out in frustration. (Likewise, it would demand monumental spiritual resources in the family to be able to understand and help the affected person.)

"Temporal lobe personality." Certain personality patterns are also found in temporal lobe disorders. While persons rarely demonstrate them all, parts of a cluster tend to be very common. Included are (1) "stickiness" or a compulsive attention to detail and a difficulty "letting things go," (2) decreased interest in sex, (3) paranoia or irrational fears, and (4) increased aggressiveness and rage.

> After a head injury [with most of the damage located in the temporal and frontal lobes] at age twenty, a young man became uncharacteristically angry with only minor provocations. This would be even more apparent for a few days prior to a seizure. At these times he would fight with friends or strangers over nothing. He also developed difficulty communicating. He had always been quite talkative but very much to the point. Now he seemed to get bogged down with irrelevant details. His conversation was often so detailed that he would either lose his point or take forever to get through secondary and tertiary minutiae. Although aware of this tendency, he seemed unable to prevent it. His wife indicated that he would also get bogged down in jobs around the house—spending hours on insignificant work. To casual acquaintances he was religious and almost mystical; to family and good friends he was simply very difficult. (Blumer & Benson, 1975)

Again, "temporal lobe personality" is not an excuse for sin, but the physical problems can leave affected persons prone to certain sinful patterns.

Memory. The temporal lobe is much involved in memory. Typically, if there is decline, it will target recent memories and leave older memories intact. In degenerative diseases, these problems may be very subtle at first and the person may compensate for the problems with notes or other devices. Even when the problems become more severe, some people may be too embarrassed to admit them and may prefer to be considered lazy, too busy, or even self-centered.

Partial complex seizures with automatisms. For some reason, the temporal lobe tends to experience more seizure activity than the rest of the brain. The most interesting of these seizures are the partial complex seizures. These last from a few seconds to several minutes and may be characterized by meaningless repetitive activity (such as repeating words over and over, buttoning and unbuttoning), unusual facial movements, aimless behavior, a lack of responsiveness, and no memory of the episode. They are called "partial" because they occur in only part of the brain—

the temporal lobe in this case. "Complex" is a technical way of indicating that the person's level of awareness is impaired in some way. These seizures are discussed in the section on epilepsy (see chapter 6).

Sensory hallucinations. Because the temporal lobes are involved in processing a variety of sensory data, dysfunction may be revealed in auditory, visual, olfactory (smell), and gustatory (taste) hallucinations. Curiously, the taste and smell hallucinations are usually very foul, such as feces, "burnt rubber," and "dirty dishwater."

Occipital Lobe

The occipital area mediates vision. At worst, dysfunction in this area can lead to blindness (cortical blindness), even if the eyes themselves are fine. Other variations of occipital lobe problems include visual hallucinations, blindness, or neglect in specific areas of the visual field, color agnosia (inability to name colors), and visual distortions.

Notes

1. Problems with self-control are especially related to dysfunction in the frontal lobes. The frontal lobes send out nerve fibers that suppress brain activity. When these neurons are impaired, the rest of the brain is neuronally more active.

2. A very good book that gives a feel for a world that is full of isolated information is *The Man with a Shattered World*, by the Russian neuropsychologist A. R. Luria.

3. Technically, even if the left hemisphere is liguistically dominant, it is inaccurate to say that the right hemisphere is linguistically incompetent. The right hemisphere has some language ability, but it is not as sophisticated as that of the left hemisphere.

4. Early reports on psychosurgery suggested dramatic improvements in some patients, and Moniz won the Nobel Prize for this work in 1949. In the 1950s, however, its barbaric quality became more apparent and the accompanying personality changes were studied more intensely. As a result, prefrontal lobotomies, though still legal, are considered more ignominious than therapeutic (Shutts, 1982).

5. These details may seem irrelevant, but with the advances in CT and MRI, it is easy to know the precise location of a brain problem and, as a result, to predict more accurately the possible cognitive side effects.

5

Diagnostic Instruments

The number of technical medical procedures seems to increase daily, and a detailed knowledge of them all would be pointless for counselors. There are, however, some widely used procedures with which you should have some acquaintance.

The History, Interview, and Physical Exam

Even with all the new medical technology, skilled physicians still rely on a careful interview and history. In this they are no different than counselors. That is, while young counselors may rely heavily on psychological tests and canned techniques, skilled and experienced counselors are able to make accurate assessments simply with careful observation and good questions. Likewise, a good medical history is still the best diagnostic tool in medicine. In the hands of a skilled physician, the initial interview is an art form that is more comprehensive than the most sophisticated diagnostic tools.

The medical history and interview includes vital statistics such as blood pressure, height, and weight along with certain basic questions: Past illnesses? Previous medical treatments? When were the first symptoms? Did they emerge gradually or suddenly? Have they improved, gotten worse, or remained constant? Were there any precipitating factors? Is there a family history? This is not to say that the interview is a series of predetermined questions. In the hands of a talented physician, it is the work of a detective whose carefully chosen questions and observations can lead to elegant deductions.

If warranted by the history, or if a general physical exam is requested, the physician will usually continue by asking questions that are focused on the major organ systems of the body such as the head, heart, stomach, intestines, and kidneys. Routine screening tests often requested at this point include a chest X-ray, EKG, thyroid function test (T_3, T_4, TSH), complete blood counts (CBC), B_{12} and folate levels, screening for syphillis, urinalysis, perhaps a CT scan, and blood tests that include electrolytes, blood urea nitrogen (BUN), creatinine, liver functions, calcium and phosphate (e.g., SMA 12 or SMA 20).[1]

Some physicians will perform these tests whenever there are vague complaints that have possible organic bases. Most physicians, however, use their clinical judgment and select those tests that in their opinion have the highest probability of detecting underlying disease. Therefore, at times it may appear that physicians did not perform a thorough evaluation because they bypassed dozens of laboratory tests and CT scans. Certainly, it is possible for physicians to overlook critical data and ignore important diagnostic tests; however, experienced physicians only request tests that are warranted by the history and physical evaluation.

The Neurological Exam

If, during the course of an interview, the patient indicates that there may be subtle problems with the brain and central nervous system, the physician may conduct a neurological exam. This exam is noninvasive. Although you may get poked occasionally, there are no needles or injections. It is used to determine (1) the presence or absence of malfunction in the nervous system, (2) the location, type, and extent of malfunction, and (3) the prognosis for rehabilitation (DeJong, 1988). The neurological exam consists of tests of mental status (level of alertness and orientation to place and time) and higher cerebral functioning (memory), cranial nerves, cerebellar function (balance), motor system (muscle power), sensory system (sensation), and reflexes. Its strength is that it can reveal evidence for brain damage from many causes. A weakness is that it is poor at estimating the degree of social or vocational upheaval that may result from a particular problem.

EEG (Electroencephalography)

Developed in the 1940s, the electroencephalogram was one of the first techniques for investigating brain function. Still useful, it monitors the electrical activity in the brain. It consists of electrodes, usually glued to the scalp, that transmit electrical data from several brain sites to pens that translate the data onto a continuous paper tracing. The procedure is usually done while the patient is awake, but to have a more pronounced reading, patients may be administered drugs or be asleep.

The EEG was once the most prominent diagnostic device in neurology, but it has been supplanted by CT scans and other more recent scanning procedures. It remains, however, *the* diagnostic tool when there is suspicion of epilepsy. It isn't perfect—normal people can have abnormal EEGs and epileptics can have normal EEGs—but it is very useful in diagnosing seizure disorders and encephalitis.

A new variation of the EEG is Brain Electrical Activity Mapping (BEAM). This is roughly a sophisticated EEG that uses computerized statistical analysis. It has been reported to be useful in identifying pure dyslexia, dementia, epilepsy, and other cerebral disorders (Berg, Franzen, & Wedding, 1987), but its usefulness is still difficult to evaluate.

Angiography

Cerebral angiography is an X-ray technique that is predominantly used to examine cerebral blood flow. It gives valuable information but can be unpleasant and requires hospitalization. In this procedure a small amount of dye is injected into the bloodstream and a series of X-rays are taken. As with other techniques, CT scans have usurped some of the angiogram's applications, and because it is invasive, it is only used when absolutely necessary. Yet it uniquely exposes blocked arteries, strokes, and aneurysms.

Like the EEG, angiograms have also profited from the computer revolution. Sophisticated versions of computed angiography, such as Digital Subtraction Angiography (DSA), have added greater precision to the procedure.

CT Scans

CT scans are certainly the best known of the new wave of diagnostic devices. The abbreviation stands for Computerized Axial Tomography (CAT) or Computerized Tomography (CT). It consists of a series of X-ray beams on a rotating axis that take computer-generated pictures of different segments, or *tomos*, of the brain or body.

The principle behind CT scans is essentially the same as for an ordinary X-ray. Different tissues have different abilities to absorb X-rays: dense material such as bone weakens X-ray beams and appears white, air and liquids allow X-rays to pass through freely and are black, and cerebral

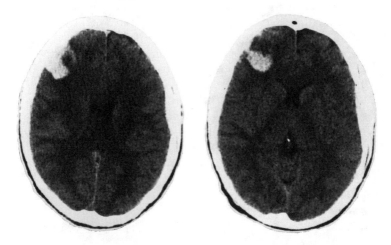

Figure 5.1. Computerized Tomography (CT scans). These identify a dysfunction in the left frontal lobe. (Courtesy of Kenneth Neigut, M.D., Germantown Hospital, Philadelphia)

tissue is expressed as various shades of gray (Figure 5.1). Instead of using a photographic plate to collect X-ray beams, CT uses a sensing device that feeds the data into a computer. More specifically, narrow beams are transmitted from one side of a rotating scanner to collecting devices on the opposite side. The scanner then circles the head in one-degree sequences until it completes a half-circle (180 degrees), taking thousands of readings that are translated by computer into a series of pictures with outstanding resolution.

The advantages provided by CT are enormous. Because of the rotating gantry, the CT avoids any "shadows" that can block important brain features. Also, pictures are clear and radiation exposure is low, about the same as a common chest X-ray. The only disadvantage is cost.

MRI (Magnetic Resonance Imaging)

Magnetic Resonance Imaging is a latecomer to the brain-and-body imaging scene, but it already is out-distancing the CT scan in some types of imaging. It was once called Nuclear Magnetic Imaging, implying that it involves dangerous nuclear reactions. In fact, it is safer than CT and involves no nuclear activity. "Nuclear" refers to the small magnetic fields generated by the spinning nuclei of hydrogen atoms. These randomly

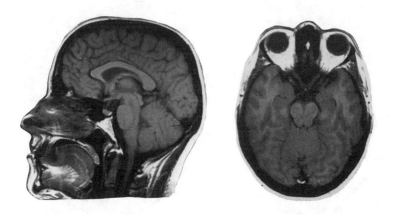

Figure 5.2. Magnetic Resonance Imaging (MRI) of the Brain. (Courtesy of Kenneth Neigut, M.D., Germantown Hospital, Philadelphia)

aligned magnetic fields become aligned in the same direction when they are influenced by the powerful electromagnets of the MRI scanner. If an appropriate radio frequency is aimed at these atoms, it changes their alignment. (This is similar to the way a vibrating tuning fork will influence strings that are tuned to the same frequency.) When the radio frequency is turned off, the nuclei realign themselves and emit electromagnetic energy that is detected by the receiver coils of the scanner and constructed as a brain image by computer.

MRI is a very expensive procedure at present, usually twice as much as CT. Some patients complain about its noise and claustrophobic chamber, but its advantages are significant. It uses no radiation, discriminates very well between the white and gray matter in the brain, shows no bone artifacts, and has amazingly clear resolution (Figure 5.2). It is an exciting procedure with considerable untapped potential.

PET and SPECT

Positron Emission Tomography (PET) and Single-Photon Emission Computed Tomography (SPECT) represent recent developments of CT. Their unique contribution is that whereas CT takes pictures of brain structures, PET and SPECT actually offer images of brain function—the brain at work. It is comparable to the difference between a snapshot and a movie.

The historical precursor of PET, which is still used occasionally, is the test to determine regional cerebral blood flow (rCBF). There are multiple methods for this procedure, but the most common is to give patients, either by inhalation or injection, oxygen that has been "labeled" with radioactive xenon or krypton (yes, krypton!). Since the brain requires oxygen for its activity, these isotopes travel to brain areas that are metabolically active and are monitored by scalp recordings. The resultant two-dimensional record does not give a clear measurement of subsurface structures, but it does allow identification of areas of decreased brain activity.

Positron Emission Tomography uses similar technology but is more sophisticated and has more applications. PET can measure either oxygen consumption or brain metabolism, in the form of glucose consumption. Rapidly decaying radioactive isotopes are "brewed" in a special machine called a cyclotron. These isotopes are injected into a patient and emit positrons wherever they flow. The positrons collide with electrons in the body, annihilate one another, and release a burst of gamma rays that are picked up by a ring of detectors around a patient's head. These messages are reconstructed by computer and produce an image of the functioning of the brain. SPECT is a variation of this process, similar in resolution and sensitivity, but more affordable in that it uses commercially available isotopes rather than those produced by an on-site cyclotron.

This technology is exciting, but its potential is still to be evaluated. Because there are too many factors that confound interpretation of the images (De Lisi & Buchsbaum, 1986), they are used more for research than everyday diagnosis. Their future could include mapping the neurotransmitter systems in the brain and examining the action of psychoactive drugs. They have already provided intriguing hypotheses on the relationship between brain activity and behavior.

Notes

1. SMA (SMAC) tests usually include either twelve or twenty different blood studies.

Part II
DISEASES THAT AFFECT INTELLECT, MOOD, AND BEHAVIORAL CAPABILITIES

6

"Must-Know" Diseases

Alas, our frailty is the cause, not we!
—*Twelfth Night*, II, ii, 32

The Bible indicates that there are four possible interactions between heart and body: the heart does not affect the body, the body does not affect the heart, the heart does affect the body, and the body does affect the heart. Of these four possibilities, this section will focus on bodily problems that can influence the work of the heart. The particular emphasis is on diseases that characteristically alter intellect, emotions, or behavioral capabilities. These diseases can impair understanding, pose limitations on the expression of the heart, provide occasions for temptation and sin, and raise unique problems for families. Therefore they should be accompanied by more active pastoral interest and counsel. Also, because they mimic spiritual problems of the heart, they are often misdiagnosed by counselors and physicians.

The diseases discussed in this chapter provide a broad sampling of those that can affect brain function. They are not the only diseases that affect brain function, but they are fairly common and probably present in most churches. The goal of this section is not to provide an encyclopedic reference of diseases. Rather, along with alerting you to possible areas for pastoral care and counseling, the goal is to provide a *method* for approaching problems and to offer a means of gaining experience in differentiating issues of the heart from physical weakness.

Each of these diseases has unique features, but there are some general, commonsense guidelines that apply to them all. First, obtain the services of a good physician, one who is attentive, understanding, and knowledgeable about a particular disease. It would be worthwhile to know if the physician will remain in your area for a while because in some cases those with the disease will consult with this person for years. Second, although it may not sound like very profound advice (and you will soon tire of hearing it), counselors should encourage patients and their families to read whatever they can about the disease and to pepper their primary physician with questions. Too often, families prefer denial to education. As a result, there is less communication between the affected person and the spouse, and children are perplexed or embarrassed by strange behavior that may accompany some of these diseases. Reading current literature can prepare families for what lies ahead, and it will provide an opportunity to understand the inner world of affected persons.

Alzheimer's Disease and Dementia

The aging of America has made dementia a critical issue confronting both the church and the society at large. Medical care, housing, responsibilities of the spouse and children, the honoring of dementing adults, role reversals—these are just a few of the potentially overwhelming problems that must be addressed by the caring community. Yet the situation is far from despairing. With education about the disease, a biblical perspective, a good diaconal team, and a family committed to ministry, the care of a dementing adult can be an edifying experience for an entire church. Here are an overview and guidelines for ministry.

Dementia

Dementia has taken over the place that the term "senility" once occupied in our vocabulary, and for good reasons. "Senility" had derogatory connotations and tended to be associated with the myth that all older people became senile. The term is still used widely today, but with a more limited meaning. "Senile" simply refers to the age period sixty-five and older. Therefore, a pre-senile dementia is one that emerges before age sixty-five and a senile dementia one that occurs after age sixty-five.

As you probably know, dementia is not an inevitable consequence of aging, and it is easily distinguishable from the dulled senses and occasional forgetfulness of old age. Actually it is a fairly generic term that refers to a deterioration of memory and intellect severe enough to interfere with social relationships and work. It may be brief and reversible, as in an alcoholic stupor or a severe hypoglycemic episode; or it may be chronic and progessive, as in the best-known dementia, Alzheimer's Disease.

Alzheimer's Disease

Alzheimer's disease (AD) is an increasingly common form of dementia that can strike surprisingly early, even in the forties. The fourth-leading cause of death in the United States, AD affects about 1 percent of the population under age sixty-five. Its statistics rise dramatically to include about 20 percent of the population over eighty. This penchant to strike older persons is especially significant because those who are eighty-five and older represent the fastest-growing age group in our population.

The changes most commonly associated with Alzheimer's disease occur in the nerve cells of the cerebral cortex. Under an electron microscope, accumulations of abnormal nerve fibers appear as tangled filaments or "neurofibrillary tangles." These were first described in 1906 by a German neurologist, Alois Alzheimer.

What you may find surprising regarding the disease is that, prior to autopsy, there are no medical tests that can definitively diagnose Alzheimer's.[1] The best that medical science can do at present is to rule out other diseases. This being so, the first agenda for those who demonstrate intellectual decline is a comprehensive medical work-up to rule out the host of diseases that can mimic Alzheimer's.

Known Treatable Dementias

Because diagnosis is not a clear-cut process, many people have been misdiagnosed as having AD when there was actually a treatable, underlying problem. It has been estimated that up to one-third of those originally diagnosed with Alzheimer's do not have the disease! For them, their families, and their friends, misdiagnosis is a tragic error.

The most frequent imitators of AD are depression and side effects of prescription drugs—both very treatable. Depression is easily misdiagnosed because, along with the difficult emotions, it is accompanied by dementia-like mental and physical sluggishness. In fact, mental and physical slowing may be the most prominent symptoms of depression, even more pronounced than complaints of feeling depressed. (Many older persons would rather admit to physical problems than emotional ones.) For the family or counselor, this means that evidence of intellectual

changes in the elderly must be accompanied by both a thorough medical
evaluation and a systematic counseling interview. A counselor may ask,
"Have there been any recent changes in your life? Death of loved ones?
Physical disability? A sense of purposelessness? What have these changes
been like for you? Have you been feeling depressed recently?" If you note
any evidence of depression, be sure to alert those who are considering the
diagnosis of Alzheimer's.

The other major offender, prescription drugs, is notorious for
causing dementia. Yet though almost everyone is aware of the potential
problems of multiple medications in the elderly, drugs are still casually
prescribed for even minor complaints.

> Mr. Lee, at age fifty-two, began to experience episodic confusion and
> intellectual decline. He was treated with medication and diagnosed with
> Alzheimer's Disease. For nine years he and his family lived under the
> Alzheimer's shroud. Finally, the family funds depleted, Mrs. Lee brought
> her husband home and chose to cut off all his medication. After suffering
> some withdrawal symptoms, Mr. Lee improved dramatically. He recov-
> ered—largely a result of the resilience of his relative youth—and,
> amazingly, went on to teach college math. (Larimer, 1989)

The scenario goes like this: older people are already taking
medication for chronic illnesses. Then, when they experience drug-
related fatigue, depression, mild memory problems, or sleep loss, they are
often prescribed more medication. Not infrequently this medication will
have side effects, so it is deemed necessary to prescribe more medication
again. Perhaps a young adult can withstand this chemical deluge, but
older persons, with their more fragile metabolism and fatigued kidney and
liver function, are slow to excrete the drugs. The gradual accumulation of
psychoactive drugs can then produce a downward intellectual spiral that
mimics the untreatable Alzheimer's.

One way to prevent this form of dementia is to keep a list of every
drug a person is taking. Then make certain every physician involved in
the medical treatment is aware of the list. Also, know why someone is
taking a particular drug and what the proper dosage is, and question the
primary physician if you suspect a prescription is unnecessary.

There are many other treatable forms of dementia. Figure 6.1 lists
some of the treatable dementias merely to remind you that intellectual
decline in the elderly does not necessarily mean AD or some other
untreatable dementia.

Table 6.1. Sources of Some Known Treatable Dementias

Toxins and Drugs
   Prescription and over-the-counter drugs
   Street drugs
   Alcohol
   Toxic substances encountered at work

Infections
   Brain abscess
   Meningitis (bacterial or fungal)
   Mononeucleosis

Endocrine and metabolic disorders
   Thyroidism disorders (myxedema, Grave's disease)
   Parathyroid disorders
   Liver disease
   Wilson's disease
   Cushing's syndrome
   Renal failure, uremia
   Respiratory failure
   Hyperglycemia and hypoglycemia

Trauma
   Subdural hematoma
   Heat stroke and hypothermia

Vascular disease
   Stroke
   Multi-infarct dementia

Deficiency states
   Pellagra (niacin)
   Vitamin B_{12}
   Wernicke-Korsakoff's syndrome
   Anemia
   Marchiafava-Bignami disease

Other diseases
   Brain tumor
   Normal pressure hydrocephalus
   Whipple's disease
   Fever
   Depression
   Dehydration
   Hearing-aid dysfunction

If you are aware of subtle intellectual changes in a family member, consult a doctor in whom you have confidence—someone who will listen, answer questions, and, if warranted, pursue a series of medical and intellectual tests. These tests may include the following: chest X-ray, skull CT scan, EEG, EKG (electrocardiogram), urinalysis, stool testing, liver function tests, thyroid function tests, arterial blood gases, electrolytes (sodium, potassium, calcium, magnesium), basic blood tests, CSF exam, fasting blood sugar, vitamin deficiencies, and review of current medications. Most work-ups will also include an evaluation of memory and intellectual function.

The Course of Alzheimer's Disease

The course of AD is progressive, but the rate of decline is unpredictable. It can last anywhere from three years to more than fifteen. Its incessant progress is not prone to plateaus, yet some families experience different stages of the disease.

The early stage. The onset of Alzheimer's disease is usually insidious. It may begin as "forgetfulness" apparent only to fellow workers or a spouse. What makes it even more difficult to detect initially is that workers may cover up for the dementing adult, and families are quick to deny any significant changes. Consider this report written by a son:

> Over the period that we worked together, I became gradually aware that the fine edge of his intellect was becoming dull. He was less clear in discussion and less quick to make the fine jump from a new piece of evidence to its possible significance. He spent more time over his work and achieved less; and he found it increasingly difficult to get his work ready for publication. He tended to become portentous and solemn about his subject, as though one small corner of knowledge nearly filled his world and the wider horizons were narrowing in. The change was so slow as to be barely perceptible, and the signs vanish when I try to pin them down: they were like those faint stars which are seen more easily when they are not in the direct line of vision. I was left with a feeling of uneasiness which I could not justify. (Anonymous, 1950)

This early stage, lasting two to three years, is characterized by progressive changes in memory, decreased intellectual efficiency, and spatial disorientation. That is, affected persons may get lost or be uncertain in previously familiar surroundings. Then, as they become overwhelmed with tasks that were once easily manageable, they may begin to withdraw in an attempt to adapt to a confusing world. After a diagnosis of AD, families immediately tend to see changes previously considered to be eccentric or humorous. Now, instead of bounced checks being attributed to "forgetfulness," families interpret them as harbingers of quick cognitive deterioration, and the initial tendency is to take control of and from those with AD. Caregivers, however, must constantly maintain a goal of maximizing the person's spiritual gifts and physical abilities, and AD patients must be given as much say as possible in their care.

The key biblical principle is to honor the elderly. Honor them by listening, understanding their perspectives, helping them maintain relationships with friends, being honest with them, and working creatively to serve them. Also, within safe boundaries, give them decision-making responsibilities and ongoing ministry.

One of the most difficult decisions during this time regards driving privileges. For many adults, to rescind this is to rob them of freedom, and they may respond with anger along with absolutely brilliant strategies to get use of the car. Some families actually dismantle parts of the engine whenever they are not using the car. Most of this kind of activity can be avoided if families receive counsel from others, offer specific facts that indicate a poor driving record, and look for transportation alternatives.

Financial management poses another problem. If the person with AD is the financial manager, a spouse or relative will gradually have to perform that function. Paying bills, balancing checkbooks, locating important financial documents, and reviewing wills are all part of this financial package. At this stage, legal advice is helpful.

Later in this stage, symptoms become more obvious. For example, an adult may have difficulties recognizing and interpreting previously familiar objects such as a showerhead. As a result, a simple shower may be misinterpreted as a rainstorm and the person may belligerently seek to escape to a safe place. Self-care is increasingly difficult, and the person soon needs full-time supervision. The family can minimize difficulties by establishing a structured daily routine.

For the family, perhaps the most difficult part of this stage is the patient's emotional lability. Emotions are unpredictible and range from anger, suspicion, depression, and transient crying episodes to silliness and childish elation, all without a moment's notice. Family members are alternately perplexed, angry, and guilt-laden as they are swayed by these emotional swings. This is often when families realize their need to be educated about dementia and AD (don't forget to be familiar with the brain-behavior relationships). During this time, families should be reading everything they can about Alzheimer's.[2] Through the plethora of good available literature, local support groups, and biblical studies on the elderly and honoring parents, both parents and children are in a position to understand the strange behavior associated with AD and grow in faith.

At this point, if not sooner, families must begin to develop available resources. Specifically, they must begin looking toward other family members, the church, and perhaps community resources. The church's participation can be invaluable at this stage. Along with providing encouragement and counsel, deacons and friends can provide supervision during nights or weekends out. Also, if possible, other family members can help. Usually, there is one "responsible" child who oversees parental care, but that child must be encouraged to enlist family support. This can be difficult and it can be an opportunity for old family problems to surface. But if possible, the AD patient could spend a few weeks each year with other family members. If not, the church diaconal team and community day-care centers may have to function in place of the absent or disinterested extended family.

The middle stage. As the disease progresses, patients seem to regress; they become like dependent children. They avoid anything but a towel bath, personal toilet care is inadequate, incontinence becomes a burden on the family, emotional outbursts—occasionally precipitated by hallucinations—are frequent. Fortunately, by this time, denial and intellectual incompetence protect affected individuals from a full awareness of their problem. Families, however, don't have this recourse. Instead, they may wrongly but understandably choose to let emotional ties diminish and distance themselves from the patient.

A curious problem in this stage is sleep disturbance. It is as if the biological day-night rhythms of affected patients parallel the confusion of their intellect. These persons may stay up all night, despite the pleas of their caregivers, and sleep in their favorite chair during the day. A variation of this is called "sundowning." Demented persons may show very little confusion during the day, but at night, when the sun goes down, they become confused, agitated, and difficult to manage. Some of these changes may be treatable, and caregivers should consult with the primary physician. Causes for sundowning include medication, pain, urinary tract problems, depression, caffeine, and frequent daily naps. Along with treating these causes, exercise and nightlights are often helpful.

At this time, often after episodes of frightening and irrational behavior, many families feel incompetent to deal with any further decline, and they will consider placement in a nursing home. Along with consulting the pastor and others regarding a nursing-home decision, families should speak with the primary physician. If the patient's behavior is blatantly out of control, some doctors suggest psychoactive drugs, specifically an antipsychotic drug. These drugs can subdue some of the more difficult symptoms, but they must be used with caution, for they can dull the remaining alertness of the person.

The late stage. In this stage, dementing adults produce very few comprehensible words, have difficulty walking and coordinating movements, and may not appear to recognize family members. They may seem so far removed from reality that families may think that times of talking and touching are inconsequential. Human contact, however, is important and meaningful. Families need to be reminded that although the ministry seems unappreciated, it has both temporal and eternal significance.

To shed a ray of hope and offer a reminder that moral responsibility and faith are not intimately related to cognitive abilities, consider the following case.

A sixty-five-year-old woman, an avowed atheist with three married children, was widowed at age forty-seven and struggled with chronic depression from that time on. Her symptoms were unchanged until, at age sixty-two, she was fired from her job. Seemingly overnight, some uncharacteristic behaviors became apparent. With no previous history of anything illegal, she was arrested for shoplifting, and strangely, she had no recollection of the event when apprehended. (Her children concluded that she must have been lying.) She also frequently lost her car in parking lots, and she was increasingly "forgetful."

At the insistence of her children, she had a medical exam in which a team of doctors, with only one dissenting vote, said, "Alzheimer's disease." Not surprisingly, the children immediately rejected the majority opinion, but they couldn't help being alerted to further signs of AD. For example, their mother participated at a senior citizens center, where she was consistently yet uncharacteristically angry. She would scream in others' faces, would ask for more coffee and doughnuts when she had just had some but had forgotten, and would often wander aimlessly. When the center indicated it couldn't handle her, the children accepted the diagnosis of Alzheimer's and decided that their mother would live with the oldest daughter and her family.

During this time most people were unaware of the intellectual changes in this woman because she had a few stock phrases that made her appear socially aware and friendly. But the progress of the Alzheimer's disease was relentless. She zealously guarded "her chair," and when the children were close to it, she sometimes hit them with her cane. Auditory hallucinations were constant. She wandered away from the family at stores, was up at 2 A.M. with the TV blaring, and always forgot to turn off the stove. To prevent wandering outside, she had to be locked in the house with bolts on the outside of the doors! But the most striking feature of her dementia was this, that in spite of all her intellectual changes, she never lost her disdain for the gospel. Her clearest words were, "I don't want your Jesus."

This continued until one day, on the way home from a church service, she seemed to come momentarily out of her stupor and said, "I need to be forgiven for what I have done to them [old friends]." The daughter and her husband seized the moment and explained the forgiveness of Jesus expressed through the cross. Their mother not only accepted Christ, but even told others. Her ability to communicate her faith verbally did not last long, because her dementia robbed her of communication skills. However, other family members, who did not claim faith in Christ, were amazed at the joy they found in their mother's face and the peace in her demeanor. She became a living example of how the outer person wastes away but the inner person can be renewed—even when faced with seemingly insurmountable physical obstacles.

Multiple Sclerosis

Among North Americans and Northern Europeans who are in the prime of life, multiple sclerosis (MS) is the most common disease of the central nervous system. As such, MS patients are found in most churches and counseling practices. The disease is best known by the physical weakness and paralysis that may be apparent in the later stages. Yet there are also significant counseling issues that may accompany the disease. Some of these difficulties, such as a tendency toward hopelessness and depression, are characteristic of any chronic, restrictive disease, but some of them are endemic to MS.

MS is a chronic, slow-growing neurological disorder which has its usual onset between the ages of twenty and forty; onset is rare before age twelve and after age fifty. It is characterized by neurological symptoms that remit and recur over a period of twenty to thirty years or more. For example, in the early stages of the disease, the only symptoms may be transient episodes of blurred vision, double vision, or an unusual weakness in one side of the body. These symptoms may improve in a few days and not recur for years. However, many MS patients are left with permanent neurological changes with each recurrence of the disease, upon which future episodes are superimposed. This progression may result in eventual paralysis, incontinence, pain, bedsores, and intellectual decline.

Yet the disease is not necessarily synonymous with prognostic despair. Even though it is presently untreatable and chronic, it is *unpredictable* rather than lethal. The duration of the disease is variable, but up to 75 percent of affected persons live in excess of twenty-five years following the diagnosis and up to 50 percent live over thirty-five years after onset. At the end of twenty-five years, one-third of MS patients continue to be vocationally active in their chosen profession, and two-thirds of those surviving are still ambulatory (Kurtzke, 1970).

Since the disease is characterized by unpredictable fluctuations, diagnosis is problematic. And, indeed, the uncertainty surrounding the initial diagnosis is often a time of confusion and frustration for patients and their families. MS is diagnosed largely by way of careful history-taking and observation. Presently there are no laboratory tests which offer a definitive diagnosis. The unusual clarity of Magnetic Resonance Imaging (MRI) offers support to the diagnosis, but, in the early stages, clinical judgment and experience reign. This lack of diagnostic certainty makes misdiagnosis commonplace. For example, one of the few studies to investigate misdiagnosis in MS found that out of 142 MS patients, thirty-one (22 percent) originally were misdiagnosed. Furthermore (and of special interest to counselors), the symptoms were usually considered to be functional—psychiatric rather than medical (Currey, 1982).

Symptoms of MS

About 40 percent of affected persons have an episode of *optic nerve inflammation* (optic neuritis) that may be manifested by spots of blurred vision. One-third of these individuals recover completely, one-third show considerable improvement, and one-third demonstrate no improvement. If there is recovery of function, it will usually occur within two weeks. *Disorders of sensation* are often reported by MS patients. Tingling in the arms and legs, pain around the jaw (*tic douloureux*), facial anesthesia, burning on the hands and feet, and Lhermitte's sign are common. Lhermitte's sign is a sudden electric shock sensation spreading down the body, usually occurring after tipping the head forward.

Urogenital disorders consistent with MS include *impotence* as well as *bladder dysfunctions* such as difficulty holding urine (incontinence) and hesitation and urgency associated with urination.

Other classic symptoms of MS include double vision, weakness, dizziness, poor coordination, frequent hesitations in speech (scanning speech), and hand tremors. The hand tremors tend to appear during purposeful movements but are absent while the arms and hands are at rest (intention tremor). Paralysis is common in advanced stages of MS, usually appearing first in the legs and then traveling up the body to affect the trunk and arms.

Of particular interest to counselors are the changes in emotions and intellect. Especially in the later stages of the disease, emotions may become very exaggerated, as if they were difficult to control. Patients may laugh or cry with little or no provocation. Curiously, these emotions are often unrelated to what people with MS actually feel. For example, a person may cry but not actually feel any sadness, laugh but experience no joy. Most often, the expressed emotion is cheerful acceptance or euphoria. Yet this apparent sense of well-being can be misleading. It might represent a form of denial or mask underlying depression. Most often, however, it is a symptom of intellectual changes.

Some studies have found memory changes and impaired conceptual ability in about 65 percent of MS victims (Surridge, 1969). In the majority of these cases, the deterioration was slight, but even slight changes can have social and vocational repercussions. As a general rule, the intellectual decline parallels the physical problems. That is, the greater the physical problems, the more likely there are to be some intellectual changes.

Mr. Dean, a single forty-five-year-old man, has a ten-year history of MS. He was diagnosed after a series of unexplained episodes of weakness that were accompanied by facial numbness and tingling sensations. Four years after the diagnosis, Mr. Dean was admitted to the hospital with difficulties controlling his bladder and complaining, "I feed bad, I've lost all my strength." At that time his IQ was 93 [average is 100], but it had clearly declined from a previous level. During the past three years, Mr. Dean's disease has progressed unremittingly, leaving him paraplegic and with nothing more than gross movements in his arms. As a result of these problems, as well as his incontinence, he has been forced to live in a nursing home. Now Mr. Dean's IQ score is 79. He denies any changes in his emotions or intellect but, when pressed, he briefly acknowledges depression and a sense of hopelessness.

Causes and Treatment

The neurological symptoms of the disease are caused by the patchy destruction of material known as myelin, a fatty substance which insulates the neuron. When the myelin sheath breaks down, the conduction of the nerve impulses along the now exposed axon is disrupted, thus leading to the various physical signs of the disease. Eventually, scar tissue forms and produces the hard plaques (sclerosis) for which the disease is named.

MS is about eight times more common in immediate relatives of affected persons than in the general population, but there is no known consistent genetic pattern. Of particular interest is the geographical dispersion of the disease: the incidence rate is three to eleven times higher in more extreme latitudes. That is, there is more MS in Alaska than there is in Florida. Furthermore, if a person lived in a high-risk latitude prior to age fifteen and then moved to an area of lower risk, the person would carry the risk associated with living in the more extreme latitudes. Although a definitive cause for MS is elusive, this geographical data may suggest that MS is the result of a slow-growing virus that may lie dormant in the nervous system.

Unfortunately, even though there is a very active research effort, there is no definitive treatment or cure. Affected individuals are encouraged to exercise and be followed by a neurologist who is current on new developments in the field.

Counseling

There are numerous counseling issues related to MS. But like all persons who are struggling with chronic diseases, affected individuals should not be viewed as cases. Rather, with their unique experiences, they are in a position to learn biblical truths that are hidden from many people. As such, we should be encouraging them to be leaders—

examples of men and women who are learning to live by faith. These people have a great deal to teach the church, especially a church that is filled with comfortable Christians. Indeed, MS can be used by God to bring revival to affected individuals as well as to the larger church community.

But this is not to deny their unique struggles. People with MS often go unnoticed because of their cheerful disposition and apparent acceptance of the disease process. However, the disease inevitably has consequences for both affected individuals and families.

The diagnosis. MS is characterized by unpredictable fluctuations of neurological symptoms. Therefore, the initial diagnosis is not a straightforward process. Many counselees indicate that the early years of the disease are marked by diagnostic confusion, and they are often referred to counselors to treat their mysterious symptoms.

> "Many new diagnoses each new admission. . . no one could clearly explain my symptoms. . . The doctor made arrangements to have me transferred to the psycho unit. I had to call my lawyer and block this sort of treatment." The patient saw a psychiatrist "more than 10 times between 1960–1976." The patient also received "hospitalization, shock treatment, drug therapy, Thorazine, and Mellaril" costing "over $1,500." (Currey, 1982, p. 496)

Counselors must be aware that counselees who have a history of vague neurological complaints that remit and recur may have MS. These counselees should be evaluated medically by a good general practitioner or neurologist.

At the same time, other counselees may have an unwarranted diagnosis of MS. Perhaps a physician or other medical professional suggested possible MS years ago but the counselee is symptom-free. A real problem with misdiagnosis is that people may make decisions based on the possibility of future disability. For example, they may avoid marriage or physically demanding jobs. This can be avoided by second opinions or regular medical evaluations.

The least that can be said about the very early stages of MS is that it is a time of confusion, misunderstanding, and lack of direction. Counselors can be used to give hope and encouragement.

The uncertain course. Closely allied with the diagnostic problems is the unpredictable course of MS. Affected persons never know when, for how long, or with what severity the various symptoms will emerge. As a result, some forsake all plans and retreat in depression and despair. Biblical teaching can allow affected individuals to see that purpose and productivity are consequences of faith, not physical health. From an eternal perspective, there is nothing more powerful and significant than seeking God's kingdom daily by using present gifts, by faith, to the glory of God.

It is also worth mentioning that anxiety, which is common in the face of unpredictability, has been observed to provoke flare-ups of the physical symptoms.

Sexuality. MS patients often mention sexual problems. In men this may take the form of impotence, in females the inability to reach orgasm. Only a small percentage report no changes in their sexual life. Thus, this is an area that requires attention and frank discussion. Open discussion of these issues will go a long way toward the discovery of solutions. Also, impotent men should consider a thorough urological exam and available treatments for impotence.

Role changes. Any change in a person's role in the family or job can be particularly difficult. Perhaps a husband is suddenly in the unwanted role of househusband, or the independent woman is now dependent on her family for basic needs. Role changes need to be discussed biblically.

Emotional and intellectual changes. You are already aware of the emotional or intellectual changes that may accompany MS. This awareness can be put to use by being very specific and concrete when counseling with a declining MS patient. If intellectual changes are apparent, families need to be informed. When families realize that behavioral changes are a consequence of intellectual decline, they are usually more understanding and patient.

Remember, persons with MS tend not to be complainers. As such, they can slip through the cracks of pastoral care. Make a point to meet with them, ask them specific questions, and don't accept superficial answers.[3]

Parkinson's Disease and Related Disorders

Parkinson's disease is a "must-know" disease because it is a chronic, debilitating disease that imposes significant physical limitations, and it can be accompanied by both emotional and intellectual changes.

Symptoms

This by no means rare condition is characterized by tremor, fatigue, muscular rigidity, slow movement, an expressionless face, and a stooping posture. The average age of onset is fifty-five, with the majority of cases beginning between the ages of forty-five and sixty. Life expectancy is diminished in Parkinson's disease, but some patients may show very gradual progression and be relatively active even after twenty years.

> . . . to know what Parkinsonism is you must know the surprise of finding yourself standing in a sloping position as though you were trying to impersonate the leaning tower of Pisa. You must know the bewilderment of finding yourself prisoner in your own clothes closet, unable to back out of it. . . You must live with the near panic which you face when you walk into a roomful of people, and the uneasiness of the questions you ask yourself: Do I just imagine that I can't seem to turn over in bed anymore? How will I get my feet moving when they want to stay glued to the floor? (Bourke-White, 1963, p. 31)

Movement disorders. Tremor is the first sign of the disease in about 75 percent of cases. It may initially begin as a slight, rhythmic tremor in the fingers or a leg, and it may progress to include the arms, jaw, tongue, and occasionally the legs and head. Along with this tremor there may be "pill-rolling" tremors, so called because affected persons seem to be rolling a pill between the thumb and index finger. All these tremors are most obvious when the body is at rest (but not asleep), and they are commonly lost during voluntary movement and sleep. Also, they are exaggerated by fatigue, anxiety, and excitement.

Along with the noticeable tremors, muscular stiffness affects the limbs, trunk, and neck. People with Parkinson's seem physically rigid. In fact, they demonstrate constant resistance to movement, even during sleep. If you try to put their limbs through certain movements, there may be an intermittent change in resistance, called "cogwheel" rigidity; otherwise, the stiffness is persistent.

Slowness and lack of movement are perhaps the most characteristic and problematic features of Parkinson's. It is as if affected persons are moving with the brakes on! It can be seen in slowness to initiate action, near absence of normal arm swing when walking, infrequent blinking, monotonous and mumbling speech, poor handwriting, constipation, and the characteristic expressionless or "mask-like" face. The gait is increasingly affected throughout the disease. It gradually becomes slow and shuffling, often with a tendency to accelerate (festinant gait), and there are marked difficulties in starting, turning, and balance. Patients are often afraid to walk for fear that they will fall, and indeed, they can be a bit unsteady and have a tendency to fall backward. As with the other movement problems, this overall slowness seems to be profoundly affected by emotional states: depression will exaggerate it; excitement may temporarily disguise it.

Other symptoms that occur in Parkinson's disease include a stooped posture, urinary problems, excessive salivation, subjective discomfort, and fatigue. Of particular concern to counselors are reports of intellectual decline and depression.

Depression. Depression is very common in Parkinson's disease, present in over half the patients. Therefore, if families or affected persons want counseling, it is usually for depression. Since the incidence of depression is so high, you should ask patients if they feel depressed—even if they do not actively seek help.

The feelings of depression come from any one of at least four sources (Figure 6.2). First, fatigue and physical slowness, hallmarks of the disease, simply feel like depression. Not only is it difficult for observers to differentiate between physical lethargy and depression, it is also difficult for affected persons to tell the difference! To complicate this dilemma, when Parkinson's patients diagnose themselves as depressed, they begin to look for explanations. Some may blame it on children leaving home, losing old friends, or marital discord (even though these may be present) when the real culprit is a physical sluggishness misinterpreted as depression. If this is the case, counselees can be served by simply helping them reinterpret their depression as Parkinson-induced slowness of movement.

Depression associated with Parkinson's disease may also be a result of the disease itself. It is likely that the disease can affect the brain in such a way that many patients experience depression. (Remember, depression, in itself, is not sinful). Therefore, affected persons may be living by faith and wisdom but still experience depression. In such cases, the best

Figure 6.2. One Possible Interaction Between Heart
and Body in Parkinson's Disease

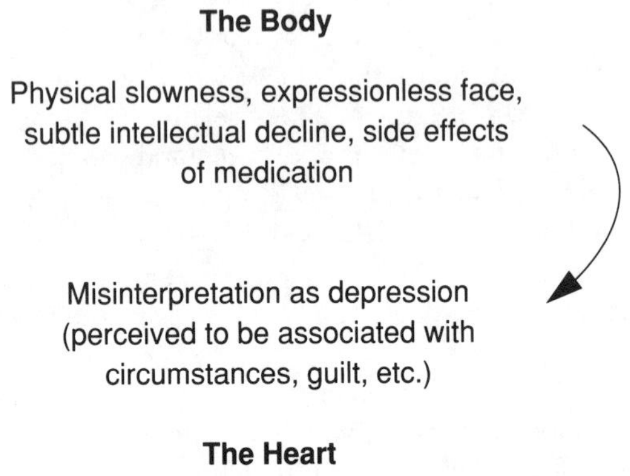

The Body

Physical slowness, expressionless face,
subtle intellectual decline, side effects
of medication

Misinterpretation as depression
(perceived to be associated with
circumstances, guilt, etc.)

The Heart

counsel available will not appreciably alter their depressed mood, but counselors still have important ways to serve. They can remind patients that the feelings of depression are not necessarily indicative of difficult circumstances or underlying spiritual problems. Also, they can provide daily encouragement for patients to look to Christ, interpret their situation by faith, and grow in eternal hope (Heb. 11, 12). As Parkinson's patients grow in faith through their trials, they can have significant counseling ministries themselves.

A third possible cause of depression, or at least something that mimics depression, is intellectual decline. Both may appear as withdrawal, physical and intellectual sluggishness, and rapid emotional fluctuations. The presence and extent of intellectual decline in Parkinson's disease is still debated. Yet most researchers agree that, in some persons, there is demonstrable intellectual decline, imitating a frontal lobe syndrome (Stern & Mayeux, 1987). This means that you must understand those with Parkinson's and make sure their tasks are compatible with their abilities. It is not unusual for families to be frustrated by mistaking intellectual decline for obstinacy, moodiness, and a general lack of concern. When they realize that the cause is intellectual decline rather than personal choice, families are often more sympathetic and supportive.

One other source of depression—the medication used for Parkinson's disease—is discussed below.

Causes and Treatment

Although London physician James Parkinson first described the disease in 1817 (*Essay on the Shaking Palsy*), the cause of Parkinson's disease is not yet fully known. It has been well established that with the disease, there is a marked deficiency of the neurotransmitter dopamine in the basal ganglia area of the brain. This deficiency, however, is indicative of a more basic, underlying dysfunction that remains a mystery.

Despite the unknown cause of Parkinson's disease, in many cases the symptoms of the disorder, including depression, are effectively relieved by medication. Until recently, the most effective medication has been levodopa or L-dopa (e.g., Sinemet). This often provides considerable relief from Parkinson's symptoms. But even though it has been a tremendous benefit for many people, it is not a cure. First, there is no evidence that it stops the progression of the disease. If the medication is stopped, the symptoms will reappear with increased severity, thus demonstrating that the medication is masking the disease process and not treating the underlying disorder. Second, the drug only works for about a year, after which it loses some of its effectiveness even if the doses are increased. As such, the treatment has been described as "trying to patch a leaky boat."

Another problem associated with L-dopa is unwanted side effects. In a review of studies on levodopa treatment (Goodwin, 1971) it was reported that adverse psychological reactions occurred in 10 to 50 percent of those treated. These reactions included confusion, agitation, delusions, hallucinations, euphoria, and depression. Therefore, if you notice these or any other abrupt psychological changes in a person undergoing treatment with levodopa, encourage the family to immediately contact the primary physician. The physician, if necessary, can prescribe another anti-Parkinson drug.

Of the physical side effects of levodopa, one of the most difficult is poor coordination.

> Imagine the embarrassment of eating in a restaurant while you are dyskinetic [poorly coordinated]. With great concentration, you are able to order your muscles to begin to cut your steak; but as you finish the cut, the hand and arm holding the knife seem to escape your control. Your hand shoots out wildly, flinging a piece of pink meat onto the lap of your dinner partner. (Dorros, 1981, p. 196)

Because of the inadequacies associated with L-dopa, there is an active research campaign to find new treatments. The most promising is the drug deprenyl (marketed as Eldepryl). Although possible side effects are not well known, there is good evidence that this drug significantly slows the course of the disease, providing a major breakthrough in Parkinson's treatment. Other treatments remain in the experimental stages but will probably emerge within the next five to ten years. Ongoing contact with a good neurologist is the best way for families of affected persons to keep current on bona fide, new treatments.

Counseling

Along with general suggestions such as encouraging patients to be followed by a good physician and to read as much as they can on their disease, [4] Parkinson's patients also can benefit from regular exercise. This will probably not slow the progress of the disease, but it will minimize the extent of the physical disability. The church can assist by having members volunteer to "work out" with those who have PD. Exercise can be boring alone, and those with PD are rarely highly motivated to do physical activity. The primary physician can suggest a manageable exercise routine.

Another suggestion pertaining to any individuals with a chronic or progressive disease is that they need teaching about a biblical sense of purpose. Any progressive disease that limits activity is an opportunity to reevaluate issues such as success, personal goals, the future, and personal impact. Usually, like everyone else, those with Parkinson's disease accept the cultural myth that purpose is based on productivity in the marketplace rather than faith.

Other counseling suggestions and cautions follow from understanding the changes that are peculiar to Parkinson's:

—Don't mistake fatigue for apathy or lack of facial expression for indifference.

—Ask about depression, and realize that it may have at least four different causes.

—Be alert to medication-induced depression or mental changes.

—Be patient when trying to understand the sometimes garbled speech.

—In light of the possible intellectual changes, be certain that patients understand you.

Other Parkinsonian Symptoms

Parkinson's disease is not the only disease that presents a Parkinsonian cluster of symptoms. Other diseases and drugs that affect the substantia nigra section of the brain can also produce the same symptoms. The most common "secondary" cause of Parkinsonism is the side effects of prescription drugs, especially antipsychotic drugs. These drugs are commonly used in the treatment of schizophrenia, severe depression, psychosis, and other profound psychological changes. The Parkinsonian side effects usually occur within three months after beginning drug treatment, and they usually subside within three weeks after stopping the drug. Again, if you observe these symptoms, encourage affected persons to have their medication reviewed by a physician.

There are other conditions that mimic Parkinson's, but most of them are not medically treatable. For your information, some of these include lack of oxygen due to a heart attack, carbon monoxide poisoning, Alzheimer's disease, Wilson's disease, and cerebral arteriosclerosis. Perhaps the one you are most familiar with, and may have observed, is Parkinson's symptoms that are the result of repeated head injuries from boxing.

Seizures and Epilepsy

"Seizures" have been long associated with demon possession, evil, the mysterious, and the bizarre. Described by Hippocrates about 400 B.C. and well known in New Testament times (e.g., Matt. 4:24), they are certainly one of the most easily recognized of all medical problems. Their violent "fits" continue to be very unpredictable and frightening. And medical science is still a long way from fully understanding their causes.

Most people think of seizures only as the dramatic fits of the grand mal attacks: "He often falls into the fire or into the water" (Matt. 17:15). Yet seizures actually consist of a very broad spectrum of disorders that can have many different causes and many different modes of presentation. Some seizures may be imperceptible even to the trained observer. What unifies this motley array of symptoms is that they are all characterized by changes in the electrical activity of the brain.

During a seizure, the communication of neurons—a low-level electrical brain chatter—is disrupted and suddenly transformed into a united, resounding chorus. When this abnormal firing spreads throughout the entire brain and includes both hemispheres, as in the case of a grand mal seizure, it is called a *generalized seizure*. When the seizure remains localized, affecting only a circumscribed area of the brain, it is called a *partial seizure*. *Epilepsy* means that the seizures, generalized or partial, tend to recur.

Generalized Seizures

Generalized seizures include grand mal seizures, technically known as generalized tonic-clonic seizures (Gastaut, 1970), but they also include other seizure types. Perhaps best known of these are the subtle petit mal seizures. Found only in children, petit mal, or absence seizures, last from a few seconds to half a minute. During the seizure, children exhibit a vacant, motionless stare, absence of speech, and normal balance and posture with maybe a drop of the head. When the seizure is over, affected children immediately resume their normal activities. These seizures usually disappear by adolescence, although in about 50 percent of these cases the petit mal seizures are replaced by grand mal seizures (Trimble, 1988).

Also included under generalized epilepsy are two, very brief seizures: akinetic seizures and myoclonic jerks. Akinetic seizures consist of a brief loss of muscle tone, and generalized myoclonic jerks are brief but often violent movements in the neck, arms, or legs. Chances are you have experienced myoclonic jerks—or have been kicked by someone who has. These are often experienced by nonepileptics when falling asleep, yet if they occur during the day, they may indicate an underlying brain disease and the person should be medically evaluated.

The most common and well-known generalized seizures are the grand mal (big bad) or tonic-clonic seizures. Up to 5 percent of the population will experience this type of seizure at some time in their lives, and about 1 percent of the population is epileptic. Yet among this large group, there is no one underlying cause. Head injury, medical illness, fever, CNS infection, alcohol abuse and drug toxicity, abnormal venous structures in the brain, and brain tumors are only a few of the potential causes of seizures. Many epileptic conditions still have no known cause.

Grand mal seizures are characterized by the following symptoms: the aura, a cry, a fall, a tonic-clonic phase, incontinence, and post-seizure (postictal) confusion or lethargy. An aura, reported in 30 percent of seizures, is a kind of warning sign that may last for hours or even days before the seizure. It may consist of nausea, headache, mood changes, gastrointestinal discomfort, or simply feeling "different." The seizure itself begins with an epileptic cry—a sometimes blood-curdling sound that occurs when the initial, resounding discharge of neurons constricts the muscles in the chest. Since the brain is not functioning at this time, unconsciousness is immediate and a horrible fall can follow. Persons with recurrent and unmanageable seizures will probably report a history of injuries that occurred during the fall. In fact, although long-term brain damage from seizures themselves is rare, if there is brain injury, it is usually a result of the many head injuries sustained during the attacks.

Following the fall, seizures progress into a phase of muscle constriction, or tonic phase, and then continue into the most infamous of the symptoms—the violent spasms of the clonic phase. These phases can last up to a few minutes, during which time affected persons are often incontinent of urine or feces. After this time of incredible physical exertion, people are left exhausted, sleeping, or temporarily confused. Headaches and muscle pain can last for days.

Fortunately, most epileptics can take medication that controls seizures. Tegretol (carbamazepine), Dilantin (phenytoin), Luminal (phenobarbitol) and other medications have been used successfully. These medications are, however, associated with side effects such as sedation, intellectual decline (Hartledge & Mains, 1981), nausea and vomiting, and liver toxicity. Furthermore, there are some epileptics who are not helped by the medication.

Counseling implications. Perhaps the most obvious counseling issue associated with uncontrolled epilepsy is the fear of another seizure. Epileptics live in an unpredictable world where they may lose control at any time. Without warning, they may find themselves waking up on a sidewalk, incontinent of urine or feces, and surrounded by fifty transfixed onlookers. Friends might treat them differently, employers are reluctant to hire them, and, often the most difficult aspect of epilepsy, automobile privileges are suspended for at least a year. Not surprisingly, depression is commonplace and suicide rates for epileptics are five times greater than those of nonepileptics (Lechtenberg, 1982). Therefore, always ask uncontrolled epileptics about depression and suicidal thinking.

Counselors should also be alert to possible undiagnosed epilepsy. If a person has experienced a grand mal seizure, or a counselee mentions blackouts, they *must* undergo a medical evaluation. This should include a thorough history, a neurological exam, and EEG, and, if warranted, a CT scan or MRI. Perhaps there will be no apparent explanation for a seizure, but seizures, especially if they occur for the first time after age thirty, are frequently the first symptom of a treatable but potentially lethal brain tumor.

After his discharge from the army, Tom's life was characterized by poor decisions, legal problems, poor or few relationships, and unpredictability. He separated from his wife and was soon arrested for car theft. Six months later, he was again arrested but on a much more serious charge—his wife's murder. However, the coroner's report was inconclusive, and he was released from jail. Two months later he stole another car in order to "find my son" and was given probation with the stipulation that he not leave the state. He left almost immediately, "borrowed a car," drove 2000 miles to "find my son" (with no idea where he might be), decided to go see Mount St. Helen's [after the eruption], and was apprehended for speeding in a state that was nowhere near a logical route to Washington State. He was given a two-year jail sentence.

Within one week of entering prison, he experienced a violent grand mal seizure. CT scan revealed a huge tumor that dominated his right frontal lobe. It was likely that his erratic behavior was a consequence of spiritual issues as well as frontal lobe symptoms (distractability, poor ability to plan. . .). He died six months later.

Misdiagnosed epilepsy also has counseling relevance. Some people are wrongly diagnosed as epileptics when they consciously use seizures for secondary gain. People actually fake seizures. Both those who have epilepsy and those who do not can stage the dramatic grand mal symptoms to obtain certain perceived privileges. For the dramatically inclined, these faked seizures are near photocopies of the real thing—indistinguishable even to experts. They are suspected when seizures consistently occur at convenient times, when there have never been injuries associated with the falls, or when there has been a history of grand mal attacks, yet no urinary incontinence. Consult with a physician if these signs are present.

Compliance in taking medication is another recurring issue with epileptics. Remember, between seizures, epilepsy is relatively silent, so affected people see little reason to take medication. Also, since medication may have unwanted side effects, epileptics might feel as if they have good reason not to take medication. If you find that counselees take medication "when I remember it," refer them back to their physician for reevaluation or instruction.

Finally, both generalized and partial seizures may be precipitated by sensory and possibly emotional stimulation. This is certainly not the case with all epileptics, yet some people may experience seizures only in the presence of some specific stimuli. Astute counselors may pinpoint the epileptic trigger and perhaps help a person avoid future attacks. These triggers will be discussed more fully under partial complex seizures.

Partial Seizures

Partial seizures affect only part of the brain. Therefore, their symptoms are less obvious than those of generalized seizures. But what they lack in drama they make up for in variety and eccentricity. For example, if you happened to talk with a young man who was seeing the head of a barking dog—always on the left—but heard no bark, and who was seeing a woman sitting in a chair, in the TV, but knew she was not part of the program because she was there during commercials, you would immediately question his sanity. These symptoms, however, are definitely organic—they are a result of partial complex seizures.

Elementary seizures. The two types of partial seizures are called *elementary* and *complex*. During elementary seizures (also called simple or focal seizures), a person is usually conscious and responsive and can describe the episode in detail. Their symptoms depend on the brain area affected. Therefore, the best way to detect elementary partial seizures is to know the behavioral correlates of the four lobes of the brain. For example, seizure activity in the motor strip might produce involuntary movements in the limbs (Jacksonian epilepsy) or twitching in the face or hand. The parietal lobe might be responsible for sensory changes such as numbness or tingling. The temporal lobe tends to produce the most unusual symptoms, such as hallucinations of offensive tastes or smells. And elementary seizures in the occipital lobe can be reported as visual hallucinations, such as flashing lights or moving spots. These symptoms last from a few seconds to several minutes.

One diagnostically fascinating example of an elementary seizure was that of a man who, during a routine medical check-up, happened to mention that he occasionally smelled "burnt rubber." The physician, alert to a possible organic symptom, decided to pursue the patient's comment. "Is there a reason for you to smell burnt rubber? Do you smell it when other people smell it?" The gentleman indicated that he lived in the desert and there was no obvious source for such a smell. Immediately, the physician scheduled a CT scan. Diagnosis: temporal lobe tumor.

Fortunately, the physician knew that smell or taste hallucinations, especially when they are disagreeable, can betray a physical problem. Because of his prompt diagnosis, the man's tumor was treated and he recovered quickly.

Complex seizures. With all due respect to elementary partial seizures, the complex partial seizures are easily the most intriguing of the partial seizures. And along with their unusual symptoms, they offer some theological challenges for counselors because they are allegedly associated with rage and explosive anger.

During elementary seizures, a person is alert. During complex seizures mental awareness is blurred in some way. The person is not completely unconscious: they may hear sounds or perform automatic, purposeless acts, but they are temporarily unresponsive to their surroundings.

The seizure. Seizures last from a few seconds to several minutes. If you ask epileptics what they remember of a complex seizure, they may draw a complete blank. Sometimes, however, they may recall some peculiar changes in thoughts or emotions. People have described terrifying but irrational fears (Macrae, 1954); irrelevant thoughts that seem to persist (obsessional thoughts); intense anxiety, depression, or anger; a feeling of familiarity with unfamiliar events (déjà vu); and a feeling of unfamiliarity with things that should be familiar (jamais vu). Other strange experiences include running, uncontrolled laughing (gelastic epilepsy), orgasm, a feeling of indigestion, and dizziness! It is no wonder that partial complex seizures are easily misdiagnosed as "psychological problems."

> Before his seizures [during the aura] a man experienced dizziness, a bell ringing, and a compulsion to think of "number two" before losing consciousness. The obsessional thought was probably a result of having been fecally incontinent until the age of six. At that time, he called feces "number two." (Lishman, 1978)

> A twenty-one-year-old woman had experienced two generalized [grand mal] seizures as a child—one at age three, one at age four. At age ten, episodes of fear began that lasted from two minutes to twelve hours. She appeared afraid, perspired, and did not want to be left alone. She would say she was "scared" and continually looked back over her shoulder. When she was older, she had frequent seizures in bed, consisting of crawling around the bed, rubbing the pillow, lighting a cigarette, moaning, chewing, and

salivating—usually with a fearful expression. After surgery and medication, she had no further episodes. (McLachlin & Blume, 1979)

Epileptics also report bizarre yet fascinating hallucinations. Geometric designs, flashing lights, musical tunes, unpleasant odors or tastes such as feces or dishwater, mechanical sounds, and changes in the perceived size of a body part (Currey, 1982). These can occur in any sensory modality (taste, touch, sight, sound, smell), and are distinguished from schizophrenic hallucinations in that they tend to be impersonal, nondirective, stereotypic, and not part of a delusional system.

"All of a sudden I developed many unusual symptoms, including bending over in a park and vomiting, mental blocking, confusion, writing backwards, inability to see certain colors. There would be waves on the wall, wall and curtains would turn wavy or into water. I'd get deja vu or walk two blocks away and not know how I got there. I was talking to someone from five years ago when really I was talking to my husband. . . I was diagnosed as schizophrenic and hysterical. . . Finally I had an abnormal EEG in the right temporal area." This woman was finally treated with an anti-seizure medication and her symptoms largely disappeared. (Currey, 1982, p. 498)

If you ask observers what they noticed, they will usually indicate that epileptics performed some repetitive activity such as chewing motions, lip-smacking, grimacing, spitting, repeatedly buttoning and unbuttoning, picking at one's clothes, or incessant pouring and drinking. The key is that they act like robots. They may appear to be moving about in a normal manner, but behavior is random—without any goal—and there is only spotty recollection of events. As a result, although the complex partial seizure is often used as a legal defense, it is rarely effective.[5]

Legal disappointments notwithstanding, there is increasing enthusiasm among researchers for associating complex seizures (temporal lobe seizures) with violent anger. The "disease" has been called episodic dyscontrol syndrome (also limbic rage) and it is "characterized by recurrent attacks of uncontrolled rage, usually without provocation and often completely out of character" (Elliot, 1984, p. 113). People report feeling out of control—"I didn't know what I was doing." In some cases, these symptoms are reportedly calmed with medication (Inderal, Tegretol, Dilantin).

The postseizure (postictal) period. Unlike the elementary seizures, complex partial seizures are often followed by a short time of confusion or poor responsiveness, usually lasting no more than ten minutes. Some observers have reported postictal violence, but this is probably related to confusion more than purposeful violence. The confusion gradually lifts and victims are left with memory gaps, but only of the seizure itself.

The period between seizures (interictal). An area of active research and debate is the behaviors of epileptics during the interictal period, or the period between the actual seizures (Bear & Fedio; 1977; Tucker, Price, Johnson & McAllister, 1986). To summarize, persons with complex partial seizures tend to have a higher incidence of counseling-type problems than the nonepileptic population. They seem to have increased emotional intensity from elation to anger, unusual emotional fluctuations, decreased sexual interest, extensive and compulsive writing (diaries, autobiographies), unusual but deeply held religious beliefs (Tucker, Novelly & Walker, 1987), and compulsive attention to detail.

A twenty-five-year-old woman had seizures that had begun at the age of ten. The seizures were usually generalized, often beginning with twitching in the left arm and face, and on some occasions, were associated with lip-smacking and chewing movements that were followed by urinary incontinence and tongue-biting. She had begun to write extensively when she was fifteen years old, often spending hours per day writing. She was constantly writing lists: items of food and furniture in her house, her records and books, her friends, songs her father could play on the harmonica. She recounted having recurrently written "at least hundreds of times" the words to a song she had learned when she was seventeen. At the age of twenty-one, she began to experience auras before her seizures. They took various forms. Sometimes they consisted of nausea and a feeling of fear before her seizures. Other times, they were visual hallucinations of colored flashing lights that moved from left to right. Interestingly, the woman became devoutly religious and experienced at least five religious conversions. On one occasion, she described her conversion as "like seeing God." (Waxman & Geschwind, 1975)

Epileptic triggers. A curious aspect of seizures, both generalized and partial, is that some of them can be induced by different types of stimuli. About 6 percent of epileptics have seizures that are called reflex or sensory-precipitated seizures (Mavor, 1980; Fenwick, 1981).

Visual stimulation is probably the most common provoker of seizures. In fact, some physicians, when testing for seizures by way of an EEG, will try to induce a mild seizure with strobe-like flickering. Usually, the stimulation must have some rhythmic features such as flickering lights, strobe lights, or video games. Some children have been known to pass their hands repeatedly in front of their eyes while looking at the sun, or to jump up and down while looking through Venetian blinds, possibly with the intent of producing a mild, pleasurable seizure (Robertson, 1954).

Other unusual yet fascinating precipitants include specific tones or types of music (e.g., church bells), rubbing or touching a place on the body, seeing a safety pin, performing arithmetic calculations, strong emotions, and observing Hebrew letters. It is likely that the triggering quality of some of these objects and events results from their association (in the mind of the patient)with some emotional experience (Feldman & Paul, 1976).

A thirty-nine-year-old man had seizures from the age of ten. His peculiar aura consisted of nausea, raising a hand above his face, and saying "Don't hit me Dad, please don't hit me." He also described a scene of his father threatening him with a poker. A person who knew this man and his father stated that the father had actually struck the patient with a poker just before his first seizure. (Lishman, 1978)

A woman had her first seizure in an anxious situation after having lived in a desolate war environment. Her aura consisted of a scene of a city in ruins accompanied by a strong sense that she had been there before (deja vu). Many years later it was still possible to provoke an abnormal EEG by inviting her to remember the pre-seizure scene of the city in ruins. (Lishman, 1978)

Diagnosis and treatment. When physicians suspect seizures, they usually conduct a battery of tests that include blood studies, CT, EEG, and a neurological exam. The electroencephalograph (EEG) is an older device that painlessly measures electrical brain activity. It remains the diagnostic cornerstone, but it is not perfect. A normal EEG is possible in an epileptic, and an abnormal EEG is possible in a seizure-free adult.

Like the grand mal seizures, partial seizures are often controlled with medication. Yet medication does not always work, and there are potential side effects.

Counseling. Partial seizures are perhaps the best example in medicine of an illness that is frequently misdiagnosed. The unusual symptoms are commonly mistaken for nonmedical phenomena. Therefore, counselors should be aware of the basic characteristics of partial seizures and, when suspecting seizures, be quick to get corroborating data from persons who know or live with possible epileptics. The key to detection is that the symptoms are usually brief and without any clear provocation. Other alerting symptoms include: (1) blurred or clouded consciousness: epileptics usually have a hazy recollection of events; (2) rapidly rising, unprovoked emotions; (3) hallucinations; (4) brief obsessional thoughts; and (5) ritualistic or repetitive behavior.

The second significant counseling issue concerns the interictal behavior of some epileptics, and, more importantly, allegations that complex seizures can make people violent. This area is particularly challenging to Christian counselors because counselors have always been persuaded that anger was the Scripture's purview, not medicine's. Now, our theology is being tested. Can seizures make someone sin? Can people be morally unresponsible during seizures?

The evidence for episodic dyscontrol syndrome began in the animal laboratory. Researchers found that when they electrically stimulated certain parts of an animal's limbic system, they could provoke rage responses. This planted an idea. "Perhaps," some physicians surmised, "some of the anger we see in our patients is a result of electrical activity in the limbic region of the brain." Thus a new disease was born.

Before you jettison a biblical model, however, realize that there are some problems with the diagnosis; dissenting views exist both from scientific and biblical quarters. From a scientific perspective, it is perplexing that almost all cases of limbic rage are directed toward family members. While at work or with other people, these individuals are fine, but with family they demonstrate explosive anger. A second problem is that there are no documented cases of actual brain seizure activity during a rage episode. Granted, it would be almost impossible to hook up a person to an EEG before a rage attack, but without that evidence, the case for seizure-induced rage is weakened. Third, in most cases, there is no evidence for a distinct or consistent abnormality in the brain.

From a biblical perspective, there are two basic problems. First, although animal experiments can be very helpful, there are significant differences between animals and humans. Humans are created in the image of God while animals have no apparent moral dimension in their lives. Animals are not commanded to obey God's law—they are not commanded to refrain from sin in their anger—but humans are. Animal studies cannot always be directly translated into human experience.

The second problem is that sinful anger is an issue of the heart, not

Figure 6.3. Possible Interaction Between Heart and Body
in Episodic Dyscontrol Syndrome

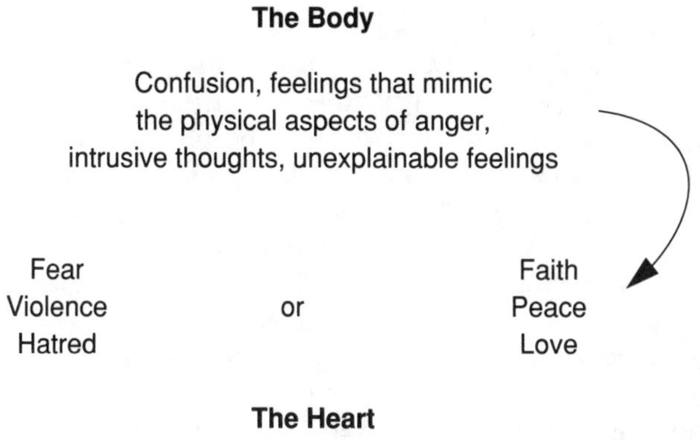

The Body

Confusion, feelings that mimic
the physical aspects of anger,
intrusive thoughts, unexplainable feelings

Fear   Faith
Violence   or   Peace
Hatred   Love

The Heart

the body. The body can provide stumbling blocks for the heart, but it cannot force someone to sin. Furthermore, the biblical model isn't surprised when people report that they feel out of control with their sinful behavior. That is simply the nature of sin. People actually *are* out of control. They need help from another source, but they remain responsible for their behavior.

This does not mean that there is no possible connection between complex seizures and explosive anger. As Figure 6.3 represents, seizures may impose experiences that make it more difficult to resist sin. If these physical experiences encounter a heart that is unprepared, they can easily provoke sinful responses. As such, even though the research on limbic rage is unclear, counselors can refer some people for medical evaluation and possible medication if they seem to struggle with rage. The best candidates for referral are people who have had some obvious brain injury.

Stroke, or Cerebral Vascular Accident (CVA)

Strokes are well-known causes of brain damage that result in a plethora of difficulties. Foremost among these is the difficulty in understanding the effects of strokes on personality, emotions, and cognitive functions.

An emerging theme in this book is that families are inadequately prepared for the changes that occur after a brain injury. Strokes are no exception. Families usually have an unwarranted assumption that cognitive damage will improve at the same rate as other physical disabilities. This, however, is rarely the case. Physical problems such as severe weakness or paralysis may abate while disruptive psychological difficulties stubbornly persist. Furthermore, these cognitive changes tend to be most apparent to families after the physical problems improve.

In the early stages after a stroke, families are mostly concerned about blatant physical problems; psychological changes tend to be ignored or masked by optimism and the controlled environment of the hospital. When physical problems stabilize or improve, psychological changes can take families by surprise. Unfortunately, by this time friends and churches believe there has been a full recovery and everything is back to normal— no more help is needed. In fact, it is not uncommon for churchgoers to be rejoicing over physical recovery while families are quietly suffering over emerging personality, emotional, and cognitive changes. When help and counsel is needed most, it may not be there, and families are often reluctant to ask for it.

Types of CVAs

Stroke and cerebral vascular accident (CVA) are general terms that refer to a disturbance of the blood vessels or arteries in the brain. Strokes occur when the blood fails to get oxygen to brain cells. The disturbance is usually a sudden, dramatic development with distinct neurological deficits such as paralysis or pronounced weakness. However, it may have a very slow, insidious onset, and in its mildest form it may consist of only subtle physical changes that go unnoticed.

There are two general classifications of stroke: ischemic and hemorrhagic. Ischemic strokes are the result of obstructions that reduce the flow of blood. Brain cells are then deprived of oxygen and there is resulting "infarction, " or cell death. Hemorrhagic strokes are caused by tears in cerebral blood vessels. The subsequent bleeding disrupts rather than kills brain cell activity.

Ischemic strokes
Cerebral thrombosis. Cerebral infarction due to thrombosis is the cause of approximately 60 percent of strokes. A thrombosis is a clot (occlusion) in a blood vessel that restricts or prohibits the flow of blood. It is usually a result of fatty buildup called atherosclerosis, but it can also

be related to trauma, obesity, sickle cell disease, smoking, lupus, diabetes, and other diseases that affect the cerebral blood vessels. The course of thrombotic strokes is more variable and perhaps less dramatic than other strokes. In the majority of cases, it is preceded by minor neurological changes called transient ischemic attacks (TIA). During a TIA, the affected artery is only partially blocked and allows intermittent blood flow. The results vary depending on the affected brain area, and attacks last from a few seconds up to eight hours with the average being less than ten minutes. Since 35 percent of TIA victims are likely to experience another stroke in the five years following their TIA, detection should lead to immediate medical referral. Anticoagulant medicine is often the first treatment and "balloon" surgeries are becoming increasingly popular.

The stroke itself may develop in one of several ways. In 60 percent of the cases, there is a single attack that develops over a few hours. Other cases may demonstrate a step-like or intermittent progression where symptoms wax and wane until, over days or even weeks, a full stroke develops. The stroke often occurs during sleep and is apparent shortly after rising.

Predicting improvement in stroke victims is still a very imperfect process. In adults, improvement may begin within hours and continue up to two years. Some severe deficits, however, show little or no improvement. If some recovery does not begin within two weeks, prognosis is guarded. After five to six months, motor problems such as paralysis tend to improve very little while difficulties with speech (aphasia and dysarthria), walking, and psychological functions may show improvement for up to two years.

Cerebral embolism. Embolic strokes result from the sudden blocking of an artery by a clot or obstruction which has been transported to its place from another part of the body. Accordingly, CVAs due to emboli usually develop without warning. The stroke is often related to heart disease because irregular heart contractions can dislodge potentially obstructive matter from vessel walls. These emboli gradually find their way to the smaller arteries of the brain and produce an infarction (cell death). After the stroke they can move from their resting place and produce yet another stroke in another area of the brain.

Hemorrhagic strokes
Cerebral hemorrhage. Strokes from hemorrhages, or ruptured arteries,

can result from high blood pressure, ruptured aneurysms, bleeding disorders and arteriovenous (blood vessel) malformations. The stroke is often preceded by a situation that raises blood pressure, such as straining with a bowel movement, coughing, sex, violent emotion, or heavy eating. The bleed may be small and slow or relatively large and explosive—symptoms develop accordingly. The symptoms usually progress in a gradual, steady fashion, taking perhaps days to reach their peak.

Since it is very difficult to stop major bleeds in the brain, up to 70 percent of hemorrhagic patients die within a few hours to thirty days. Of those who survive, however, there is a greater tendency to regain function. This is probably due to the fact that hemorrhages disrupt rather than destroy brain tissue.

Dorothy, a sixty-year-old oriental grandmother who was a practicing Buddhist, collapsed suddenly and was rushed to the hospital. She was comatose for twenty-eight days but was left with only insignificant physical disabilities. Her left eye muscle was impaired and her eyelid drooped, she moved slowly, dragging her left foot, and she had little normal arm swing with her left arm. The most alarming repercussions of the stroke were not these, but the loss of short-term memory, the near absence of voluntary actions, depression, and psychosis.

Dorothy moved in with her son and his family and was immediately disruptive. She would try to escape out of windows, perhaps in obedience to or to escape her fearful hallucinations. For example, at dinner, she would occasionally ask for more food than she could eat and secretly put it on the floor. "You are starving him [her hallucinatory companion]," she would respond when questioned, and she was furious when restrained from putting the food on the floor. At other times she would hide behind the curtains saying, "That thing is here! There it is!" Due to her almost complete loss of short-term memory, she would repeat questions endlessly. Most of the time, they concerned the whereabouts of loved ones: "Is he home yet?" (Her grandson once counted this question forty-six times in less than an hour.) Her lack of voluntary movement was also difficult. She could carry out basic maintenance tasks such as brushing her teeth, dressing, and eating, but she needed incessant reminders. As a result, she needed an attendant at all times. Her moods were completely unpredictable. Some days she would get up and, for no apparent reason, start weeping, sometimes asking, "Where is my Mom? I want my Mom." During these times she was inconsolable. Only exhaustion and sleep would help.

During this time, Dorothy's family continued to pray for her. They taught her about Jesus and even started teaching her John 3:16. To their surprise, she memorized it and recited it with only a few hints. Later, with her limited vocabulary, she began to tell people that she believed in Jesus. She would also tell people about Jesus—even though she could not consistently recognize her own children. Those who have known her are amazed at the revival of her spirit and the obvious growth in joy and peace. At her request, she was baptized.

Multi-infarct dementia. Multi-infarct dementia is second only to Alzheimer's disease as a cause of intellectual impairment in the elderly. As its name indicates, it consists of multiple infarcts, or many small strokes, and is common in people who have high blood pressure or some evidence of cerebral vascular disease. The disease usually progresses in an unpredictable but stepped fashion with one neurological problem overlaid on another. The progression, however, can be so subtle that it leaves no obvious physical changes—only psychological manifestations such as depression, psychosis, and intellectual deterioration (Cummings, 1987).

One interesting symptom in some cases of multi-infarct dementia is emotional lability, or rapid emotional changes that seem unwarranted by the circumstances.

Mr. Hughs is a relatively active sixty-nine-year-old who entered the hospital after a suspected heart attack. He had experienced some severe chest pain while chopping wood and was taken to his local physician, who found Mr. Hughs's blood pressure to be 200/120. Immediately, he was sent to the hospital.

Except for the high blood pressure he was given a clean bill of health, but something was not quite right. After the first day in the hospital, he enumerated many emotional, social, and family problems in a very tearful manner. They seemed to be related to his recent retirement. However, on subsequent visits, he was not interested in talking about these previous concerns at all! Yet his emotional intensity was unabated. He would swing from joy and elation to irrepressible tears within one sentence, without any provocation. When asked about this, Mr. Hughs indicated that he had been having problems controlling his emotions. Furthermore, he indicated that there were times when he displayed emotion while he was emotionally unmoved. His wife corroborated this. She also reported that the labile emotions had been apparent for at least two years, and they were accompanied by lots of "silly" and inappropriate comments and poor memory.

Counseling

The symptoms of strokes vary depending on the location of the brain damage and its severity. A large stroke in the left frontal lobe will produce obvious problems such as paralysis on the right side of the body and a Broca's aphasia. A smaller stroke in the right hemisphere may simply make the left side of the face droop and appear expressionless, but it may leave a patient otherwise symptom-free. A stroke in the occipital lobe may leave a person blind but with no other apparent physical or psychological symptoms. In order to understand the stroke patient, you should review the behavioral changes associated with the damaged area (chapter 4).

Sexual relationship. I will underline only two problems that are often associated with strokes: sexual problems and speech problems. Sexual issues are often neglected because of embarrassment (for the counselor or counselee) or, in the case of older patients, because of the myth that "older people aren't interested in sex." But stroke patients, if sexually active before the injury, usually desire to be sexually active afterward. One study indicated that of 102 stroke patients, there was about a 60 percent decrease in sexual activity but only a 14 percent decrease in sexual desire (Lavin, 1985). With medical consultation, sexual activity can be resumed as soon as the patient's symptoms are stable. The impediments to satisfactory sexual relationships after strokes tend to be fears more than physiology. More specifically, sexual changes are often related to fear that a stroke may recur, fear of being perceived as unattractive, depression, and a sense of personal inadequacy.

Granted, sexuality is a bit complicated with more severe strokes. Patients may have a very poor memory and have little knowledge of previous sexual activity. In fact, this knowledge may be wiped out altogether! If the stroke victim has been spared from a Wernicke's aphasia (difficulties comprehending), spouses might have to give specific directions and, perhaps in conjunction with pastors or counselors, reeducate their stroke-affected partners.

A different kind of sexually related problem is when spouses are baffled by the patient's emotional and cognitive changes and are uninterested in sexual intimacy. Many spouses report, "This is not the person I married." In such situations, thoughts of intimacy might actually be repulsive, and divorce is commonplace. Certainly, pastors and counselors have critical functions during this time. Along with offering a biblical perspective on the relationship, counselors can begin to explain the cognitive changes that underlie the apparent personality changes. Also, counselors can encourage families to focus less on weaknesses and more on the uncompromised moral ability and remaining gifts of stroke patients. As a rule, stroke patients are usually desirous and capable of having a sexual relationship—some even have better sexual relationships after the stroke. The "mechanical" problems due to paralysis or spasticity can often be circumvented. Be assertive in asking questions and getting information from counselees, and be quick to get medical consultation regarding physical limitations to sexual activity.

Speech and communication difficulties. A second problem commonplace in strokes involves language and comprehension difficulties. Broca's aphasia, for example, relatively common among stroke patients, spares many intellectual processes but may severely compromise normal communication.

Bernice, at age forty-two, collapsed to the floor with a left-sided cerebral hemorrhage. She was left with a right-sided paralysis and was unable to speak. After four months this determined, college-educated teacher could walk with a distinct limp and use her right hand, but she could say only three words. "For two years I spoke one word, two words. Then it started to come, a little bit at a time. I was determined to speak." After six years she was, with some word-finding difficulties, able to converse, but only one-to-one. "Three or four people—two conversations—forget it." Her reading and writing were similarly affected. "I have one word at a time for reading, one word. Then I go back and reread it." When she writes to a friend, "it's difficult, because I can't write sentences. One word. But then the week ends—and I will mail the letter."

Her friends, except for one or two, seem to have drifted away, and in their place she has substituted stroke clubs. "I listen, I read, but it's not the same as the stroke clubs. I enjoy people." But interestingly, she has noticed that the stroke clubs often consist of male victims with their wives, while the female victims come alone. "The women! The women sit at home and stare. I went two days ago to a stroke club. There were four women, and eleven or twelve men with their wives. Women by themselves—men with wives."

Now divorced with a grown son, Bernice is working in clay to strengthen her hand and has been producing some fine art work. But life has changed. "I can't explain the difficulties. I was full of life and now I'm withdrawn. I was a teacher, and now it's the other way around! I would love to do something. I would love to live downtown and go to the theaters and the concerts. I would like to go to Italy to study the marble. I would love to teach—but it's not possible." (Shultes, 1985)

This type of story is easily duplicated. Divorce is common. Friends disappear. The wife of a mildly aphasic man may invite old friends over because her husband enjoys the company. But soon she realizes that her husband is always sitting alone, or people begin declining her invitations. A stroke patient may love to have someone to go fishing with, only to find that no one is ever interested. Those who do approach a stroke patient are often startled and back off when the patient begins to laugh or cry uncontrollably or when the patient uses an occasional swear word.

Here are a few suggestions for communicating with those who experience Broca's aphasia. Basically, the comments are just common sense. But, strangely, common sense somtimes goes by the wayside when interacting with a stroke patient.

—Look at the person while you are talking.

—Try to get the main idea. As illustrated by Bernice, not all the words are used correctly, but you can still get the message.

—Don't try to supply the word for the person. Just be patient.

—Realize that profanity may uncharacteristically slip into the remaining vocabulary. Don't be alarmed. For some reason, it is relatively common among stroke patients.

—Ask questions if you don't understand. If you can't get the idea, suggest that you come back to the topic later.

—Realize that you can communicate with people who cannot talk. If comprehension is a problem, communication will be very difficult. But if the problem is limited to Broca's area (and language production), they can understand you and can communicate through gesture and facial expressions.

—If asking questions, try to ask closed questions more than open ones. For example, rather than "Can I get you anything?" ask, "Can I get you coffee or tea?"

—Be creative. Look for things you can do together than don't require much conversation.

—Physical affection and touch always go a long way. (Shultes, 1985)

One final reminder: if you haven't actually experienced a stroke in your family, it is impossible to understand the struggles. Do everything you can to understand both the world of the stroke patient and that of the family. Read whatever you can; you can even ask families for a list of readings that would help you understand them. Also, don't forget that these family struggles usually emerge after an initial honeymoon period. At the outset, families report that they are simply delighted that the injured member is alive and getting better. When the person comes home, and the psychological changes appear in full bloom, families often feel frustrated, overwhelmed, or guilty. They are reluctant to discuss these problems except with the closest friends for fear they will sound like complainers. Without question, there must be long-term pastoral interest and diaconal care for the brain-injured person and the family.

Brain Tumors

We are moving into an era in medicine when a discussion of brain tumors is no longer filled with fear and prognostic pessimism. Advancements in treatment emerge monthly, and longevity statistics are constantly being updated. No longer is the diagnosis "brain tumor" the signal to immediately settle your affairs.

Medical Overview

Tumors, also called neoplams, are either benign or malignant. Cancer is synonymous with malignant tumors. These abnormal proliferations of cells invade and destroy surrounding healthy tissue.[6]
There are many types of malignant brain tumors, each with a distinctive signature. Some grow like a plant, with an extensive "root" system that infiltrates other areas. Others might have clearly defined boundaries. These are called encapsulated tumors and, if accessible, can be removed surgically. Tumors are also categorized by the type of glial cell involved, the location in the brain, or the particular characteristics of the cell (e.g., blastoma). The most frequent malignant gliomas are the glioblastoma multiforme (23% of brain tumors), astrocytoma (13%), and oligodendroglioma (2%). Other common brain tumors include meningiomas (16%), pituitary tumors (8%), and metastatic tumors (13%).[7]

Counseling

As with most diseases that affect the brain, counselors encounter brain tumors in two ways: counselors may be involved in follow-up after a diagnosis has been made and treatment given, or they may suspect an organic component to counseling problems and be instrumental in procuring an accurate diagnosis of brain tumor. If pastors and counselors are involved after diagnosis and treatment, there are many counseling needs experienced by patients and their families. Families are rarely warned about the possible cognitive, social, and vocational changes that may accompany brain tumors, and they are usually reluctant to ask questions. Counselors can confer with the medical team, encourage the family to ask questions of the team as well as rehabilitation therapists, and, armed with an understanding of the relevant brain-behavior relationships (chapter 4), offer practical, biblical counsel.

Because of the subtle beginnings of many brain tumors, counselors might also be involved before a diagnosis is made. Don't be deceived by the fairly low incidence rate of about one in 10,000 in the general population; brain tumors are common in medical and psychiatric populations. Estimates of the overall incidence of brain tumor in general medical hospitals is 1 to 2 percent (Cushing, 1932); in psychiatric populations the range is from 2 to 14 percent (Ausman, French & Baker, 1974, Williams, Bell & Guy, 1974). Therefore, counselors will see people with brain tumors more frequently than the incidence rate in the general population suggests. Furthermore, it has been estimated that two-thirds of all internists miss brain tumors when their symptoms first appear (Aronson & Aronson, 1972), and up to 55 percent of those misdiagnosed or undiagnosed are usually labeled with a psychiatric disorder (Patton & Sheppard, 1956).

> Bill was initially seen by a physician at age thirty for double vision, difficulties with coordination, a dilated right pupil, and a drooping right eyelid. His symptoms gradually resolved and he was given a tentative diagnosis of Multiple Sclerosis. Two years later he was admitted with similar complaints, except they were all more severe and he was having trouble walking. His diagnosis was changed to third cranial nerve palsy.
>
> While in the hospital, he fell and bumped his head. And from that time on there was a dramatic turn in his mental abilities—his memory was atrocious, he could not understand why he was in the hospital, and he became increasingly belligerent. A CT scan showed that his ventricles were enlarged and there was a large mass obstructing the flow of cerebral spinal fluid. Diagnosis: inoperable tumor of the brain stem.
>
> Amazingly, after going undetected and misdiagnosed for two years, chemotherapy and radiation sent the cancer in remission. Seven years later Bill was healthy, with only traces of his original symptoms.

Brain tumors are frequently misdiagnosed, and people may come to pastors or counselors before physicians because brain tumors often begin with subtle personality changes. Some changes may be quite rapid and noticeable, especially if they are accompanied by a grand mal seizure. Yet most are insidious and barely detectable. These relatively silent tumors often develop over years, leaving some victims increasingly reticent, indifferent, depressed, and listless. Others may exhibit the opposite symptoms. Instead of a lethargic pattern, affected individuals may be anxious, restless, irritable, and have unstable and rapidly fluctuating emotions (emotional lability).

Along with these personality changes, intellectual changes may also occur. And these, too, may emerge quite subtly. They are most apparent in persons with intellectually demanding jobs that demand ongoing decision-making. Yet these changes might be masked as co-workers "cover" for a boss or peer who is making unusual mistakes. For example, one middle-aged couple came for counseling because of marital problems, ostensibly because the children were leaving home and their relationship was struggling. In the course of counseling, some evidence for personality and intellectual changes began to emerge in the husband, but the wife was adamant that her husband was no different either at work or home. Furthermore, she indicated that she was constantly getting good reports about her husband's work from his co-workers. This temporarily assuaged thoughts of an organic problem until the husband's uncharacteristic anxiety about work suggested that he was experiencing some sort of change. After receiving permission to talk with co-workers, a sad tale began to emerge. A good friend and co-worker stated that the counselee had been essentially incompetent in his job. The little work he did was poor in quality and riddled with mistakes. Apparently, his co-workers respected this man highly and wanted to help him through some "emotional problems." The man was subsequently diagnosed as having a large frontal lobe tumor.

Intellectual changes take on many shapes, but common manifestations include (1) memory impairment, (2) impaired ability to learn, (3) poor attention and concentration, (4) difficulty thinking abstractly, (5) fatigue after mental effort, and (6) impaired judgment.

A fifty-eight-year-old man came to a physician with a twelve-month history of extravagance, boastfulness, excessive drinking, marital discord, unrealistic planning, and several changes of job. He has previously held a

Table 6.4. Symptoms of Brain Tumor

Symptoms of brain tumor	First symptom (%)	Symptom present at some time (%)
Headache	33	67
Seizures	19	35
Personality change	12	43
Vomiting	10	70
Movement problems	9	44
Speech problems	6	27
Visual changes	5	17

The second column ranks the most frequent initial symptoms. The third column indicates how frequently those symptoms emerge over the course of the tumor (Walker, 1975).

responsible job in a senior position. He showed a happy, confident manner and believed he was rich, but he was self-neglectful and grossly lacking in insight. After a medical exam and brain scan, his diagnosis was brain tumor: a left olfactory groove meningioma. (Avery, 1971)

To screen for brain tumors and other organic problems, counselors should first be alert to any changes from a previous level of functioning. Is a person who was once functioning well on a job now struggling with decision-making and ordinary problems? Is the once gregarious housewife now withdrawn and reticent? Although these changes can be caused by organic or functional problems, they should at least encourage counselors to maintain the possibility of organic impairment. Cautious counselors might want to recommend an immediate medical consultation if these changes are apparent. It is more common, however, to refer these persons when there are no other explanations for the uncharacteristic changes (see chapter 10).

As a more specific screen, if subtle personality or intellectual changes are accompanied by headache or nausea and vomiting, then medical referral is critical (see Table 6.4). If there is a medical evaluation, a review of symptoms, a neurological exam, and perhaps a CT scan may be used to rule out brain tumors.

Head Injury

Of all the *must-know* diseases, perhaps no other affects individuals and families as tragically as severe head injuries. Even more than with strokes, families have very high expectations for loved ones who have survived head injuries. And there are reasons for their enthusiasm. Victims of head injury are usually young and active, and head injuries rarely slow them down for more than a few days. Families have every reason to believe that cognitive function will be as normal as the rest of the person's physical functioning. But if the head injury has been fairly severe, rarely are expectations fully met.

As introduced in the previous section, *physical recovery is not the same as psychological (cognitive, perceptual, emotional) recovery.* When one part of the body is healthy, other organ systems may be impaired or diseased. People with great kidneys can have weak hearts. Likewise, although the rest of the body may be in peak form, the brain and its associated functions may be significantly impaired. If counselors and families presume too close a link between all the systems of the body, especially the brain and other systems, then cognitive abilities of those with paralysis will be underestimated, and cognitive abilities of those who experienced traumatic brain injury will be overestimated.

There are three critical issues with head injuries. The first is understanding head injuries and the almost inevitable resultant psychological changes; the second is understanding the impact of head injuries on families, and the third is rehabilitation.

Overview of Head Injuries

Head injuries are not evenly distributed throughout age groups. As you might guess, because of automobile and motorcycle accidents, they are highest among males between the ages of fifteen and twenty-five. The rates are so high, in fact, that head injuries have become one of the most common neurological disorders in the United States.

They can be broadly classified as either penetrating or closed head injuries. In penetrating injuries, an object such as a bullet penetrates the skull and brain tissue, and it leaves dead nerve cells in its wake. The consequences of these wounds depend on the size and location of the damage. Since they are more localized, they tend to have predictable and discrete consequences.

Closed head injuries result from a blunt impact to the head that might be experienced after a fall or automobile accident. They are more common than penetrating wounds and are usually more problematic. Whereas penetrating injuries usually affect only a specific area of the brain, closed head injuries affect the entire brain, doing their most severe damage to the psychologically complex frontal and temporal lobes. After a blow to the head, the brain smashes into the skull and hits some bony protrusions in the frontal and temporal lobes. But the damage doesn't stop there. Since the brain is fairly soft and is suspended in cerebrospinal fluid (CSF), it whiplashes or rebounds, causing further damage. Finally, the subsequent swelling or bleeding can dangerously raise the CSF pressure in the brain and produce even further damage. It is these closed head injuries that are of particular interest to counselors.

The immediate effects of closed head injuries range from a momentary daze to prolonged coma. Along this continuum, there are two methods of establishing severity: the Glasgow Coma Scale (GCS) and post-traumatic amnesia (PTA). The Glasgow Coma Scale is a popular fifteen-point standardized test for assessing neurological responsiveness. It assesses eye-opening ability, physical responsiveness, and verbal responsiveness. GCS scores of 13–15 indicate a mild head injury, 9–12 moderate, and 8 or below severe. Rather than familiarizing yourself with the Coma Scale, an easier measure and almost as helpful in establishing a prognosis is the post-traumatic amnesia.

The post-traumatic amnesia is the length of time between the trauma and the return of ongoing memory function. This includes a coma but is not limited to it. Patients can be responsive and seemingly alert for weeks, yet they may not remember who visited them a few hours earlier or what they had for breakfast. The end of the PTA is like "waking up" to many people. Ongoing memory returns. If you are counseling someone who had a severe head injury, the easiest way to determine the length of the PTA is simply to ask, "What was the first thing you remembered after the accident? When was that?"

Severity of head injury. A mild head injury is characterized by a post-traumatic amnesia of less than an hour. Physical and neurological exams are typically normal in these injuries, but it is likely that there is subtle nerve damage. The consequences vary. Some people experience no noticeable problems, whereas others report chronic difficulties that emerge within a few days or weeks of the injury. Most frequent complaints include headaches, memory problems, difficulties with work or school, fatigue, dizziness, reduced concentration, insomnia, anxiety, and depression. These might be followed by related problems such as feeling incompetent, personal frustration, and work-related problems. Like all head injuries, obvious improvements may occur for up to one to

Table 6.5. A Brain-Injury Continuum

Head injury:	Mild	Moderate	Severe	Catastrophic
PTA:	0 1 hour	24 hours	7 days	Months
Psychological changes:	Minor or none	Noticeable to patient	Noticeable to family and friends	
	Transient	Lingering	Permanent	

two years. Some persons, however, report that their symptoms never appreciably lessen.

A moderate head injury is characterized by a PTA of one to twenty-four hours. These injuries also express themselves in various ways. Some people may seem unimpaired, others may demonstrate permanent physical and cognitive changes. When the PTA is less than twenty-four hours, most people recover full intellectual and other psychological functions. If the PTA is more than twenty-four hours, persistent difficulties are the rule. Therefore, in severe brain injury, where the PTA is seven days or longer, profound, enduring cognitive changes are commonplace (see Table 6.5). Chapter 4 reviews these changes in detail.

Catastrophic head injuries are accompanied by prolonged comas— up to several months in duration. After the coma, these people typically have little interaction with or awareness of the world around them and need long-term nursing home care. These head injuries clearly have far-reaching consequences for families, and biblical counsel and diaconal care are critical. However, they do not demand any special knowledge of the subtleties of brain dysfunction; there is nothing subtle about these horrible disabilities. Because of this, the next section will focus instead on moderate to severe head injuries.

Psychological changes after head injury. Although physical disabilities may exist after moderate to severe head injury, the most burdensome problems for families are the unexpected psychological changes.[8] Most of these changes are a result of cognitive changes such as poor concentration, decreased abstraction, and planning and organizational difficulties, as well as changes in personality style and sexual desire. But since head injury sits at the confluence of brain and heart, there are other factors that contribute to the extent of the characterological changes.

Most families who observe the results of head injuries remark that the same old behaviors are present, but in an intensified, exaggerated form. Someone who struggles with lust will either do it more openly or act on it. Someone who was angry on the inside but apparently pleasant on the outside might become more openly hostile, demanding, and critical. As such, it is not surprising that one of the best predictors of postinjury problems is preinjury character. The cognitive impairments of persons committed to biblical living will rarely lead to the same frustrating changes that are obvious in others. Secular research and case studies, even though they use different language and descriptions, support this conclusion (Shontz, 1975).

The patient who was apparently concerned about others rather than consumed with self, and who was responsible in work and family was most likely to escape severe character changes after a head injury. (Kozol, 1946)

People who pity themselves instead of accepting and dealing more actively with problems or stress continue the same pattern after head injury. (Gruvstad, Kebbon & Gruvstad, 1958)

A forty-eight-year-old male employee was mugged on the way to make a bank deposit for his firm and was briefly unconscious. For the following twelve months, although physically and intellectually fit, he was constantly depressed and anxious, and his ability to function at work appeared to be unaccountably impaired. It was later discovered that he had a series of vocational setbacks and was now employed—in a humble job—by his successful younger brother who ran a flourishing business. It appeared that many years of resentment and hostility magnified the consequences of the injury. (Lishman, 1973)

A forty-five-year-old woman was disabled for many months by a number of vague complaints after surviving a car crash. The accident resulted in a minor head injury with some short-term visual problems, but there were no other injuries. Her persistent psychological complaints were curious because she seemed to deal effectively with most problems before the accident. She eventually confessed to a long-standing secret liaison with the husband of a friend, in whose company the accident had occurred. She determined to end the relationship—as penance in return for regaining her sight—and she was trying to keep her end of the bargain. It is likely that the injury became a focus for long-standing conflict and guilt. (Lishman, 1973)

When affected by underlying sin, cognitive problems are often translated into childish behavior, unwillingness to be taught, irresponsibility, impulsiveness (especially financial), unusual emotional fluctuations, depression, and irritability. It is typical for head-injured individuals to appear cooperative and calm until they feel incapable of performing certain tasks. Then they can become rude, evasive, and sometimes aggressive. This is compounded by a lack of awareness or denial of problems. When this is present, affected persons underestimate the work involved in rehabilitation and they can get very angry at "childish" tasks they must perform.

Two other factors contribute to postinjury personality and character changes. One is the possible gain, either tangible or intangible, that might accompany obvious problems. Changes tend to be most pronounced when there is a financial pay-off for demonstrable disability. In our litiginous society, there are millions of dollars at stake in having incapacitating problems, and this appears to be sufficient motivation to exaggerate disabilities (Miller, 1969).

One other contributor is the status of the family or supporting network. An intact, supportive, knowledgeable, and cooperative family has a significant, positive effect on rehabilitation (Fowler, 1981). Unfortunately, divorce, frustration, anger, and other forms of abandonment are the norm.

Advice to Families

Families are inevitably unprepared for the consequences of brain injury. They typically receive very little information about cognitive and behavioral changes that exist after moderate to severe brain injury. Instead, they are often told by the hospital staff that the person will "recover," and families therefore expect that, when the physical rehabilitation is over, the affected person will be back to normal in all respects. This expectation is supported by the fact that many of the cognitive and behavioral changes are masked in the intensive care-giving environment of hospitals. This being the case, most families never really see the psychological changes in action until the patient gets home.

This lack of information may be coupled with "faith" and "hope" that are little more than presumption and denial. Families interpret physical healing as a sign from God, foretelling complete social and vocational recovery. Any contrary information is ignored. As a result, counsel is avoided and family members respond not to the changed person in front of them, but to the person they remember. It may take months and even years before families come to the end of themselves and are open to a more realist view (Lezak, 1978, 1986).

Families typically go through a series of stages when faced with brain

injury (Lezak, 1986). Initially they are delighted that the family member
is alive and they expect full recovery within a year. After a while, as the
months begin to drag on, families begin to blame the lack of change on
either themselves or the brain-injured person. Shared blame easily moves
to frustration or anger with the brain-injured person. Now, family
expectations are lower because they perceive the patient to be "unmoti-
vated, " "irresponsible, " "self-centered" or "lazy." And families often feel
trapped and despairing. It is at this point that divorces are likely to occur.

These experiences can be avoided, but only with a family that is
committed to understanding the affected family member and being
educated in the consequences of head injury (Diehl, 1983). The
following suggestions are by no means exhaustive, but they offer some
practical guidelines for families.

During the hospitalization

1. Get as much information as you can. Ask questions of the
primary physician, talk to the social worker, have a family conference
with the rehabilitation counselor, go to the library and get information,
contact community resources (e.g., local chapters of the National Head
Injury Foundation). Understand the physical problems and learn about
the impending cognitive and behavioral problems.

2. Decide how much time you should spend at the hospital. Round-
the-clock vigils are not always wise. Yet if the family believes it is
important, get someone from the church to coordinate diaconal concerns
(meals, baby-sitting, taking care of pets). If the brain-injured person
remains comatose for more than a few weeks, it may be helpful to gently
encourage family members to get into a more normal routine.

3. Discuss rehabilitation with the hospital staff. Since there are so
many difficulties that emerge after moderate to severe head injury, a
reputable and experienced rehabilitation program is critical. This does
not have to be provided on an in-patient basis. Programs run the gamut
from long-term in-patient care to day care to in-house consultation. The
follow-up needs are dependent on the resources of the family and the
extent of the injury. But usually there must be some access to a
multidisciplinary team sophisticated in cognitive and behavioral changes
as well as vocational rehabilitation.

At home

1. Try to maintain time schedules and predictable routines. This

should ease the brain-injured person's confusion and also encourage participation in home activities.

2. Realize that families are plagued by a host of emotions. Feeling trapped and isolated is not unusual (Lezak, 1978; Bardach, 1969). A sense of guilt is also common when families feel responsible for the lack of change in the affected person. Other related issues include sexual frustrations (if the head-injured person is a spouse) as a result of the head-injured person's lack of empathy and sensitivity, embarrassment, and a feeling of abandonment. Families may seem like paragons of strength on the outside, but this may belie unspoken grief, frustration, and loneliness. Pastors and counselors must recognize that many families perceive their difficulties as spiritual failures and are reluctant to share their burdens with anyone. Ministry support must be able to respond without being asked.

3. Low expectations are as problematic as impossibly high expectations. Families must constantly understand and help maximize patients' abilities.

4. Never allow brain injury to be an excuse for sinful behavior. And when dealing with this behavior, recognize that there are various causes and methods to encourage change. Perhaps the family member is simply modeling and imitating the tenor of the house! The treatment, then, would be for the family to ask the affected member's forgiveness. Other sinful behaviors may be changed by simple, gentle, and loving feedback, leaving the room, or changing the subject. They cannot be confronted with anger. Sometimes family members must learn to give firm and clear comments or instructions, often with an exaggeration of gestures or tone of voice. But they must surround their interactions with the fruits of the Spirit. Finally, don't get locked into power struggles with the person. Remember that you have more mental flexibility and can see alternatives that the brain-injured cannot.

5. Teach skills in more than one setting in order to maximize generalization.

6. Keep simple goals in mind, as you might with children. For example, most children, like ourselves, have all sorts of problems they must work on. But a wise parent usually focuses on one or two specific issues at a time. That is not to say that the other issues are irrelevant, but they must be constantly prioritized. Some initial goals with a head-injured person might include basic aspects of biblical communication or specific vocational or avocational goals.

7. The church should be an extension of the family. Are friends still involved socially with the family? Old friends are usually scarce within a few months after the accident. Does the family get time off if needed? Occasional meals? There are numerous gaps that can be potentially filled by the church.

8. Expect the unexpected. This doesn't mean that you avoid planning, but it does mean that at times you will have to hold onto those plans and goals lightly.

Rehabilitation

Rehabilitation is a burgeoning field. But approaches to cognitive rehabilitation are still debatable and experimental. There are two general approaches in the research literature, and most programs have a combination of both. One has as its goal the restitution or recovery of lost functions. Programs with this goal tend to develop exercises that occasionally seem very academic, intended to strengthen a function.

The other approach has a goal that is more limited, but perhaps more realistic. It is concerned with assisting the afflicted individual to function as well as possible despite handicaps (Miller, 1984). For example, rather than developing exercises to improve memory function, a more ameliorative approach would discover strategies to help a person cope with situations despite a poor memory. Perhaps the person would learn to make lists—of names, shopping items, and so on.

In younger adults, rehabilitation is focused on vocational reentry and job placement. It is surprising how a creative rehabilitation team and family can pinpoint abilities that can be used in the marketplace. Many victims of moderate to severe head injury can hold a job and have some measure of independence. There are, however, many individuals who never hold any kind of job. Sometimes this is a result of severe cognitive deficits, but usually it is the result of cognitive deficits that are overlaid with spiritual issues. Denial or unrealistic appraisal of handicaps, fear of failure, unwillingness to take a lower position, and simple laziness are some of the counseling issues that leave people unwilling to do anything.

Diabetes

Everyone knows something about diabetes—or someone with it. It is common knowledge that the incidence of diabetes is high, it affects young and old, and it often leads to those miserable, daily, insulin injections. Otherwise, most people think that diabetics are relatively free of more distressing symptoms, especially those that may have counseling significance. But the difficulties associated with severe or long-term diabetes are very significant. Very few people, apart from diabetics themselves, are aware of the constant problems inherent in this prevalent disease.

It is difficult to say why the impact of diabetes is so understated. Perhaps it is because we usually hear of the less severe diabetes that begins in older age. Perhaps the disease seems somewhat innocuous because we rarely hear of someone dying from or even complaining about diabetes (even though it is a major killer). Whatever the reason, most people are unaware that severe diabetes can be a horrible disease. Its victims are almost forced to be obsessed by their diet; they must tolerate multiple daily injections; they can, without warning, become confused, incoherent, and comatose; and they are aware of possible long-term complications such as impotence, kidney failure, and blindness.

Medical Overview

Diabetes Mellitus occurs in about 2 to 6 percent of the population, a figure that will double in the next fifteen years, with older persons much more likely to be affected than younger. After age sixty-five, the incidence rate is over 10 percent. Its name means "siphon" (diabetes) and "honey" (mellitus) and is a reference to increased urination and urine sweetened by voided glucose (sugar).

Although the precise physiological mechanism behind diabetes is still unclear, most authorities agree that inadequate insulin secretion is a significant part of the underlying picture. Insulin is a hormone, released by the pancreas, that insures efficient use of glucose (sugar)—an ever-present nutritional need in the body, especially in the brain and retinas. Insufficient insulin appears to have at least three basic effects: (1) Since insulin is critical in transporting glucose from the blood to cells in the body organs and tissues, insufficiency leads to decreased glucose in the body cells and increased glucose left in the blood; (2) When glucose is no longer available in the body cells, the body will break down its store of fats to create the necessary nutrients. This abnormal metabolism of fats leads to increased fatty deposits on blood vessel walls and, therefore, atherosclerosis; (3) Protein is less available because it must be used as a source of energy in the place of unavailable sugars.

Diabetes is usually classified as juvenile or maturity-onset. Juvenile diabetes, a genetically linked condition which leads to insulin dependence, usually begins before age forty and often appears in childhood or early adolescence. It is often detected by the classic symptoms of excessive urination and thirst, weight loss in spite of increased appetite, and easy fatigability. Occasionally, it may be first noticed by some of the long-term complications (e.g., impotence, eye problems) or "ketoacidosis." Ketoacidosis is an acidic condition that can result when the body relies on stored fat rather than glucose for nutrition. Fats break down into ketones which can be toxic in high concentrations. Symptoms include nausea and vomiting, rapid respiration, confusion, disorientation, coma, and even death.

Maturity-onset diabetes tends to develop gradually in middle to late life. Unlike those with juvenile onset, maturity-onset diabetics are usually obese and may be initially without symptoms. Their high blood glucose level may respond to diet and weight loss alone; insulin injections are often unnecessary. When medical treatment is needed, maturity-onset diabetics will often, at least initially, be given oral medication rather than injections.

Diagnosis of diabetes is fairly straightforward. Physicians look for physical symptoms, high levels of blood glucose, and an abnormal glucose tolerance test. Physicians differ on the actual values of the blood tests, but most will diagnose diabetes if the whole blood glucose level is consistently 140 mg per 100 ml or higher, or the plasma glucose level is about 160 or higher (plasma levels are about 14 percent higher than those of whole blood).

Long-term complications. Within fifteen to twenty years, poorly controlled diabetes usually takes its toll. Long-term complications include diseases of the large and small blood vessels, and nerve cells (neuropathy). For example, large blood vessels become atherosclerotic and make the diabetic more susceptible to strokes. In fact, up to 75 percent of the strokes in the United States are related to diabetes. Other large vessel problems include high blood pressure and associated heart problems, as well as gangrene and other circulation problems. Four out of five amputations are performed on diabetics.

Disease of smaller blood vessels is rampant in poorly controlled diabetes. This is usually first apparent in the eyes. Retinopathy, or disease of the retina, is commonly found in diabetics who have had the disease for twenty years or more. More specifically, some studies indicate that after ten years 47 percent of patients have difficulties with vision; after fifteen years 63 percent; and after twenty-five years 80 percent (Burditt, 1968; Kahn & Bradley, 1975; Dorf, 1976). Diabetic retinopathy is probably the leading cause of blindness, surpassing cataracts and glaucoma.

The organs that are affected by small vessel disease are the kidneys. In fact, in juvenile onset diabetes, kidney failure is the most common cause of death. Renal disease may be signaled by routine blood and urine tests or by symptoms such as nausea and vomiting, occasionally accompanied by increased diarrhea and fecal incontinence. It is treated by a rigid, low-protein diet, kidney transplant, or dialysis. If dialysis is the best available treatment, then there are other problems that diabetics face. They are dependent on a mechanical method of cleansing the blood, probably three times each week, and there are potential complications from the procedure.

Neuropathies, or disease of nerve cells in the body, involve tingling and discomfort in the legs, muscular atrophy, foot ulcers, numbness, increased or decreased pain sensitivity, as well as foot sores and infections as a result of decreased tactile sensitivity. But of particular importance for counselors is the nerve dysfunction that results in impotence. If the person has any neurological changes from diabetes, chances are there will also be impotence and bladder problems. As such, impotence may be the first, and only, obvious physical change with the disease. These problems may reverse with better nutrition and diabetic control; however, if impotence is a result of true nerve damage, the impotence is irreversible. Affected men, if concerned, should speak with their diabetes physician or urologist about treatments.

Curiously, female diabetics are spared sexual dysfunctions. Sexual desire and frequency of orgasms are relatively unchanged. The principal sexual complications in women are recurrent vaginal infections.

Insulin treatment. Although counselors should be aware of the potentially hazardous course that lies before the diabetic, many symptoms that have counseling relevance will actually be a result of the treatment! Virtually every insulin-requiring diabetic experiences *hypo*glycemia (low blood sugar) as a result of the complexities of glucose level maintenance. These symptoms are very difficult in themselves, but, if untreated, they can result in more serious problems such as brain damage, heart attacks, and even death. Also, neglected hypoglycemia will eventually make the diabetes worse!

When blood sugar level is low from too much insulin, the body secretes various hormones to raise it. This "epinephrine response" makes the diabetic weak, famished and shaky—thus giving the diabetic a warning that a potentially dangerous hypoglycemic condition is mounting. The diabetic can then drink something with enough sugar to quickly raise the glucose levels. Within one to two years of the onset of insulin-dependent diabetes, however, these hormones are less responsive, and the diabetic may not have the early warning signs of hypoglycemia. The new cues become drowsiness, and confused or incoherent thinking. If these symptoms are not recognized and treated, they may proceed to loss of consciousness.

Emotions and Diabetes

A considerable amount to research shows that emotionally stressful experiences, in diabetics and nondiabetics, can produce fluctuations in blood glucose and ketone bodies (Hinckle & Wolf, 1952a, 1952b; Tattersall, 1981). Some studies even suggest that stressful experiences actually cause diabetes. However, a less controversial position would be to claim that emotions influence the cause of diabetes.

For example, consider the case of an adolescent girl from a difficult home who had twelve hospital admissions for diabetic acidosis and coma over five years. These episodes all followed acutely stressful life situations.

> Her diabetic problems usually began with some type of stress—fights between her parents, arguments with her mother, change to a new school, the departure of her sister ("the only one who loved me"). These experiences were first followed by resentment, then by symptoms such as excessive thirst and urination, signs of ketoacidosis, and coma. This pattern was typical in that the exacerbations of the diabetic state were in all instances closely related to situational and interpersonal conflicts. (Hinckle & Wolf, 1952b)

Counseling

Diabetes is another disease where counselors are involved both before and after the diagnosis and treatment. Before the diagnosis, counselors may be the first to learn of sexual frustrations that are a result of impotence. Timely referral to an internist could then have a significant positive impact on the course of the disease.

After the diagnosis, especially in severe or juvenile diabetes, there are a host of potential issues. Questions that can accompany the occurrence of any chronic disease include, "Why me?" or "How do I live by faith in the midst of a chronic disease?" These are critical questions that deserve thoughtful, biblical answers. Other issues that are more endemic to diabetes are equally important. In light of the rigid diets, constant self-monitoring, avoidance of sweets, and daily injections, diabetics can profit from learning and practicing a biblical approach to self-control that is rooted in faith. Counselors should also be alert to fear or worry about possible long-term complications. Worry is always an issue that counselors can address, but in diabetes, since worry can exacerbate the course of the disease, biblical assistance is most important.

In younger children, juvenile diabetes affects families and other relationships. For example, juvenile diabetics may be pampered by overanxious parents, siblings may become jealous, and affected children may use their diabetes to shield themselves from difficulties in growing up. Also, diabetics often demonstrate anger by mismanaging their disease, or they may purposely bring on dangerous side effects in order to avoid unpleasant situations.

In juveniles, the first year is a particularly important time for counseling. They face immediate restrictions, needles, and hypoglycemic episodes, and their families can go into a tailspin.

Finally, diabetes is a disease that is tailor-made to bring challenges to one's faith. Its incessant reminders of a complicated life and bleak future provide rich soil to sow seeds of either faith or unbelief. Those who respond by faith can carry a powerful testimony of Christ to the entire church; those who respond in unbelief need to hear of the compassion of Jesus on those who are hurt, and they need to understand the relevance of the gospel to their unique situation.

Female Hormonal Changes

Of all the *must-know* diseases, female hormonal disorders receive the most popular attention. Premenstrual syndrome, postpartum depression, and menopause are very relevant topics. Newspaper articles, popular women's magazines, and court reports abound with personal experiences and summaries of the current medical position. In light of their fame and the frequency with which they appear, Christian counselors must develop a firm biblical position.

A firm position, however, will not include having a clear understanding of the causes of these problems. Controversy surrounds each of these areas. In fact, for some medical researchers, even using "hormonal" in the title is debatable. Therefore, the goal is to understand some of the current thinking on these problems and then organize and recast that material from a biblical perspective.

Premenstrual Syndrome (PMS)

Subtle changes in mood and thinking often accompany the end of a woman's menstrual cycle. This is inarguable. What is not so clear, however, is the meaning of PMS. At a popular level, PMS has sometimes been so broad a label that it has become meaningless. Rage, anger, tension, negativity, problems at work or home—no matter when they occur—can all be attributed to "that time of the month." Because it is used to explain just about any unpleasant symptom, some researchers prefer to eliminate the term altogether (Speroff, 1988). In its place, they suggest a simple description of menstrual-related changes: "I feel very tense today, for no apparent reason. I am in the third week of my cycle." Yet regardless of the term, some women definitely experience cognitive and emotional changes (only at the end of their menstrual cycle) that are severe enough to potentially disrupt relationships and work.

The typical menstrual cycle lasts roughly twenty-eight days. During the first five days, menstrual bleeding is accompanied by the release of follicle stimulating hormones (FSH) from the pituitary gland which stimulate ovary maturity. The next phase, the *follicular* phase, lasts about a week to nine days. At this time estrogen is secreted from cells in the ovary and stimulates both the preparation of the endometrium and the secretion of lutenizing hormone (LH) from the anterior pituitary gland. On day 14 ovulation occurs. The week after ovulation is called the *luteal* phase because LH transforms the remains of the matured follicle into a corpus luteum. This temporary gland is a producer of estrogen and progesterone. Progesterone prepares the uterus for reception of the fertilized ovum. If the egg is not fertilized, the corpus luteum shrinks and breaks down, and the levels of estrogen and progesterone fall severely. The time when these hormones are falling is the general time when PMS is said to occur. As such, it is also called Late Luteal Dysphoric Disorder.

PMS was first mentioned in the medical literature in 1931 (Frank, 1931) and was subsequently the focus of small but steady interest. Popular interest skyrocketed in the early 1980s when the research was disseminated to the general public and the American Psychiatric Association was considering PMS as an official diagnostic category. Although still not an

Table 6.6. Common Symptoms of PMS

Emotional	Cognitive
Sadness	Indecision
Lability	Sensitivity to rejection
Anxiety	Decreased concentration
Anger	
	Behavioral
Pain	Withdrawal
Headache	Impulsiveness
Other	Fluid balance
Food cravings	Weight gain
Fatigue	Bloating
Acne	
Hot flashes	

official diagnosis, PMS remains a subject of keen interest to feminists, researchers, lawyers, and those who experience the symptoms.

It is defined as occurring in the last week of the luteal phase and remitting within a few days after the onset of the follicular phase. Of the more than 150 symptoms that have been reported (Rubinow, Hoban & Grover, 1988), some of the more frequent ones are emotional lability, irritability and anger, anxiety or tension, depression, lack of energy, poor concentration, changes in appetite, and changes in sleep (Table 6.6— Steege, Stout & Rupp).

With so many symptoms reported, the list of alleged causes for PMS is extensive: explanations range from traditional hormonal theories to exclusively "psychological" theories (expectations, cultural norms). All these theories can find some support, but none of them is applicable to every affected woman. One approach and theory might help one woman but not another. Presently, no endocrine or physiological markers have been found to consistently distinguish women with the syndrome from unaffected women. Instead, PMS is a cluster of symptoms with different causes.

As a result of the different possible causes, physicians and researchers have suggested many different treatments. Usually, affected women are asked to keep a daily diary for at least two months. The diary typically includes fluctuations in mood, physical symptoms, diet, and exercise. Then, if warranted, physicians try to rule out symptoms that could be related to chronic underlying diseases. Lupus, anemia, electrolyte imbalances, and many other disorders can masquerade as PMS. If

Figure 6.7. Interaction of Heart and Body in PMS

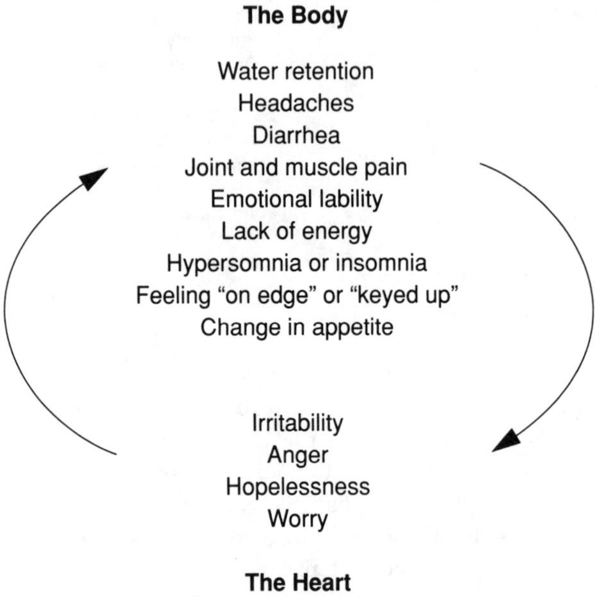

The Body

Water retention
Headaches
Diarrhea
Joint and muscle pain
Emotional lability
Lack of energy
Hypersomnia or insomnia
Feeling "on edge" or "keyed up"
Change in appetite

Irritability
Anger
Hopelessness
Worry

The Heart

there is no evidence for underlying disease, treatment suggestions begin with daily exercise and a change in diet—sugar, salt, caffeine, alcohol, and cigarettes are notorious for exaggerating PMS symptoms. If symptoms persist, physicians might prescribe magnesium, tryptophan, Efamol (evening primrose oil), over-the-counter analgesics, psychoactive drugs (antidepressants, antianxiety drugs), or vitamin B$_6$. For those who have significant bloating, a diuretic and low-salt diet is recommended.

If symptoms are still extremely bothersome, physicians may try other medicines that have questionable value. Or physicians may be asked by patients to prescribe something that worked for a friend. Progesterone is the most requested, but its effectiveness is probably overstated. Like most treatments, it may help some women, it may help others by way of a placebo effect (that is, positive changes are not directly attributable to the medicine), and it will not help most (Keye, 1988).

From a biblical perspective, the symptoms of PMS can be grouped according to those associated with the body and heart (Figure 6-7).

PMS typically begins with bodily symptoms that are not a

consequence of problems of the heart. True PMS has physical causes.[9] In these cases, while counseling may help women to grow in faith during their symptoms, the bodily symptoms will probably persist. Yet counseling is still important because bodily symptoms (*asthenia*) can make it easier to respond sinfully, and affected women need encouragement as they face these temptations. Counselors can allow affected women to see the spiritual battle that is taking place and give them encouragement to stand by faith. To be more specific, consider the following recommendations:

1. First, try to assess whether the symptoms are really related to the menstrual cycle. Some women complain of PMS every day of the month; this is not PMS (but it may be related to a chronic disease). Encourage women to keep a diary of their cycle and symptoms. This will help both them and their families prepare for some of the changes.

2. If symptoms are severe or if they don't follow the menstrual cycle, refer the person to a GP for a physical exam. If a gynecological exam is indicated, the GP can make a referral to a gynecologist.

3. If appropriate, offer some initial dietary and exercise recommendations. Are there dietary excesses with sugar, alcohol, caffeine, or salt? Is the person sedentary? Is the person overweight? Commonsense suggestions may be very helpful. Although not absolutely necessary, some counselors prefer to let physicians make these suggestions. If in doubt, make a referral to a GP.

4. Teach women to prepare themselves for the symptoms. They should know the weaknesses on which the enemy preys. Women might say, "Okay, I know I'll be struggling with being negative over the next few days. I usually feel like the world is out to get me. I must recognize that some of these feelings can't be trusted, so I'm going to have to self-consciously live by faith—what I know to be true—rather than how I feel."

5. Encourage husbands to "know their wives." Husbands can take more responsibility around the house during the most difficult days.

6. Remind women that, by faith, they have power to resist temptation. Encourage them to view the PMS period as a time for testing faith and spiritual growth.

> I first struggled with PMS around three years ago. I was away at college and under a lot of stress. There was one week a month where things just got worse. I was crying at the drop of a hat. My circumstances looked overwhelming. Things seemed so bleak and dismal for that week each

month. Then as suddenly as it came it was gone, and I was left to put back the pieces that I had torn apart the week before.

Finally, I realized that I couldn't go through life being a jerk one week out of every month. As much as PMS seemed to control me, it didn't. I couldn't let myself go into automatic drive. PMS didn't cause me to sin. I had a choice to make. I could give in and let it take over, or I could fight it. PMS is like my thorn in the flesh [2 Cor 12:8, 9]. It's a weakness I have. I need to learn to view it as an opportunity for Christ's power to shine through me, and that is exactly what God is helping me do.

Postpartum Emotional Changes

Another counseling issue that is specific to females is postpartum emotional changes. Three kinds of problems are described as occurring during the postpartum period: the short-lived baby blues or maternity blues, depression that may be longer and more severe than the blues, and the rare yet sensationalized postpartum psychosis.

Baby blues. The baby blues is a poorly defined condition that is experienced by 50 to 70 percent of women in the first week to ten days postpartum. Rarely severe, it begins within the first three days and might be experienced as sadness, depression, feelings of wanting to cry, or rapid and unpredictable emotional fluctuations. To those who experience these emotions, the triggers are often felt to be insignificant. In fact, many women will not actually feel sad when they cry!

Like PMS, there are no known, consistent, biological abnormalities that distinguish between those who experience maternity blues and those who are symptom-free. But the characteristics of the emotional experience and the association with the physically demanding experience of childbirth make a physical cause unmistakable.

Are there nonorganic influences with some women? Yes. "Pessimism," ambivalence toward the pregnancy, and exaggerated prenatal fears can contribute to the experience of the blues (Condon & Watson, 1987). But nonorganic factors, if they are present, are secondary to physical causes. The physical intensity of labor and delivery and the accompanying biochemical changes (and surgery in the case of C-sections) are sufficient explanation for these transient emotional fluctuations. Women who have experienced the trauma of major surgery can experience similar phenomena (Levy, 1987).

Women who struggle with the baby blues rarely seek counsel. After giving birth, they are usually too busy with the new infant, and by the time things settle down, the blues are gone. If husbands are concerned about their spouses' fluctuating emotions or excessive tearfulness, let them know that the experience is very common and usually passes in the first week or two. However, if pastors or counselors hear about such symptoms, it would be wise to keep track of emotional progress. There are some occasions when the baby blues persist and become a longer-lasting depression.

Postpartum depression. More severe and of longer duration than the blues, postpartum depression (PPD) occurs in about 10 to 15 percent of all mothers (Pitt, 1968; Watson, Elliot, Rugg & Brough, 1984). Indistinguishable from other forms of depression, it can last anywhere from two weeks to a year.

Although investigators agree on its incidence rate and longevity, there is much less agreement on possible causes and risk factors.[10] At this time, because our understanding of the brain is still in its infancy, specific biological or endocrinological causes remain elusive. While some presume that hormones are the culprit, other researchers declare hormonal theories as "widespread but unproven" (Kendell, 1985, pp. 8–9).

In light of the complexities inherent in medical research, most investigators are looking for nonmedical causes of PPD. As a result, most of the theories tend to stress "heart" issues over body. For example, investigators frequently point to a relationship, observed in *some* women, between PPD and marital dissatisfaction, worry, or a prepregnancy history of depression (Kumar & Robson, 1984; Kendell, 1985). These studies, however, do not prove that PPD is an issue of the heart. Since PPD is time-limited and triggered by a fairly dramatic physical event, biological causes are virtually certain. The nonmedical studies simply indicate that some women have interpersonal problems that coexist with physical problems, perhaps magnifying the physical problem.

If a woman experiences a post-partum depression that lasts for more than one month, and it is painfully severe, she should be encouraged to consult with her physician. Although there are not many treatments available, antidepressant medication is one possible alternative. If she does try medication—since PPD usually lasts a year or less—it is best to be medically reevaluated at least once every two to three months. After a few months to a year, medication is often unnecessary.

Medical consultation does not lessen the pastoral and counseling task. Depression often makes people feel like God is distant, and those affected are particularly prone to hopelessness. They need ongoing, daily encouragement to know the love of God in Christ and the anticipation of Christ's return.

What if, during the course of counseling, there are biblical or sinful issues that emerge in the depressed person's life? Are there marital problems? Is she feeling overwhelmed with responsibility and a sense of inadequacy? Is she afraid she will be a horrible mother? Is she viewing herself and her world by faith? If counselors become aware of biblical issues, they would approach those with PPD symptoms the way they would anyone: knowing that they are prone to the same problem, they humbly and lovingly bring the problem out into the open. One caution is that we remember that whatever the problem might be, it is not likely to be the cause of feelings of depression. It may make the experience more severe, but it is probably not the instigator.

Postpartum psychosis

In April 1988, Michelle Remington, twenty-nine, shot her six-week-old son Joshua with a .22 caliber handgun and then attempted suicide. She was declared by a Bennington, Vermont District judge to be not guilty by reason of insanity.

On January 7, 1989, Tanya Dacri drowned her two-month-old infant son, Zachary, in the family bathtub. She then is accused of dismembering the body, stuffing the body parts into plastic bags, and tossing them into Philadelphia area rivers. Her trial is pending, but her lawyers have already stated that Tanya was insane—suffering from postpartum psychosis.

Postpartum psychosis (PPP) is a dramatic phenomenon that is distinguishable from postpartum depression (PPD). It is much rarer than PPD, occurring about twice in every 1000 cases of childbirth. It usually begins later, sometimes from six weeks to three months after childbirth; and it tends to be brief—in some cases the symptoms can abate within two to three weeks (Kendell, Chalmers & Platz, 1987).

There are different variations to the symptoms, but they tend to be characterized by confusion and increased activity—very similar to symptoms of schizophrenia and mania.

A twenty-eight-year-old woman developed psychotic symptoms after the birth of her first baby. The nursing staff noted, "she is completely oblivious to her surroundings; she appears disoriented, unaware of being in hospital, thinking she is at home; she is bewildered, lost, and says everything is moving too fast; she thinks the staff are her family, and her baby boy Christopher is called Louise." (Brockington et al., 1981)

Although their symptoms are distinguishable from each other, postpartum psychosis and PPD share the same theories (or lack of theories) about their cause. The main difference is that since PPP is so rare, there has been less research, and, as a result, even greater uncertainty regarding what it is and why it happens. It is safe to say that PPP is a real experience. It is not a convenient, manipulative way for a mother to avoid responsibilities. Instead, it is a painful and unpredictable physical weakness *(asthenia)*. Affected women can experience confusion or despair that makes incredible demands on the resources of the heart.

Can spiritual issues contribute to or intensify these problems? From a biblical perspective they certainly can, and, from the perspective of the research literature, in some cases they do. Symptoms of PPP are more common in women who have a history of social or vocational problems, or have difficulties coping with being unmarried, a Caesarean section, or the death of an infant. Yet it must be underscored that not everyone who has had symptoms of PPP has a particularly difficult past or present. The trigger is most likely physical, and the physically induced symptoms can be intensified (poorly controlled) because of spiritual problems.

Since the symptoms are so rare, pastors and counselors will probably only hear about a person with PPP symptoms—or you will mourn as you read about PPP after mothers have killed their newborns. Therefore, PPP might have more interest from a legal perspective than a counseling one. From this perspective, the significant question has to do with the insanity defense. Is the insanity defense biblically permissible in cases of murder? Are these women responsible for any criminal acts performed while they were most likely asthenic? Both the United Kingdom and the United States have spoken unequivocally to this. Their jurists almost unanimously avoid charges of first-degree murder, and they might even drop all charges. But the fact that mental confusion or insanity does not erase moral ability or personal culpability makes those decisions open to biblical reevaluation.

Menopause

The other common diagnosis that is often related to hormone changes is menopause. Usually occurring between the ages of forty-five and fifty-five, menopause refers to the last bleeding from the uterus.

Sometimes you will hear it called climacteric. Climacteric, however, is broader, encompassing the physical and emotional changes occurring both before and after actual menopause.

Biologically, menopause is initiated by a decline in the number of mature, encapsulated eggs (graffian follicles) in the ovaries. In order to stimulate their development, the pituitary secretes more follicle stimulating hormone. Follicles, however, respond irregularly and they gradually disappear, accompanied by an overall decline in estrogen, progesterone, and other hormones. After cessation of menses, hormone levels remain relatively stable since they are not prone to the fluctuations associated with ovulation and menstruation.

There are certain well-established physical consequences to menopause, but these are not cognitive or emotional and they are rarely severe enough to cause complaints. The two most frequent symptoms are occasional "hot flushes" or "hot flashes" and mild atrophy of the breasts, uterus, and vaginal area.

Menopause deviates from the emerging pattern in the "hormonal" problems discussed so far. Whereas PMS, the baby blues, PPD, and PPP have an obvious physical root along with nonphysical contributions, menopause seems to have more obvious nonphysical causes along with physical contributions. The bulk of the research on menopause has focused on cultural, social, and personal factors.

Cross-cultural studies suggest that in cultures that foster a positive view of menopause, women tend to have few or no menopausal symptoms. For example, in India, postmenopausal women of the wealthy Rajput caste are released from their veils and seclusion from men. Also, older people are revered for their wisdom and experience. Apparently, as a result, these women demonstrate no significant menopausal symptoms (Flint, 1979). Similar cross-cultural observations have been made in Arabia, Iran, and Africa (Dennerstein, 1988). Perhaps there are also cultural components to the apparent downturn in menopausal symptoms in the United States. Women are less invested in families and more in jobs. As a result, what was once a regrettable loss of reproductive function is now a relief at the loss of concern over pregnancy, contraception, and menstruation. Of course, since cross-cultural studies are so difficult to interpret, these are best thought of as suggestions.

Other studies and personal observations suggest that menopausal symptoms vary according to social class. Although not always a consistent pattern, poorer women tend to have more symptoms than affluent women

(Van Keep & Kellerhals, 1974; Naylor, 1976). This finding was even more consistent when women worked. That is, poor, menopausal women who worked had more symptoms than their wealthy counterparts. The best explanation for these findings is that wealthier women as compared to poorer women tend to find more meaning in tasks other than childbearing or child rearing.

Along with possible cultural and sociological factors, researchers have tried to find personal factors that are related to emotional difficulties during menopause. Chief among these are marriage problems. Although these problems are certainly not unique to those who experience menopausal depression, there are significant differences in marital satisfaction between nondepressed menopausal women and depressed menopausal women (Raymond, 1988). This raises and does not answer the question of which came first, depression or marital dissatisfaction, but, at least, it alerts counselors to the possibility that if there is menopausal distress, there might also be marriage problems.

After marriage problems, the next most common accompaniment of menopausal emotional changes is a previous history of depression. If women had a tendency toward depression prior to menopause, they are more likely to report depression after menopause. Other factors include concern about physical beauty or health, lack of goals and direction, and despondency about children leaving home. In some ways, the personal factors sound like those associated with the male counterpart of menopause, the mid-life crisis.

As a result of studies such as these, the growing sentiment within the medical community is that menopause does not cause depression.

> Rather, it appears that it is the small group of women who already are depressed from which originates the bulk of complaints physicians receive about menopause and the popular stereotype of the menopausal blues, according to investigators. (Raymond, 1988, p. 352)

Biological theories and treatments are not forgotten, however. The medical theory is that a lack of certain hormones is responsible for emotional changes. In its defense, it is true that, in some women, hormone replacement alleviates symptoms such as depression and anxiety, as well as physical symptoms. But the number of women who are thought to be helped by replacement therapy is probably overestimated (Dennerstein, 1988).

Given that nonphysical factors seem to be more involved with menopausal emotional changes than biological factors, it is usually appropriate to overview biblical issues of the heart rather than encourage immediate medical consultation. Causes can include concern over fading youth or beauty, lack of impact in home, church, or society; marital turmoil, or personal regrets and guilt. All these can be directly and powerfully addressed by Scripture.

Referral to a physician, however, may be warranted in some cases. When symptoms are severe and persistent, or if they are accompanied by embarrassing or difficult physical problems, then hormonal treatment or even antidepressant medication may be helpful.

Notes
Alzheimer's Disease

1. This may change soon. SPECT is proving to be a valuable diagnostic tool for Alzheimer's disease. Unlike CT and MRI, which can rule out other medical problems, SPECT may actually detect the disease. It should be generally available in 1992.

2. Local libraries are usually loaded with books on Alzheimer's. If not, the following books and resources may be helpful:

The Loss of Self: A Family Resource for the Care of Alzheimer's Disease and Related Disorders. Donna Cohen and Carl Eisdorfer (New York: W. W. Norton, 1986). This very helpful book includes an extensive bibliography.

Understanding Alzheimer's Disease: What Is It? How to Cope with It, and Future Directions. Available through the Alzheimer's Disease and Related Disorders Association, 70 East Lake Street, Chicago, IL 60601.

The 36-Hour Day: A Family Guide to Caring for People in the Home. N. L. Mace and P. V. Rabins (Baltimore: The Johns Hopkins University Press, 1981).

Nursing Home Ministry: A Manual. Tom McCormick and Penny McCormick (Grand Rapids: Zondervan, 1987).

The Alzheimer's Disease and Related Disorders Association, 70 East Lake Street, Chicago, IL 60601, is a very helpful resource.

Multiple Sclerosis

3. Other sources used but not specifically cited are Lishman (1978) and Scheckenberg (1979).

Parkinson's Disease

4. Most local libraries have popular level books. A good one, although becoming a bit dated, is by Roger C. Duvoisin (1978), Parkinson's Disease: A Guide for Patient and Family (N.Y.: Raven Press). There is another by Sidney

Dorros (1981), *Parkinson's: A Patient's View* (Washington, D.C.: Seven Locks Press).

Seizures and Epilepsy

5. A sad but relatively unknown exception was the murder of fifteen-year-old Randolph Evans by police officer Robert H. Torsney. On Thanksgiving Day 1976, the boy was shot and killed, but Torsney, after pleading insanity, was acquitted. His legal defense was that "he was insane because of an epileptic psychomotor seizure suffered at the time of the crime" (Szasz, 1984, p. 131).

Brain Tumor

6. Helpful information is available from the American Cancer Society and The Association for Brain Tumor Research, 6232 N. Pulaski Road, Chicago IL 60646.

7. Some tumors have the potential to "seed" or metastasize to other sites of the body. That is, cancer in one part of the body can cause the development of the same cancer in another part. Brain tumors rarely metastasize to other parts of the body, but tumors in the body, such as the liver or lungs, can metastasize to the brain.

Head Injury

8. These symptoms are related to the extent and location of the injury and the age of the victim. For example, frontal lobe injury tends to have the most severe cognitive and behavioral consequences, and older persons improve less than younger.

Female Hormonal Changes

9. Even though there is no universally recognized, medical cause, we do not have to wait for a full understanding of causes before we categorize them as such. Many of the symptoms align with the biblical category of the body and bodily weakness.

10. Disagreement is largely a result of different researchers looking at different factors (medical journals prefer new ideas more than replication or confirmation of old ones).

Part Three has a slightly different focus from that of Part Two. It will focus on the potential problem of misdiagnosis—confusing spiritual and physical problems—rather than understanding specific diseases. Part Two generally presumed that a disease had been diagnosed and medical treatment initiated. Its focus was to alert counselors to the psychological accompaniments of different diseases. Part Three will present a group of common counseling *symptoms* that may be rooted in known diseases. The assumption will be that no medical diagnosis has been made—or if it has, it was inaccurate. A section on misdiagnosis is important because many diseases, including those in Part Two, start by imitating counseling problems, and affected persons are often referred to friends, pastors, or counselors, even by their physicians. Therefore, counselors must be able to make some basic screening decisions, and know when to recommend medical evaluation or a second medical opinion.

Contrary to popular belief, physicians, like counselors, are fallible. They make mistakes. Also, physicians may be unaware of the different ways diseases can manifest themselves as counseling problems. Some studies estimate that anywhere from 5 to 46 percent (Hall et al., 1978; Scheinbaum, 1979; Currey, 1982) of persons who have been given a non-organic diagnosis by their medical doctor (that is, told that there is nothing physically wrong with them), do in fact have an underlying physical disease that is a significant cause of their counseling problems. The average is about one in ten. This means that about *one out of every ten* counselees may have a physical cause underlying their problems rather than a spiritual one. To complicate the issue, there is no such thing as a test or series of tests that will rule out every possible physical disorder.

A wise counselor should not be terribly troubled by these statistics. It does not mean that you have been wrong in counseling 5 to 46 percent of your counselees. If you study your counselees and encourage them to change where the Scripture encourages them to change, you have ministered well. But you can minister better. You can be sensitive to the possibility of organic disorder and, as a result, prevent fatalities or the progression of a disease. In so doing you can be instrumental in alleviating significant suffering.

The answer is not to refer every counselee for a physical exam. Routine physical exams rarely catch underlying medical disorders. And they are just plain expensive! The answer is to have a few questions that help you screen for medical problems, to be alert to the most common diseases, and to realize that there are diagnostic alternatives for what appear to be functional problems.

7

The No. 1 Culprit: Licit and Illicit Drugs

A medicine is always directly hurtful;
it may sometimes be indirectly beneficial.

—Oliver Wendell Holmes

The most common cause of counseling problems with an undiagnosed physical origin is drugs: prescription, over-the-counter, and illegal. This may not surprise you. What may surprise you, however, is that of these drugs, the most frequent offenders are prescription drugs, not illegal drugs.[1] Certainly street drugs and illegal drugs are often the root of cognitive and personality changes, but *legal* drugs are the biggest culprit— if only because they are more prevalent. The popular myth is that U.S. Food and Drug Administration-approved medicines are safe and without side effects. But these remedies can cause more problems than the symptoms they were intended to cure! Remember, there is no perfect drug. Every drug in the world can have some type of cognitive or behavioral side effects, even when taken at prescribed dosages.

To compound the problem of prescription drugs, most people take many medications simultaneously. This makes the medications' effects and interactions less predictable and leaves patients more vulnerable to side effects. Studies report that inpatients in general hospitals take from three to eight medicines, and many consume them for either unknown or grossly incorrect reasons. In nonhospitalized persons, it is common to consult more than one physician, not telling the second about medications given by the first. Results can be dramatic or even fatal. It is estimated that, in a general medical population, 2 to 3 percent of those

177

taking medications experience unwanted emotional or cognitive (psychiatric) side effects (Currey, 1982).

Even though there is popular awareness of this problem, it is
expected to get worse. American patients seem to demand medication
whenever they enter a physician's office—even if the problem has
nothing to do with poor health. Also, physicians themselves are
bombarded with drug advertisements. If you look at any medical journal,
you will find that almost every other page proclaims the drug companies'
solutions to physicians' most pressing problems. And the pharmaceutical
companies make their offers more appealing by giving free samples and
presenting advertisements that are as slick as those of the alcohol
industry.

The following section introduces some of the drugs that are typically
found in counseling populations along with their possible emotional and
cognitive side effects. The categories include drugs that are typically
prescribed by psychiatrists, general prescription and over-the-counter
medications, caffeine, and illegal drugs.

As you peruse this chapter, avoid being sidetracked by the sheer
number of drugs and side effects. The basic point is that any drug can
have unwanted emotional and cognitive side effects in any person. The
lists are intended to provide a source of reference as well as to flesh out
this basic point.

Psychiatric Prescription Medication

Since their serendipitous discovery in the 1950s, psychiatric drugs
have become a staple of the medical community. These are the drugs that
are predominantly used with schizophrenia, mania, depression, and
anxiety (sometimes called "psychiatric problems"). For some people they
are very helpful, but they are not without negative side effects. In fact,
they can even have paradoxical effects—they may produce the symptoms
they were intended to cure (see Appendix B for a complete list of current
psychiatric drugs).

Antipsychotics[2]

Psychosis is a vague and outdated term that refers to profound
difficulties in understanding "reality" and thinking logically. The best
known psychosis is called schizophrenia. This problem will be discussed in
the next chapter as well as under hallucinations (chap. 9). For now,
recognize that schizophrenia is *not* multiple personality. Rather, it is a

very general term that includes symptoms such as hallucinations, delusions, and peculiarities in thinking and speech. Other psychotic problems include mania, severe depression, and organic brain problems in the elderly.

Antipsychotic drugs are a group of drugs intended to impose boundaries on psychotic thinking and behavior. Curiously, they also are used to treat Tourette's syndrome, nausea and vomiting, and hiccoughs. Their predominant use, however, is with symptoms that can be classified under the category of schizophrenia.

Extrapyramidal side effects. Those who take antipsychotic drugs sometimes complain about bothersome cognitive changes. Some have even called these drugs "chemical straitjackets." But cognitive and emotional side effects are rarely the most disconcerting problems. The most frequent concerns are about involuntary movements called extrapyramidal (EP) side effects.[3]

Up to 30 percent of people taking antipsychotic drugs will experience at least one of the four types of EP side effects (Tyrer, 1982). They include acute dystonic reactions, akathisia, Parkinson's syndrome, and tardive dyskinesia. Although these names are strange, it would be useful to become familiar with these symptoms. With the exception of acute dystonic reactions, you will probably see them in the course of a traditional pastoral or counseling practice.

If acute dystonic reactions occur, they are usually the first of the EP side effects, emerging within four to five hours of starting the medication. They consist of odd and sometimes startling muscle spasms or upward rotation of the eyes. Neither lethal nor permanent, the symptoms usually pass as the blood levels of the drug fall. In severe cases, physicians will inject a muscle relaxant that effectively stops the symptoms.

They are infrequently observed in counseling because they occur so quickly after starting medication. Families usually recognize that the strange movements are related to the medication and they call the prescribing physician immediately. But if affected persons or their families are accustomed to getting counsel from pastors or nonmedical counselors, then these families may rely on this nonmedical advice. In such cases, immediate referral back to the prescribing M.D. is necessary.

Chronologically, akathisia may be the next side effect to emerge. Its literal meaning, "no sitting," aptly describes the symptoms. It is characterized by a subjective compulsion to be in motion. Persons may constantly shift their legs, tap their feet, or pace incessantly. When counseling these individuals, it would be wise to give them freedom to move around. If akathisia is particularly troublesome, refer persons back to their physicians. Prescribing physicians may stop the medication or suggest one with fewer side effects.

Parkinsonism may develop within a few months after starting the medication. These symptoms are carbon copies of Parkinson's disease. Accordingly, they are characterized by slow, rigid movements, tremors, and a blank, expressionless, "zombielike" face. Most affected persons don't complain about these symptoms, but some find them very irritating. Families of affected persons especially can find them disconcerting. If Parkinson symptoms are apparent, be sure that affected persons have psychiatric consultation. The side effects are reversible—especially if they are treated quickly—and there are a variety of strategies that physicians use to limit them: they can decrease, change, or stop medication, or prescribe one of a group of drugs that can relieve the symptoms.[4]

The fourth EP side effect, tardive dyskinesias or "TDs," emerges after at least three to six months of uninterrupted drug ingestion. Estimates of their prevalence vary widely, and the severity of the symptoms is dependent on both the person and the drug. A reasonable estimate is that of those who take antipsychotics for over two years, 20 percent will experience TDs. They consist of unusual movements of the lips, cheeks, tongue, and jaw, such as lip-smacking or trembling, chewing, puckering of the lips, sticking out the tongue, and puffing the cheeks. These may be very embarrassing, and persons have been known to spend their life savings on alleged cures. Also, the side effects can be so severe that breathing and swallowing become difficult. The most troublesome aspect of TDs, however, is that in up to one-half of those who demonstrate the symptoms, they may be irreversible. Therefore, if you detect these symptoms in someone taking antipsychotic medication, refer them immediately to the prescribing physician.

Autonomic nervous system side effects (anticholinergic). Because antipsychotic drugs inhibit the neurotransmitter acetylcholine, another bothersome problem may be anticholinergic side effects. These result from the suppression of parasympathetic nervous system activity and the resulting unchecked activity of the sympathetic nervous system ("fight or flight"). Therefore, people can experience blurry vision, dry mouth, increased heart rate, delayed or retrograde ejaculation,[5] constipation, and urinary retention. Toxic side effects are much more severe. They can include mental clouding and confusion, anxiety, disorientation, and hallucinations. Older persons or persons taking more than one anticholinergic drug are particularly prone to these toxic effects.

A twenty-three-year-old mentally retarded man was taking Haldol, Mellaril, and Cogentin. His anticholinergic side effects were so severe that he was admitted to a hospital disoriented to time and place, violently agitated, and having visual hallucinations. He also had a dry mouth and a pulse rate of 120 beats per minute. (Granacher & Baldessarini, 1977)

In extreme cases, these side effects might be treated with a drug called physostigmine—a drug that can have other side effects.

Antidepressants and Lithium

Antidepressants, as their name indicates, are used to alleviate symptoms of depression. But they are no longer limited to these symptoms. Today, it seems as if antidepressants are being tried with just about everything—and with some success. They are reportedly helpful with anxiety, agoraphobia, panic attacks, obsessive-compulsive problems, anorexia, and bulimia. They seem to be the new class of wonder drugs. They are among the safest of the psychoactive medications, but there are side effects with which you should be familiar.

Antidepressants are usually divided into two broad classes: tricyclics and monoamine oxidase inhibitors (MAOIs)— (see appendix B). The more popular tricyclics, like the antipsychotics, have anticholinergic properties, so they may cause cognitive problems such as difficulty concentrating and planning, along with other problems such as muscle weakness, fatigue, nervousness, headaches, agitation, tremors, and excessive sweating.

Of particular importance for counselors are the occasional paradoxical reactions. Patients have reported anxiety and worsening of depression, insomnia, nightmares, mania, and even psychotic reactions.

A twenty-four-year-old woman with a five-year history of manic-depression was admitted to the hospital with symptoms of agitated depression. That is, she complained about feeling very depressed, but she was often physically active, pacing back and forth. All her medications were removed for two weeks but there was no improvement in her symptoms. She was then placed on lithium and imipramine (an antidepressant) and within forty-eight hours reported improvement in her depression. The dose of imipramine was increased after twelve and eighteen days. By day 22 she deteriorated rapidly, and imipramine was increased again. Her speech became slow and fragmented, she started moving around excessively, her concentration was poor, and her behavior was so disorganized that she needed constant nursing care. She was unable to even feed herself and on several occasions urinated in her clothes. On day 27 after beginning imipramine, the medication was discontinued, and within two weeks she was back to normal. Interestingly, hospital records from five years before indicated a very similar experience. (Meador-Woodruff & Grunhaus, 1986)

Of course, as is the case with all side effects, paradoxical responses do not appear in the majority of people taking these drugs. Overall, the tricyclic antidepressants are fairly safe. But side effects can occur and are often misdiagnosed. Furthermore, when side effects are misdiagnosed, the new diagnosis is inevitably a psychiatric one—a label which may become an inescapable, permanent brand. Then persons may be treated with more medications that exacerbate their symptoms even further.

MAOIs are often helpful with depressed, lethargic people, but they are less popular than the tricyclic antidepressants because they have more associated side effects: dizziness, agitation, insomnia, drowsiness, impaired memory, and confusional states, to name a few. Toxic reactions can be particularly severe and may not appear for eleven or more hours after ingestion, thus making the connection between the drug and the symptoms less apparent. With smaller overdoses there may be nausea and rapid heartbeats. Larger overdoses lead to severe cognitive changes, convulsions, and, eventually, coma.

Lithium is rarely used as an antidepressant, but it is the original psychiatric wonder drug because of its effectiveness in mania or bipolar disorders (manic-depression). For many people it seems to limit manic episodes and protect from future episodes. Lithium tends to be fairly safe, but there is a slim margin between therapeutic and toxic doses. Therefore, physicians will usually monitor the blood levels of lithium. At therapeutic doses, the most common central nervous system side effects are mental dullness, decreased memory and concentration, headache, fatigue, and tremor (Bassuk, Schoonover & Gelenberg, 1983). These symptoms usually remit quickly. With chronic administrations of high dose lithium, the nervous system slows. Sleepiness, slurred speech, and mental sluggishness may be early signs.

Antianxiety Drugs, Sedatives, Tranquilizers, Sleeping Pills

Antianxiety drugs and prescription sleeping pills are so popular that they are almost cultural institutions. But popularity does not mean that they are either safe or effective. There is increasing evidence that these drugs can be habit-forming, even when taken in prescribed doses, and they also can have unpredictable and unpleasant side effects.

Benzodiazepines. The largest class of antianxiety or sedative drugs, and the one I will focus on, is called the benzodiazepines. A latecomer in the psychoactive drug circuit, benzodiazepines were first synthesized in 1955 but were not marketed in their present form until the introduction of Valium in 1962. They were initially proclaimed as totally safe sedatives, and they took the Western world by storm. In fact, in the early 1980s, 15 percent of the United States population used a benzodiazepine during a one-year period (Frances & Franklin, 1988). The old joke was that physicians seemed to be treating us for a widespread Valium deficiency. Problems emerged only recently.

Not unlike a pill form of alcohol, the most significant problems revolve around tolerance, dependence, and withdrawal. *Tolerance* is diminished responsiveness to a drug as a result of repeated administrations. That is, the drug at the same dosage no longer has the same effect. As a result, persons may increase their dosage and begin a pattern that leads to dependence. *Dependence* is characterized by a felt compulsion to take a drug in order to experience its psychic effects or to avoid the discomfort of its absence. *Withdrawal* symptoms accompany abstinence and usually consist of effects opposite of those from the drug. Therefore, withdrawal from antianxiety drugs or sedatives—as well as withdrawal from alcohol or other depressants—may result in a morning "hangover," agitation, insomnia, or more dramatic signs of overactivity such as seizures.

Dependence and withdrawal are most common when high doses, typically two to five times the recommended dose, are taken for at least two weeks (Relkin, 1966; Woody, O'Brien & Greenstien, 1975). However, normal doses of benzodiazepines can also lead to withdrawal symptoms, especially after ingestion for several years. More specifically, after taking normal dosages for six months, 5 to 10 percent of those taking benzodiazepines develop dependence and withdrawal symptoms. After two to four years, 25 to 45 percent do so, and after six to eight years, 75 percent. Since the drug remains in the body for a period of time after the drug is stopped, the withdrawal syndrome may not be evident for seven to ten days. When it occurs, affected persons can experience severe sleep disturbances, irritability, panic attacks, tremors, difficulty concentrating, and even psychotic reactions (Petursson & Lader, 1984).

A thirty-year-old woman experienced episodes of anxiety, tension, and depression since adolescence. First prescribed diazepam [Valium] at age seventeen for agoraphobia, she took 15 mg daily for many years, although she felt the drug lost its effect after roughly six months. When her marriage started to break up, she increased the dose to 50 mg a day and gradually to 90 mg daily. (She received her prescription from a GP and an additional supply from a friend.) Only after a serious car accident did she indicate a desire to stop the drug. Her own previous attempts to withdraw lasted only a few days and resulted in intolerable panic attacks. (Petursson & Lader, 1984)

There are many other side effects of the benzodiazepines, such as tearfulness and depression, or paradoxical responses of agitation and restlessness. These side effects, coupled with the emerging evidence that antianxiety drugs may be no better than having a friend and no medication, certainly render their extended use suspect.

Their use as a sleep aid is limited because of the problem of tolerance: they tend to lose their effectiveness after one month. Taken for a long period of time, they can actually disrupt sleep.

Buspirone. Buspirone, or Buspar, is a new drug in the anti-anxiety category that seems to avoid many of the pitfalls of the popular benzodiazepines. It is not prone to abuse, dependence, or use as a sedative. However, it is used less frequently because it is a new drug and its action is not well understood. Also, in contrast to the almost immediate effect of benzodiazepines, it usually takes about two weeks to have any helpful effect. At this point, the main side effects are increased restlessness and nervousness.

General Prescription Medication

The list of general prescription drugs that can affect thinking or emotions is enormous. The following comments highlight only a limited number of the more common categories.

Medications with Known
Psychoactive (Mind-affecting) Qualities.

Antihypertensives
Cardiovascular drugs
Antihistamines: Tagamet
Anti-inflammatory drugs
Anticholinergics
Respiratory drugs and nasal decongestants
Diet pills
Oral contraceptives

Antihypertensives. With the recent warnings about the dangers of high blood pressure, antihypertensive medications abound. These drugs are sometimes associated with depression. Also, diuretics, often the first line of treatment for high blood pressure, can deplete the body of sodium and potassium (electrolytes). Without replacement of these chemicals, the resulting electrolyte imbalance may result in confusion and psychosis (Flaherty, 1979).

Cardiovascular drugs. Cardiovascular drugs seem to be ubiquitous among the elderly—a group whose nervous systems are already quite sensitive to drugs. Digitalis (digoxin), one of the most popular of these medications, will cause some kind of cognitive or emotional change in at least 20–30 percent of patients. The most typical symptoms are headache, weakness, and apathy; more severe symptoms include profound confusion and visual hallucinations (Whitlock, 1987). People have reported blurred vision, flashing lights, and seeing everything in yellow. Other heart medications have also been implicated.

Antihistamines: Tagamet. Antihistamines are frequently used for treatment of hay fever and other allergies. Their most common side effect is drowsiness, but they can have other psychological effects. The best-known drug in this class, however, is not used for allergies. It is the popular drug Tagamet (cimetidine) that is effectively used in the treatment of peptic ulcer.

There have been numerous reports of depression, mental clouding, confusion, and hallucinations following administration of this drug (Johnson & Bailey, 1979). Furthermore, these can occur in both young and old.

Table 7.1. Drugs with Anticholinergic Effects

Antidepressants	Antihistamines
Elavil	Ornade
Triavil	Benadryl
Sinequan, Adapin	Phenergan
Aventyl	
Vivactil	Anti-Parkinson drugs
	Cogentin
Cold and sleep medicines	Artane
Triaminic	
Exedrin-PM	Antipsychotic drugs
Sleep-Eze	Phenothiazines
Sominex	
Neo-Synephrine	
Actifed	

Anti-inflammatory drugs: Corticosteroids. Steroids are used in respiratory problems such as asthma as well as many other diseases: lupus, rheumatoid arthritis, and ulcerative colitis, to name a few. They are one of the few classes of drugs that report *positive* emotional and cognitive changes after administration. Patients often report a sense of well-being, increased energy, and improved concentration and creativity during steroid treatment. However, this subtle euphoria, when magnified, can move to emotional lability (rapid, unpredictable fluctuations), anxiety, and manic excitement. A wide variety of other counseling-type symptoms have also been reported. The most prevalent are depression and hallucinations (Haskett, 1987).

Anticholinergic drugs. Anticholinergic drugs have already been discussed under both antipsychotics and antidepressants, but there are many other drugs that have similar side effects (Table 7.1, from Granacher & Baldessarini, 1975). These side effects do not discriminate—they affect any age or either sex. However, as already noted, they can be a particular problem in the elderly.

Respiratory drugs and nasal decongestants. Counselors are rarely aware of the presence or absence of respiratory drugs. Sometimes this is because they haven't asked about the use of any medications at all. In other cases, the counselees don't report the use of these drugs, thinking them unimportant. Counselees do not believe these drugs are treating a chronic disease and, since they are often bought over-the-counter, most people are persuaded that they are safe. Fortunately, the incidence of cognitive and emotional reactions to respiratory drugs is fairly low, but they can be severe.[6]

> A four-year-old girl had episodes of marked visual hallucinosis and a grand mal seizure following administration of a cough medication containing phenylpropanolamine [e.g., Alka Seltzer Plus cold medicine]. (Gardner & Hall, 1982, p. 189)

> After taking phenylpropanolamine, a twenty-five-year-old woman became increasingly excited and developed disorders in concentration and sleeping. After nine days of taking the medication, she was excessively fearful and had vivid, paranoid misconceptions about her world. All of these symptoms disappeared within twenty-four hours after the drug was stopped. (Gardner & Hall, 1982)

Most of the medications have amphetamine-like effects and tend to activate the sympathetic nervous system. Therefore, agitation, "tension," and "nervousness" are common complaints. In higher doses, or over a long period of time, people have reported hallucinations, confusion, panic states, and heart problems (Hall et al., 1985).

Again, older persons tend to be more susceptible to these problems, but of interest are the number of younger children who have psychotic symptoms and hallucinations. For example, Actifed and Sudafed have led to numerous reports of hallucinatory and behavioral problems in children (Sills, Nunn & Sankey, 1984).

Diet pills. Diet pills, prescription and over-the-counter, can raise quite a few problems for counselors. Even though their effectiveness is suspect, they can produce psychotic side effects. And since those taking them do not consider them medicines, they are rarely reported.

> A twenty-year-old female college student was referred for psychiatric consultation because of a two-month history of psychiatric symptoms. She complained of feeling "uptight" and reported unusual deja vu experiences. She also felt that her mother had been trying to poison her and that people at her college were playing games on her, such as turning the clock back, because they didn't like her. Probably hallucinating, she imagined that she could speak three different languages because these languages would have dialogues inside her. She also felt as if the Holy Spirit, the Devil, and she were in conflict.

> She never had similar symptoms in the past, and she was scared and perplexed by her symptoms. But even with these indicators of organic

dysfunction, she was given the provisional diagnosis of acute schizophrenic reaction and was treated with Stelazine [an antipsychotic]. Three weeks after beginning the medication she mentioned to the psychiatrist that she had been taking diet pills for three months, beginning one month prior to the onset of the symptoms. She had not mentioned these pills previously as she did not consider them medicine. The diet pills were stopped and within three weeks she felt "back to normal." (Hoffman, 1977)

Oral contraceptives. Oral contraceptives are another group of drugs that are rarely mentioned to counselors. Sometimes women are embarrassed to do so, other times they do not even realize that contraceptives are medications because they are not treating any disease. Yet they are frequently implicated in depression, and since they are the most widely used conventional medication in history, counselors must be aware of their use.

A twenty-nine-year-old woman complained of feeling "down" for several months and even talked about suicide. Also, she was waking early, unable to get back to sleep, and becoming more and more lethargic during the day. This was accompanied by a sense of resentment and alienation from her family. Although she had a history of depression, the previous episodes seemed to be related to starting birth control pills and postpartum blues. As such, her physician suggested she stop taking birth control pills. Over the next several weeks she showed considerable improvement in her experience of depression, sleep, and family relationships. (Daley, Kane & Ewing, 1967)

Studies indicate that 10 to 40 percent of oral contraceptive users may suffer mild to moderate depression and related symptoms. Frequent complaints are sadness, tiredness, and lethargy, which are occasionally accompanied by a loss of interest in sex. Sometimes these symptoms disappear after a few months; other times they persist (Kane, 1976).

Summary of counseling guidelines. Prescription drugs are notorious for their capacity to induce unwanted symptoms. Many times these symptoms are cognitive and emotional, and they are then easily misdiagnosed as functional. The following guidelines will help minimize this problem.

1. Know what drugs people are taking. And remember, most people will underestimate their drug intake, and they will not even list either drugs that have been prescribed for many years or over-the-counter preparations. Therefore, ask specifically: "What prescription drugs do you

take—for *any* reason?" "Do you take sleeping pills or anything for your 'nerves'?" "What about over-the-counter drugs? Aspirin? Cold medications? Nasal sprays? Anything for asthma? Oral contraceptives?"

Sometimes you should even inspect the bottles and labels for all these drugs. Then you will know with more certainty what individuals are taking, and you can check to see if counselees are following the recommended dosages.

2. Make sure that counselees know what the drugs are for, their potential side effects, and the recommended dose. If they are uncertain on these issues, send them back to their physician. If they have more than one physician, each physician must know about every drug.

3. Keep a *Physician's Desk Reference (PDR)* handy. This volume, published yearly, describes all the drugs that are marketed in the United States. You can probably get an older copy from a friendly physician.

If you are unfamiliar with a particular drug, look it up in the *PDR*. Review the most common side effects of each medication. In the *PDR* side effects are listed in order of frequency, from most to least.

4. If new or different psychological changes appeared soon after taking a drug, realize that medication may be the cause and refer counselees back to prescribing physicians. But also realize that many people are side-effect free for years, but that the drug may only gradually become toxic and result in subtly emerging psychological changes.

Be particularly alert to those persons with a number of illnesses, over sixty, using multiple drugs, or getting prescriptions by phone. These people are most prone to cognitive and emotional changes induced by traditional medications (Currey, 1982).

Nonprescriptive Drugs and Stimulants

Caffeine

From 1886 to 1903, cocaine was literally a household drug, present in every bottle of Coca-Cola. Popular sentiment against cocaine caused the company to remove it, but the company retained Coke's other appealing stimulant, caffeine. Although accepted at the grass roots level, most people probably realize that caffeine acts like an addicting drug: it is associated with tolerance, dependence, and withdrawal. Take away the social acceptability of caffeine, and the person who has a need for caffeinated, morning eye-openers looks strangely like an alcohol abuser looking for a drink.

A physician suggested caffeine tablets to a woman who experienced continual physical fatigue. While the caffeine helped, she became nervous, restless, and an insomniac. Prior to a party, she took quite a few pills in order to have energy for the evening, but "she became confused, disoriented, excited, restless, and violent, shouted and screamed, and began to throw things about her room." Although religious, "she became exceedingly profane" and was finally taken to a hospital. She was diagnosed as neurotic, anxious, and hysterical.

On another occasion she took an entire box of caffeine pills and was sent to a psychiatric ward where she was initially tied to her bed because she was so manic. After almost two months on the ward, she was noticed to be drinking more than four cups of coffee daily. After she stopped ingesting caffeine, her unusual symptoms disappeared. (McManamy & Schube, 1936)

These potentially hazardous effects of coffee have been documented throughout the nineteenth and twentieth centuries. For instance, a popular 1909 medical text called *A System of Medicine* gave clear warnings against coffee. In fact, in this text Dr. Walter Dixon, one of the foremost pharmacologists of his generation, discussed the "poison" coffee while mentioning the benefits of opium pills!

I'm not promoting a crusade against caffeine. Even though addictive, caffeine is rarely a problem for most people. But some people are unknowingly affected by it and can experience adverse side effects. Counselors should be aware of these because the side effects are typically diagnosed by patient and physician as counseling-related. When it is a problem, complaints of "caffeinism" emerge after at least 250 mg a day of caffeine (Table 7.2). Symptoms include restlessness, nervousness, irritability, insomnia, and headache. Thus, if counselees have symptoms that look and feel like anxiety, it is wise to encourage them to stop taking caffeine. At the same time, realize that stopping is no easy task. Withdrawal symptoms can be unpleasant, having an effect opposite that of caffeine (lethargy, nervousness, inability to work effectively).

Street Drugs and Drugs of Abuse

Without trying to minimize the drug epidemic, it is true that the side effects of of prescription and legal drugs tend to be underemphasized, whereas the effects of street drugs tend to be sensationalized. Sometimes the differences between them relate more to the social class of the user than the actual deleterious nature of the street drug. Furthermore, many effects of street drugs are a result of their prohibition more than the

Table 7.2. Common Sources of Caffeine

Source	Approximate amounts of caffeine
Beverages	.
Brewed coffee	80–140 mg per cup
Instant coffee	66–100 mg per cup
Tea	30–100 mg per cup
Cola drinks	30–65 mg per cup
Cocoa	5–50 mg per cup
Stimulants and diet aids	.
Dexatrim	200 mg per tablet
Dietac	300 mg per tablet
No Doz	100 mg per tablet
Vivarin	200 mg per tablet
Diuretics	.
Aqua-Ban	200 mg per tablet
Permathene	200 mg per tablet
Pre-mens Forte	100 mg per tablet
Prescription medications	.
APCs (aspirin, phenacitin, caffeine)	32 mg per tablet
Cafergot (for migraine)	100 mg per tablet
Darvon (for pain relief)	32 mg per tablet
Fiorinal (for headache)	40 mg per tablet
Migral (for migraine)	50 mg per tablet
Over-the-counter (OTC) analgesics	.
Anacin	32 mg per tablet
Midol	32 mg per tablet
Vanquish	32 mg per tablet
Excedrin	65 mg per tablet
Most OTC cold medicines	15–30 mg per tablet
Small chocolate bar	25 mg per bar

chemicals themselves. That is, drug abusers are more prone to participate in illegal activities in order to get money for drugs.

Yet this is not to say they are safe. They are not. Cognitively or mentally, they can produce psychotic experiences and intellectual dulling. Physically, they can lead to death. Indeed, there are no drugs, legal or illegal, that are perfectly safe; and drugs that are taken for the sole purpose of mood enhancement are especially prone to dependence and abuse. It is true that "drugs make sick people well and well people sick."

What follows are some of the most popular street drugs and their effects on cognitive functions and emotions. Omitted are data on the effects of long-term drug abuse on bodily organs. If these were included,

Table 7.3. Street Drugs

Stimulants ("uppers")
  Cocaine ("coke," "crack")
  Amphetamines ("bennies")
  Methamphetamines ("speed," "ice")
  Diet pills (Dexatrim)
  Decongestants (Ornade, Comprex)
Depressants ("downers")
  Alcohol
  Barbiturates ("reds")
  Quaaludes
  Benzodiazepines (Valium, Ativan, Dalmane . . .)
Narcotics—Opium and its derivatives
  Morphine   Dilaudid
  Codeine   Heroin
  Darvon   Paregoric
  Demerol   Percodan
Hallucinogens   Psilocybin (mushrooms, "buttons")
  LSD   Mescaline (Peyote)
  Phencyclidine (PCP)
Marijuana (THC)
  Marijuana
  Hashish

however, the damage done by legal drugs—alcohol and tobacco—would head the list.

Street drugs (and alcohol) can be categorized in different ways. They are best arranged in five different categories: stimulants, depressants, narcotics, hallucinogens, and marijuana (Table 7.3).

Stimulants

Arguably the most dangerous of the recreational drugs are the stimulants. This group includes a wide range of drugs, all with differing potencies but the same general effect. In mild to moderate doses they produce mood elevation, a sense of increased initiative and confidence, wakefulness, diminished appetite, and an increase in mental alertness and performance on simple tasks. At higher doses they can lead to insomnia, headache, heart palpitations, dizziness, confusion, and a more depressed mood. At toxic doses, stimulants are very dangerous. They can produce an "amphetamine psychosis" that is almost indistinguishable from the most severe of schizophrenic symptoms.

Amphetamines. No longer relegated to use by truck drivers, students, dieters, or "speed freaks," amphetamines are making a comeback. They tend to alternate with cocaine as a popular drug of abuse. That is, when cocaine is popular and easy to get, amphetamines are less popular. When cocaine is more expensive or legally dangerous, amphetamines are the stimulant of choice. There is mounting evidence that many people are switching from cocaine to amphetamines—especially a smokable form called crystal meth or "ice." Amphetamines have a perceived advantage over cocaine in that they are cheaper and offer a longer "high."

A twenty-eight-year-old man, married and the father of two, had abused amphetamines since age sixteen. After his conversion at age twenty-six, he claimed to stop both the drug abuse and relationships with the drug culture. He became a model father, husband, and worker and was often called on to give testimony about his conversion. Sometimes he would seem hyperactive, but this was considered to be "the way he was."

Two years after his conversion, his wife came for counseling because her husband seemed to be increasingly suspicious and defensive. Also, he had several episodes of frightening rage. When he came for counseling, he denied using any drugs but was talking nonstop and obviously not hearing biblical counsel. The following week, still adamantly professing abstinence, he was irrational, delusional, and unable to stay on track with any conversation. At that time the counselor decided to take him to a hospital emergency ward. On the way, he confessed to amphetamine abuse—abuse that, he reported, never waned over the past few years. It was simply more covert.

Interestingly, the loudest protests against speed come from the drug culture itself. For example, in a 1965 interview with the *Los Angeles Free Press*, Allen Ginsberg, a well-known drug user and poet, proclaimed, "Let's issue a general declaration to all the underground community, *contra speedamos ex cathedra.* Speed is antisocial, paranoid-making, it's a drag, bad for your body, bad for your mind, generally speaking, in the long run uncreative, and it's a plague in the whole dope industry" (Beecher, 1972, p. 292).

Cocaine. Although all stimulants can be dangerous, cocaine is the most notorious drug in the class. Not everyone finds it attractive, but those who do are often ensnared by its potency.

The drug is administered by snorting (sniffing through the nose), smoking (freebase or crack), or injection. Although cocaine "worship" can result from any one of these means, smoking and injecting produce the more rapid and intense high. The reasons are fairly simple. When smoking, it is the lungs, not the nose, that absorb the drug, and their larger size gets more drug to the brain faster. With injection, drugs enter the blood immediately and proceed uninterrupted to the brain. Also, the smokable and injectable forms of cocaine are usually of higher quality than the cocaine that is snorted.

The pharmacological impact of cocaine is a result of its blocking the activity of neurotransmitters. After neurotransmitters cross the synapse and stimulate the neighboring neuron to fire, they are released, and usually absorbed again by the sending neuron and stored for future use. Cocaine blocks this process and leaves more of the neurotransmitters in the synaptic gap to be used immediately. The subsequent high neuronal firing rate seems to be the biological foundation for excitement and euphoria. Also, the fatigue and depletion of these neurotransmitters are the basis for the lethargy and depression that can accompany the cessation of cocaine use.

For those who find the drug pleasurable, the brief euphoria can become the most important experience in life. Addicts will do anything to get it, including lie, steal, and engage in prostitution. Although it is difficult to translate from animal studies to human experience, when monkeys develop a passion for cocaine, they will ignore everything—food, water, and sex—if cocaine is available. Their refusal of eligible females is especially interesting since most animals have a strong biological need to procreate. In Peru, the enslaving nature of cocaine has so baffled those who offer treatment that they have resorted to more experimental procedures—frontal lobotomies! Indeed, the desire for the mood-enhancing qualities of cocaine can become a stumbling block that some people never overcome. It can become a powerful idol that leaves people feeling overwhelmed and powerless.

> Cocaine is the most exhilarating drug I have ever used. The euphoria centers in the head. Perhaps the drug activates pleasure connections directly in the brain. (Burroughs, 1959, p. 249)

> She [his wife] had just caught me with cocaine again after I had managed to convince her that I hadn't used in over a month. Of course I had been tooting (snorting) almost every day, but I had managed to cover my tracks better than usual. So she said to me that I was going to have to make a

choice—either cocaine or her. Before she finished the sentence, I knew what was coming, so I told her to think carefully about what she was going to say. It was clear to me that there wasn't a choice. I love my wife, but I'm not going to choose *anything* over cocaine. It's sick, but that's what things have come to. Nothing and nobody comes before my cocaine. (Weiss & Mirin, 1987, p. 55)

A curious aspect of cocaine is that with repeated high doses, it loses its psychological impact. In fact, more than that, it can actually depress mood. Unfortunately, most abusers interpret the bad feelings as a need to do more of the drug. As a result, they increase the dose, only to become more depressed in their search for that elusive high. The reasoning makes sense: "The drug made me feel great before; it can do it again." But it is ignorant of the pharmacological properties of the drug.

Tolerance and dependence. Tolerance and dependence are problems with all stimulants. The user first develops tolerance to the stimulant's appetite-suppressant action; that is, although there is an initial appetite-suppressant effect, it is usually short-lived. The user then develops a tolerance to the mood-enhancing effects—it will take more and more of the drug to come close to the original "high." Tolerance, however, does not develop as far as the awakening effect. These drugs persistently disrupt sleep.

All the stimulants can lead to mild physical dependence. That is, over a long period of time the body will resist efforts to stop the drug. But contrary to popular opinion, the resistance is usually not that severe. Even with prolonged use of the more powerful stimulants such as cocaine or amphetamines, the physical effects of withdrawal and abstinence include only lethargy, fatigue, and mild depression. Dependence, especially in cocaine abuse, is more an issue of the heart than the body.

For counselors, the question becomes whether or not to recommend hospitalization for those who have a daily habit of cocaine abuse. Physically, hospitalization is not necessary. Persons do not die when they withdraw from stimulants. However, there are many cases where the intensity and isolation of the in-patient experience are exactly what the user needs.

Depressants

The depressants are headed by the most disruptive drug known to the world—alcohol. Its relatives are the benzodiazepines (anti-anxiety drugs) and barbiturates. The effect of depressants are fairly well known, having been chronicled in movies, TV, bars, and most city streets. Beginning with a mild euphoria, intoxication progresses to mental cloudiness, drowsiness, and loss of consciousness. As the saying goes, heavy drinkers go from jocose, to bellicose, to lachrymose, to comatose. All the depressants lead to tolerance in those who abuse them. For example, a heavy drinker may appear to function well with blood alcohol levels that would leave a nondrinker inebriated. Usually this tolerance is lost or greatly reduced within three weeks of discontinuing drinking.

Dependence is more individualized. Some heavy drinkers or depressant abusers can stop without any ill effects. Others may experience withdrawal syndromes immediately. Usually, however, withdrawal symptoms occur only when discontinuing years of heavy, chronic abuse. In mild cases, alcohol withdrawal may be apparent simply by anxiety, nausea, insomnia, sweating, and tremulousness. In more extreme cases, the tremulousness may be extreme because of the excitability of the cortex (remember, the effects of withdrawal are the opposite of the drug effects), and it may be expressed in seizures, or "rum fits," and auditory hallucinations. The most extreme form of withdrawal, delirium tremens ("DTs"), can be very dangerous and can lead to death. The features include severe apprehension, agitation, unintelligible speech, visual and auditory hallucinations, disorientation, seizures, and delirium. These symptoms typically begin between eighteen and thirty-two hours after cessation of drinking, and they subside within ten to fourteen days. Because of the potential danger associated with withdrawal, persons known to be dependent on alcohol or depressants are best observed in a hospital setting during detoxification.

Narcotics[7]

Opiates and their derivatives are known for their pain-killing action as well as their ability to produce a sense of tranquility. When injected intravenously for their psychic effects, they produce a thirty- to sixty-second "rush" followed by a period of euphoria and peacefulness that can last for hours.

Like some of the other illicit drugs, opium products are well known to lead to tolerance and dependence. Tolerance to some of their effects can develop within only a week of regular use. Degree of dependence varies depending on the type of drug, amount, length of time used, and expectations of the user. With chronic use of heroin, dependence and withdrawal symptoms emerge within six to twelve hours after the last dose. They begin with a mild craving for the drug, yawning, sweating, and some anxiety. As withdrawal progresses, there may be hot and cold flashes, muscle cramps, restlessness, and insomnia. Within eighteen to twenty-four hours symptoms intensify and are characterized by nausea and vomiting, increased blood pressure, and a mild fever. Symptoms peak by forty-eight to seventy-two hours after the last dose, and they disappear within seven to ten days. Hospitalization is not necessary for detoxification, but supervision by someone knowledgeable in the withdrawal process is helpful.

Hallucinogens

Hallucinogenic drugs are a motley group of chemicals with various effects. They might enhance awareness of body and environment, create an unusual array of perceptual distortions, give a sense of importance to the mundane, or imitate a brief psychotic experience. The varieties of experiences are a result of the strength of the drug as well as a host of factors other than the drug itself. Mood, relationships, and expectations all contribute to the drugs' effects. As such, "bad trips" might be determined more by personal and interpersonal conditions than drug characteristics.

LSD is the best known of this class. Synthesized in 1955, the drug can have significant effects in very small amounts. In fact, the original effects were discovered because minute amounts leaked through a test tube cork and the chemist probably licked his fingers! Within twenty to sixty minutes there are some sympathetic nervous system effects. Peak effects occur between two and three hours after ingestion, and intoxication usually lasts up to twelve hours.

With repeated administrations, tolerance can develop quickly— within two to four days. However, since there is no known dependence, LSD-users rarely take the drug more than once or twice a week.

Phencyclidine or PCP ("angel dust") is one of the most popular hallucinogens because it is cheap and easily made. Like other drugs, its effect varies depending on dose and mode of administration. Usually dissolved onto marijuana or tobacco (sometimes without the user's knowledge), PCP can produce perceptual distortions, auditory and visual hallucinations, and unusual body experiences. What is unusual about PCP is that the majority of abusers report unpleasant experiences such as disorientation and anxiety with each high, yet they continue to use the drug. The only explanation can be that its pleasant effects outweigh the consistently undesirable side effects. Also, it is safe to say that most PCP users are experienced drug users and they turn to PCP because they want a new, more daring experience. Tolerance occurs with chronic use, but dependence has not been reported.

Marijuana

Marijuana is by far the most commonly abused illicit drug. But popularity does not mean that it is immune from adverse effects. The marijuana of the 1980s is as much as twenty-five times more potent than that of the 1960s and 1970s. Therefore, experiences tend to be more pronounced. It has been known to affect memory, spatial judgment, and reaction time as well as cell structure and the immune system. Those who are chronic users are prone to boredom and seem to be less competent in coping with daily problems. Also, although it is difficult to measure, chronic users seem to be intellectually less sharp and generally less motivated than they once were. These cognitive changes usually reverse themselves, but, since marijuana can remain in the body for over a month, some abusers report that it may take months before they feel intellectually normal.

Although those who smoke marijuana indicate that it does not lead to tolerance or dependence, they may be wrong on both counts. There is good evidence that tolerance develops to marijuana (Nahas, 1985), and there are too many habitual smokers to deny the possibility of dependence. There are, however, no apparent withdrawal symptoms when the drug is stopped.

While the dangers of some drugs are overblown, the dangers associated with marijuana are minimized. There is growing evidence that it is a very harmful drug. And even if the evidence is not yet overwhelming, that is no reason to pronounce it safe. All drugs should be guilty until proven innocent. (Remember, it took over fifty years to develop a case against nicotine.)

Guidelines for Counselors

Illicit drug use raises a host of issues for counselors: family difficulties, dealing with peer pressures, learning how to deal with the real world, and many others. When examining the effects of the drugs themselves, however, the most important issue is not the "high" or toxic effect of the drugs, but their penchant for producing tolerance and dependence. With these problems Christian counselors should excel. After all, the Bible has the most accurate description of "addiction." It is a form of idolatry and worship. Christians know that the idol—though deaf and dumb—can be a cruel master, and only the power of the gospel of Christ can loosen its hold. Christians, however, have been slow to be wholly biblical in their understanding of drug abuse and treatment.

Although brief and incomplete, consider the following guidelines.

1. The biggest counseling problem with illicit drugs is actually knowing that there is abuse. With prescription drugs, you simply have to ask the right questions, but with illicit drugs, all the best questions will not necessarily uncover the presence of drug abuse. Many times, family members or close friends will not even be aware of the problem.

Clearly, there are no magic means of detection.[8] Wise counselors must establish good relationships with counselees, be aware of the effect of illicit drugs, and ask questions.

2. Realize that recidivism with drugs of dependence is enormous. That is, people who take drugs associated with dependence are quick to go back to those drugs. After a bad experience, abusers may swear they will never touch a substance again, but in time they usually forget the bad, remember the good, and take the drug. Then, they often lie—easily and frequently. Without question, there is not an experienced counselor alive who has not been lied to about a recurrence of drug abuse.

Presently, there is controversy about whether moderation is possible after abusing legal drugs such as nicotine or alcohol. Biblical issues abound on this question. Without reviewing the arguments, it is safe to say that if a person struggled with worshiping a particular drug, then complete abstinence from that drug would be wise, even if the drug is legal or biblically permissible.

3. Develop a biblical perspective on addiction. Most Christians have not really thought the issue through. Many say that it is sin, period, and the treatment is to repent and stop. Others accept the medical model that portrays drug abuse as an irresistible compulsion, a disease, and treatment is more an effort to boost the self-image of the abusers and figure out a way to keep them accountable and drug-free. Both extremes have some merit but are incomplete. A more accurate understanding of drug abuse realizes that it is just one form of modern idolatry. Therefore, an understanding of sin and repentance is critical. It is also important to understand the slavery experienced by idolaters. They are trapped, and in

many ways feel, and *are*, out of control. As such, all the willpower in the world will not lead to liberation. Instead, faith must replace willpower as the agent of change.

4. Realize that addiction or dependence on a drug does not occur after one experience. In many ways the process of dependence is like that in a relationship. In some cases there is an immediate infatuation. But in most cases, dependence is the result of many months of drug use. Drug abuse is to this generation what cigarette smoking and glances at *Playboy* were to previous generations. It is a dangerous experiment, but not everyone gets hooked. This does not mean that you take sporadic drug use casually. Rather, it is to say that there are many myths about drug abuse, and if you are going to do reasonable counseling or parenting, then you must have accurate and current data.

5. Be willing to follow-up. Call, meet for prayer, discuss the coming day's possible temptations, and do these things often and over a long period of time. This is where AA-type programs have been much more effective than the church. The church rarely understands the power of drugs of dependence. As such, the church is too quick to declare a person victorious over drugs. It is not uncommon for a church to hold up a former drug abuser as an abstinent "trophy" while that person is waging a covert battle with drugs, and losing.

Notes

1. A broader perspective on drugs, as defined by the World Health Organization (1974), describes drugs as "any substance that, when taken into the living organism, may modify one or more of its functions."

2. This class of drugs goes by a variety of names, none of them adequate. They may be called neuroleptics ("affecting the nervous system"), antischizo-phrenics, major tranquilizers, and ataractics.

3. The name is actually a misnomer. The word *extrapyramidal* comes from the pyramidal tracts in the brain. These tracts are between the motor strip and the spinal cord, and they are a pathway that mediates *voluntary* muscle movement. EP symptoms are problems with *involuntary* movement; thus, the old theory was that the pyramidal system is bypassed in favor of extra or nonpyramidal routes. It is now known that the pathology behind these movements is more complex and involves various parts of the brain.

4. The trade names of some of these drugs are Symmetrel, Cogentin, Benadryl, and Artane. They are sometimes prescribed for as long as a person takes an antipsychotic, but there is evidence that they are equally as effective if taken only for two to three months. Also, they have side effects of their own.

5. In retrograde ejaculation there is orgasm without ejaculation, followed by urination that has a foamy appearance.

6. Popular drugs that can produce psychological side effects include Vicks Formula 44, Sine-aid, Robitussin CF, Coricidin, Comprex, and Excedrin-PM.

7. Opium comes from the Greek word *opion* meaning poppy juice. Morphine, isolated in 1803 by a German pharmacist, was named after Morpheus, the Greek god of dreams. Heroin is a marketing name. Its similarity to the word *hero* indicates that it was once lauded as a cure-all.

8. Drugs can be detected by urine and blood tests. Also, a cursory eye exam may be helpful (see the note on this in chapter 3). Otherwise, symptoms are usually covert and difficult to detect.

8

Common Deceptive Problems: Depression, Anxiety, Schizophrenia, and Mania

Such is man that if he has a name for something, it ceases to be a riddle.
— Isaac Bashevis Singer

Depression, anxiety, mania, and schizophrenia—especially depression and anxiety—are some of the most frequent problems that counselors face, making an awareness of possible organic causes and treatments essential. There is also another reason why an update is important. These are the bread and butter of modern psychiatry. And it is here, with these symptoms, that the medical model has its cutting edge into the national psyche. Everything you read and hear—from newspapers, popular magazines, and even pulpits—proclaim that science is finally winning the war against these mental "illnesses." They are now proclaimed curable— and out of the realm of pastoral and counseling ministry.

As the research evidence regarding the effectiveness of drug therapy [as treatment for anxiety, mood disorders, and schizophrenia] has become compelling, psychologists, social workers, and pastoral counselors have found themselves in an uncomfortable position, since their training and their professional societies have not emphasized advances in systematic diagnosis, neurochemistry, and psychopharmacology. . . . Inevitably, rationalization, motivated perception, and the pocketbooks are likely to play a part in the ardent defense of the nonbiological position. . . . (Wender & Klein, 1981, pp. 40–41)

Is this true? Has medical science effectively banished nonmedical counselors from working with these "psychiatric" symptoms? Or are these medical claims coming from the medical (disease) model rather than the medical evidence?

Considering the dogmatic nature of the popular psychiatric position, and the potential scrutiny of our conclusions, we must approach these issues carefully. We want to be biblical, aware of substantiated medical work, and cautious where answers are presently unclear. It has been said that Christian responses to new scientific discoveries go in three stages: (1) "It's foolishness"; (2) "It's against the Bible"; and (3) "We knew it all the time." The last thing we want to do is to follow this historical pattern and be dismissed as simplistic, religious fanatics who only say, "It is against the Bible." Instead, our goal is to allow the Scripture to be our overarching guide and to provide a robust and practical framework that incorporates the available medical evidence.

Are They Illnesses?

The first question that must be considered is, "Are these disorders organic or functional?" That is, do persons demonstrating these symptoms have real physical disease?

"No," at this time, psychiatric symptoms have no known organic cause. If we use the strictest definition of organic, our answer would be "no," these common problems are not organic. Contrary to what is popularly suggested, there are no consistent anatomic changes, and there are no definitive chemical abnormalities in those experiencing these symptoms. The most sophisticated of medical tests will not consistently distinguish between those with psychiatric symptoms and those without, and there are no medical tests that verify the presence of "mental disease."

Evidence from diagnostic uncertainty. Without any clear biological marker, you would expect that experts might have difficulty agreeing on who has what disorder. And indeed, that is the case within psychiatry. The absence of any objectively verifiable biological problem is manifested in diagnostic uncertainty. Although most psychiatrists will agree on the *definitions* of depression, anxiety, mania, and schizophrenia, they will frequently disagree when *applying* these definitions to particular people (Hill, 1983). What one psychiatrist may diagnose as depression, another may label anxiety or "schizoaffective." Researchers have been trying to have tighter guidelines for classification (e.g., Lewis & Winokur, 1983), but psychiatry is still a long way from reliable diagnoses. In light of this difficulty, a more accurate way to understand the labels of psychiatry, along with their various and ever-changing subtypes, is that they are highly overlapping categories that are rooted as much in creative ideas for labels and cultural biases as in scientific observation.

As an analogy for this diagnostic morass, consider this attempt at classification from a ninth-century Chinese encyclopedia (Colby & Spar, 1983, p. 68). It divided animals into the following classes:

> Those that belong to the Emperor
> Mermaids
> Embalmed ones
> Those that are trained
> Suckling pigs
> Fabulous ones
> Stray dogs
> Innumerable ones
> Those that are included in this classification
> Those that tremble as if they were mad
> Those drawn with a very fine camel's hair brush
> Others
> Those that have just broken a vase
> Those that resemble flies from a distance

The diagnostic system of modern psychiatry is not quite as fanciful as this, but it is probably *less* reliable! That is, most of the ninth-century Chinese would probably agree that a certain animal was a suckling pig, but a group of ten psychiatrists would not be able to agree on a diagnosis of schizophrenia (let alone one of its subtypes) (Colby & Spar, 1983). Yet labels tend to take on a life of their own, even if they have little or no objective reality.

The present diagnostic guide for American psychiatry is called *DSM-III-R* (1987). Published by the American Psychiatric Association, this stands for the *Diagnostic and Statistical Manual of Mental Disorders, 3rd edition*, revised from the original 1980 version. It covers every disagreeable problem known to man, from disobedience to dementia. And although it claims to be only a practical description of personal difficulties, it is much more than that. It places all problems under the auspices of medicine, and it represents itself as science despite its clear cultural and unbiblical biases.

An example of these biases is the "diagnosis" of homosexuality. This was a diagnostic category prior to 1973, but it has since been removed— not because of scientific evidence but because of pressure from homosexual rights organizations and cultural changes. Admittedly, this is an extreme example, but it does illustrate how diagnostic categories are suggestions for certain types of psychiatric action rather than impartial, clear, scientific categories. In actual practice they are used more to place insurance claims than to guide practice.

So, while vigorous medical research continues, at this point there is no clear evidence that depression, anxiety, schizophrenia, and mania are distinct categories, let alone easily recognized diseases with physiological causes.

The question then arises, "Why are these problems dogmatically proclaimed to be diseases that are on the verge of being cured?" One reason is that the medical model presumes that anything that is remotely unusual—physically, cognitively, or spiritually—has its cause in biology. Another reason is that medications tend to relieve some of the symptoms of depression, anxiety, and madness. Psychiatric drugs can be very effective for some people. And whenever drugs help, we automatically believe that there is some underlying pathology or "chemical imbalance." A history of the chemical imbalance hypothesis, however, will demonstrate that the theory is not as scientific as it seems.

Evidence from the history of psychiatric treatments. The idea of chemical imbalance suggests that someone, through elaborate blood tests and pathological work, looked at chemicals in a patient's brain and found that it was deficient in certain specific chemicals. But this is far from the actual case.

All psychiatric chemical hypotheses are historically rooted in "serendipitous" events—events that occurred by "chance" or "good luck." For example, the first drug for schizophrenia was originally an anti-worm agent that had sedative qualities. Only in 1950, after a surgeon tried to enhance anesthesia with the drug, did it happen to find its way to, and help, a person with schizophrenic symptoms. There is no question that the drug was effective, but effectiveness does not mean that it was treating an underlying deficiency. It is possible that the medication worked like painkillers: it relieved the symptoms but did not treat the cause. The real cause may have been spiritual issues that led to physical consequences.

At this time, the claim of a clear, physical origin for depression, anxiety, mania, or schizophrenia is inaccurate. It is more a hope, or a prediction that future research will provide proof (Mahendra, 1987).

"Yes," aspects of psychiatric diagnoses are best classified as physical. There is another perspective on whether or not these particular diagnoses (mania, depression, anxiety, and schizophrenia) have organic features. From a biblical perspective, many aspects of these psychiatric problems are best categorized as physical rather than spiritual. For example, confused thinking, hallucinations, fatigue, feelings of depression, and shortness of breath are just some of the symptoms of these diagnoses that the Bible associates with bodily disorders. They are physical weaknesses that are not necessarily remediable by repentance, faith, and obedience.

It is possible that some of these organic symptoms have their cause in spiritual issues (e.g., Pss. 32, 38). In such cases, biblical counsel is helpful in dealing with the underlying issues, but the organic symptoms are still physical disorders that can be treated medically. For example, if someone has ulcers that seem to be related to worry, we still treat the ulcers with available medication. It is also possible, however, that these symptoms can emerge apparently unrelated to issues of the heart; they could be a result of living in a body that is wasting away. There are many known diseases and drug side effects that can cause psychiatric symptoms, and it is likely that many persons with functional psychiatric problems (where demonstrable physical problems are absent) have organic causes that are presently undetectable.

As you can see, an answer to the question, "Are anxiety, mania, depression, and schizophrenia physical illnesses?" is not straightforward. The medical evidence, having been overstated by medical model enthusiasts, is less certain than you would think. Yet a biblical perspective suggests that we do not have to wait for full medical confirmation to categorize certain characteristics of these diagnoses as organic. Although some aspects of these diagnoses are related to the heart, there are other features that are best understood as physical problems. The remainder of this chapter will begin to distinguish between the two.

Mood Disorders: Depression

Mood disorders is the *DSM-III-R* category that includes depression, mania, and manic-depression or bipolar disorder. These different experiences are lumped together because they all are accompanied by some change in emotional experiences—whether up (mania), down (depressed), or both (manic-depression). First, consider the broad category of depression. The goal is to become familiar with the traditional medical approaches, be aware of some of the diseases that can appear as depression, develop a biblical perspective that can distinguish between heart and body contributions, and provide counseling guidelines.

Medical Perspective

Even though some segments of psychiatry suggest that all depression is organic, the *DSM-III-R* distinguishes between functional mood disorders and organic mood disorders. Functional depressions are those we usually think of as depression. They are often treated with medication even though they have no clear organic cause. They cannot be revealed by blood tests, CT scans, or any of the most sophisticated devices known to medicine at present.[1]

Organic depressions are a result of demonstrable disease. Treatment, therefore, is aimed at the underlying disease rather than administering antidepressant medication.

Medical treatments of functional depression. Even though there is no clear evidence of pathology in functional depression (more technically called major depression or the less severe dysthymia), lack of medical evidence does not nullify the usefulness of medication and other medical treatments. Since depression has bodily components (e.g., fatigue, insomnia, poor concentration), and the bodily components can provide occasions for sin (Reda, Carpiniello, Secchiaroli & Blanco, 1985), counselors clearly have biblical permission for antidepressant therapies.

A rough analogy is the idea of stumbling blocks in Romans 14. The apostle Paul, in talking about weak and strong brothers, indicates that the treatment for the weak brother is not simply to say, "C'mon, weak brother, you are allowed to eat everything. Stronger brothers, you just keep eating what you want, even if it causes someone else to stumble." Instead, Paul indicates that the stronger brother should remove the stumbling block from the weak. Analogously, we don't simply say to a depressed person, "C'mon, depressed person, just believe and act." Even though the physiological "stumbling block" is not sinful in itself, it can influence some people in such a way that they are distressed and caused to stumble. If possible, we remove the stumbling blocks, the occasions for sin that may lie in the path.

There are quite a number of medical treatments for functional depression: nutrition, sleep deprivation, bright lights, and others. The ones most accepted in traditional medical practice are antidepressant medications and electroconvulsive shock treatment (ECT).

Modern antidepressant drugs have a history of little more than a generation. The first of the drugs, introduced in 1957, was a chemical variation on the antipsychotic drug chlorpromazine (Thorazine). It failed as a tranquilizer, its intended use, but it was eventually found to help some depressed persons after a few weeks of treatment. This was the beginning of a class of drugs called the tricyclic antidepressants (TCAs) (see Appendix B for a full list of antidepressants).

Like all drugs, although there may be potential benefits, they also have possible side effects. The benefits are that in endogenous depression, or depression that seems unrelated to bad circumstances, TCAs reportedly help 65 to 75 percent of affected persons (Morris & Beck, 1974; Stewart, et al., 1983). But side effects are not uncommon. Most significant are sedation and anticholinergic effects. Anticholinergic effects, as noted earlier, include dry mouth, visual difficulties, constipation, excessive sweating, heart palpitations, urine retention, and heart failure. In the elderly, the anticholinergic activity of these drugs can lead to mental confusion.

The antidepressants called monoamine oxidase (MAO) inhibitors are considered to be as effective as the TCAs but they are used less frequently because they tend to have more adverse side effects and are accompanied by a restricted diet. Lithium, best known for its use in mania, is also used as an antidepressant. But it is used much less frequently than either the TCAs or MAO inhibitors.[2]

Without question the most controversial of the medical treatments for depression is electroconvulsive shock treatment (ECT). Its modern history dates back to 1938 when convulsions—grand mal seizures—were first induced electrically. Prior to that time, insulin and other drugs were used to provoke seizures. Electrically induced seizures represented a technological advance because seizures became more controllable, but for quite a while the switch from drug-induced to electrically induced seizures did little to alleviate the barbarous and terrifying nature of ECT. Patients often left ECT with muscles and tendons torn and teeth and bones broken under the stress of intense muscle contraction. When they regained consciousness, they were usually bereft of past memories, some of which never returned. Eventually, they would begin to live in fear of the next "treatment."

There have since been dramatic improvements in the ECT procedure. Anesthesia and muscle relaxants have made the technique virtually free of deaths or physical complications. Cognitive complications, however, especially related to memory function, are common. It is generally agreed that most people after ECT experience memory problems that may last up to six months. There is some research evidence, and a great deal of anecdotal evidence, that a smaller percentage of patients have ongoing memory problems (Pettinati & Bonner, 1984).

Yet even with these side effects, ECT is a very common treatment for depression. It has been reported that 65 percent of patients would accept ECT again if advised (Freeman & Kendall, 1980), and its effectiveness in relieving symptoms of depression may be greater than the effectiveness of medication (Scovern & Kilman, 1980). In my opinion, however, if used at all, it should only be for the suicidal person (with consent) who responds neither to counsel nor medical approaches.[3]

There are many other treatments for depression. All of them are at least creative and some of them have promise. Two of the more interesting areas of research come out of observations that depression is accompanied by sleep disturbances and seasonal fluctuations.

The sleep problems of depressed people are well known: they are usually insomniacs or hypersomniacs, that is, they either sleep too little or too much. What is not as well known is that sleep *deprivation* alleviates depression in some people. Sometimes improvement from deprivation is transitory, and there is clearly a limit to how long and how often the treatment can be used. Yet the evidence suggests that some forms of depression may be related to a disturbance in circadian rhythms. Affected people seem to have a confused twenty-four-hour cycle.

Related to this are the mood changes that occur with *seasonal* rhythms. There is increasing evidence that some people experience depression during the winter months when the days are shorter, and normal moods during the summer months. A clever physician hypothesized that this "seasonal affective disorder" was a result of lack of light, so he exposed some people to artificial, bright lights with some success in relieving their depression. A larger study found an average profile for this group. They tended to be women in their mid-thirties who experienced seasonal depression yearly for about ten years. Their depression was characterized by physical sluggishness, excessive sleeping, overeating, and carbohydrate-craving.

A final treatment for functional depression, and one that has often felt like medicine's neglected stepchild, is nutrition. Nutritional approaches tend to be popular with Christians, and they do have some advantages. They rarely have negative side effects, they are usually (but not always) less expensive, and the informed, interested person can follow the nutritional guidelines without extensive medical or psychiatric follow-up. The disadvantage is that nutritional approaches usually take a few months to begin working, and their effectiveness is not always clear.

Usually called orthomolecular medicine (literally "right molecules"), nutritional approaches attempt to use vitamins and amino acids to gradually affect the amount of available brain neurotransmitters. The theory is essentially the same as that for the antidepressant medication; that is, medication is needed to rectify an alleged deficiency of a neurotransmitter. But nutritional approaches seek to "naturally" augment the amount of certain neurotransmitters by supplying basic building blocks for their production. A good example of this approach applied to depression is found in the book *The Way Up from Down*, by Priscilla Slagle, M.D. (1987). There are many other accounts that can be found in community libraries.

A variation on the theme of nutritional approaches is cerebral allergies. The allergy theory is that some people are allergic to certain foods such as wheat, dairy products, corn, or sugar. However, instead of (or along with) having rashes, coughing, watery eyes, and other common allergic symptoms, susceptible people have emotional symptoms that can imitate any of the psychiatric symptoms. Suggested criteria for spotting food allergies are: (1) evidence of food addictions or repetitive menus, (2) conventional allergy symptoms, (3) fatigue, not helped by rest, (4) marked fluctuations in weight, and (5) other symptoms of general ill health. Testing for food allergies usually includes either a fast or a systematic elimination of possible food culprits. If symptoms gradually improve, cerebral allergies are the possible diagnosis.

Nutritional approaches tend to be reported as cure-alls by devotees, and they are described as shams and placebos by some in traditional medicine. The truth is probably somewhere in between. As such, they are worth investigating.[4]

Table 8.1. Some Medical Causes of Depression

Central nervous system	
Parkinson's disease	Infections
Vascular disease (stroke)	Tumors
Epilepsy	Narcolepsy
Multiple sclerosis	Wilson's disease
Alzheimer's disease	
Endocrine	
Hyperthyroidism	Hypothyroidism
Hyperparathyroidism	Hypoparathyroidism
Cushing's disease	Addison's disease
Premenstrual syndrome	Hyperaldosteronism
Inflammatory	
Rheumatoid arthritis	Systemic Lupus erythematosis
Temporal arteritis	
Deficiency	
Folate	Niacin
Vitamin C	Vitamin B_{12}
Infections—viral or bacterial	
Other	
Postpartum depression	AIDS
Hepatitis	Kidney disease
Cardiac insufficiency	
Electrolyte abnormalities (sodium, potassium, calcium . . .)	

Organic mood disorder: depressed. Although the focus of medical attention tends to be on somatic treatments for functional depression, there are many known diseases that contribute to or wholly account for depressive symptoms (Table 8.1). That is, there are demonstrable diseases that cause symptoms of depression—regardless of the affected persons' prior spiritual preparation and vigilance. In fact, up to 30 percent of depressed persons have underlying, causative organic problems (Whitlock, 1982). And these are the people who often go misdiagnosed.

As an example of how easy misdiagnosis can be, consider the case of hypothyroidism. The thyroid gland, located in the neck, regulates the speed of bodily functions. When its hormones are low, it can produce the following symptoms:

> Loss of energy
> Weakness
> Poor concentration

Memory loss
Decreased sex drive
Constipation
Insomnia

To most counselors, these are almost unmistakable signs of depression. If they are attached to a subjective sense of depressed mood, the diagnosis is nearly certain. Yet, especially if accompanied by an intolerance to the cold or other physical signs such as heart failure and slowed reflexes, these are the classic symptoms of hyptothyroidism—a very treatable disorder that can be confused with functional depression.[5]

Not surprisingly, although many diseases can cause depression, the number one culprit remains the unwanted and unpredictable side effects of prescription drugs. The documented offenders are nearly endless. To give you an idea of *some* of the different classes and specific drugs implicated, Table 8.2 lists just a few (Cummings, 1985; Sternberg, 1986).

Biblical Perspective

Severe depression has many different symptoms that are placed together in *DSM-111-R*. From a biblical perspective, however, they fall roughly into two categories: those related to the body and to the heart (Figure 8.3).

The phenomenon of depression may be caused by the body, the heart, or both. The cause that is most familiar is the heart. When difficult circumstances encounter a heart of unbelief, responses might include guilt, anger, feeling defeated and "down in the dumps," or despair. Persons who base their meaning on personal performance (i.e., works righteousness) rather than the finished work of Christ are particularly susceptible. Then, because of the unity of heart and body, the heart might initiate a cycle that leads to bodily feelings of depression. These bodily feelings, in turn, can continue the cycle and make the heart more prone to despair.

Depression may also be caused by the body—physical processes that are unrelated to personal sin. Disease may produce bodily weaknesses such as fatigue, insomnia, poor concentration, and a sense of alienation. Then affected persons might think, "I feel depressed. Why? What has been happening to me? What have I done?" They look to the heart for answers, and, not uncommonly, the heart attributes blame to itself or bad circumstances, and the whole person plummets into despair.

Table 8.2. Prescription Drugs Associated with Depression

Class and generic name (trade name)

Cardiac and high blood pressure medication
   Propranolol (Inderal)
   Reserpine (Serpasil, Sandril)
   Clonidine (Catapres)
   Guanethidine (Ismelin)
   Lidocaine
   Digitalis (Digoxin)

Anti-Parkinson
   Levodopa (Sinemet)
   Amantadine (Symmetrel)

Hormones and steroids
   Estrogen (Menrium, Premarin)
   Progesterone
   Cortisone
   Prednisone
   Danazol
   Oral contraceptives

Psychiatric drugs (see appendix B)
   Antipsychotics
   Anti-anxiety
   Antidepressants

Antibacterial and antifungal drugs
   Sulfonamides (Bactrim)
   Streptomycin
   Tetracycline

Anticancer drugs

It is also possible that the body and heart will not obviously interact. Therefore, bodily diseases that feel like depression might not affect the heart. Persons can experience all the physical symptoms of depression but simultaneously have hearts that are characterized by faith, hope, and love. Certainly, this produces a strange and difficult experience, but it can be one that leads to spiritual growth. The other side of the coin is that the heart may leave the body unaffected. Sinful despair and hopelessness of the heart might have no bodily consequences. The body may never experience the full fury of a major depression.

Regardless of the initial cause or mode of interaction, it is obvious that biblical counseling is important. If issues of the heart make a significant contribution to the depression, then, as these issues are handled correctly, depression will lift. If bodily processes are the causative

Figure 8.3. Possible Contributions of Heart
and Body in Depression

The Body

Insomnia or hypersomnia
Poor appetite or significant weight loss
Feelings of being slowed down or restless
Fatigue, loss of energy
Real or felt problems with concentration, thinking,
    and decision making
Sense of distance and alienation from things
    once deemed beautiful and pleasant

Sad, blue, down in the dumps . . .

Feelings of worthlessness (self-obsession)
Guilt
Lack of thankfulness
Hopelessness, despair
Unbelief, or a "negative" view of the world,
    oneself, and the future (Beck, 1967)
Sense of failure
Anger

The Heart

factor, then faith and obedience might not affect the bodily experience of depression, but affected persons can have hope in the midst of pain. Like the Old Testament saints, those who experience suffering can have renewed anticipation of the object of their faith and hope, Jesus Christ. As Hebrews 12:1–2 says,

> Let us throw off everything that hinders and the sin that so easily entangles, and let us run with perseverance the race marked out for us. Let us fix our eyes on Jesus. . .

These brief and somewhat sterile comments certainly are not meant to imply that dealing with depression is easy. It never is. Regardless of the cause, finding hope in Christ can be a difficult process—a spiritual battle—when experiencing severe depression. Growth is sometimes gradual, progressing in nearly imperceptible increments. J. B. Phillips, the popular Bible translator and commentator, documents this spiritual battle in his autobiography, *The Price of Success* (1984).

> Without any particular warning the springs of creativity were suddenly dried up; the ability to communicate disappeared overnight and it looked like my career as a writer and translator was over. . . .
> After a few months, during which time I was not entirely idle, I found the mental pain more than I felt I could bear and I went as a voluntary patient to a psychiatric hospital. . . . My reason for writing this chapter is that it may help someone else who is depressed and in mental pain. It may help simply to know that one whom the world would regard as successful and whose worldly needs are comfortably met can still enter this particular hell, and have to endure it for quite a long time. (P. 97)

Depression such as this can make some friends and counselors feel helpless and ineffective, but a two-track biblical approach offers hope, both now and in the future. For example, in the case of Mr. Phillips, you could focus on the heart by reminding him of the gospel of grace in Christ, encouraging him in faith and hope, and rebuking if necessary. Also, you could refer him for a medical consultation to rule out an organic cause. If there were no apparent physical causes, psychiatric referral would be worthwhile in order to consider a trial regimen of antidepressant medication. Finally, surrounding his overall treatment would be compassion that acknowledged the difficulties of living in a world yearning for the return of Christ.

Anxiety

Contrary to popular opinion, Søren Kierkegaard did not discover anxiety with his book *The Concept of Dread* (1844). There is a wealth of biblical material on worry and anxiety. In fact, at first glance, a review of relevant medical data on anxiety seems inappropriate. After all, although depression may have a physical component and is not morally wrong *per se*, anxiety is directly forbidden in Scripture. As such, it would seem to be a wholly moral problem.

> Do not be anxious about anything, but in everything, by prayer and petition, with thanksgiving, present your requests to God. (Phil. 4:6)

Therefore I tell you, do not worry about your life, what you will eat or drink; or about your body, what you will wear. (Matt. 6:25)

Yet, like depression, our modern conception of anxiety includes both spiritual and physical elements. In popular use, worry tends to be an issue of the heart, whereas anxiety can refer to problems of the heart, body, or both. As delineated by *DSM-III-R*, nonorganic anxiety can be roughly organized into four categories: generalized anxiety and panic disorders, phobic disorders (agoraphobia, social phobia, school phobia), obsessive-compulsive disorder, and post-traumatic stress disorder. These are all functional disorders. That is, they presently have no known organic cause, but, again, medication can be helpful. The following overview will ferret out the respective contributions of heart and body to each of these experiences.

Generalized anxiety

Generalized anxiety is a somewhat generic label that includes what we would typically think of as anxiety: persistent feelings of tension and jitteriness, sweating, heart pounding, and insomnia. Curiously, this anxiety often appears for no apparent reason—circumstances can be fine—and it tends to be constant and insidious. From a biblical perspective, it can be divided according to physical and spiritual symptoms (Figure 8.4).

As the circular model suggests, anxiety has its cause in *either* the heart or the body. When anxiety has its source in the heart, it is usually from worry, a lack of confidence in the love of our all-powerful Father. Then, when worry sows its seed, it can grow into the physical problems that are often associated with anxiety: tension, insomnia, rapid heartbeat, and diarrhea. Affected persons, feeling alone and inadequate to confront their problems, have to rely on their own resources, so the body becomes mobilized for battle. It is tense, vigilant, on edge. These bodily symptoms can provide occasion for more worry, which in turn can be a catalyst for more physical symptoms. Indeed, anxiety can be a downward spiral that goes on indefinitely.

The other possibility is that bodily disorders begin the cycle. Medications or disease might arouse the sympathetic nervous system or increase metabolism (mimicking the experience of anxiety) and thus be labeled as anxiety. These bodily feelings are temptations that can lead to

Figure 8.4. Possible Contributions of Heart
and Body in Generalized Anxiety

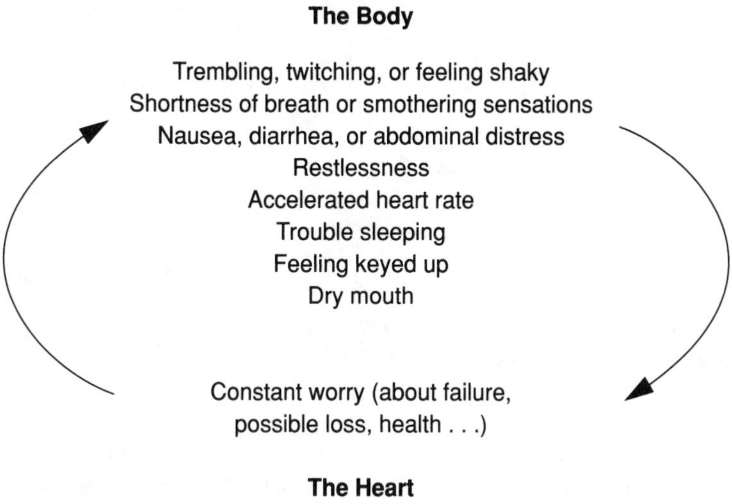

The Body

Trembling, twitching, or feeling shaky
Shortness of breath or smothering sensations
Nausea, diarrhea, or abdominal distress
Restlessness
Accelerated heart rate
Trouble sleeping
Feeling keyed up
Dry mouth

Constant worry (about failure,
possible loss, health . . .)

The Heart

ungodly worry, and the downward spiral can start again. However, it is also possible that the heart can remain firm despite the bodily feelings. In such a situation, counselors must realize that a complaint like "I feel anxious" may be a description of bodily states more than an indicator of sinful worry.

Therefore, the counseling agenda is again twofold. Counselors can provide an opportunity for anxious persons to examine their lives through faith. Many times, roots of worry and unbelief will be quickly apparent. If biblical issues are not apparent, counselors can help people distinguish bodily symptoms from sin.

A twenty-seven-year-old woman came for counseling because of severe anxiety. Prior to becoming a Christian, at age twenty-one, she struggled with fears and anxieties that would be intensified by drug experiences (mostly marijuana and cocaine), but she had been anxiety-free for over four years. Now, she was very nervous about her health. She believed her thinking was getting clouded, she would wake up at nights sweating, she was generally scared. And she was certain that it had something to do with her unbelief and, perhaps, consequences of past drug experiences. The counselor told her that there could be many issues that provoked her

anxiety, from physical to spiritual. Yet, regardless of the cause, the feeling of anxiety provided a good opportunity for her to examine her life.
    Counseling did reveal issues in the woman's life (as it would in anybody's), but she was moving forward by faith in all areas. The counselor then suggested more strongly that her anxiety might be related to physical problems. After being alerted to a physical possibility, she realized that she had cold symptoms—poor appetite, clogged ears, stuffy head. After taking some over-the-counter cold medicine, her symptoms disappeared.

If medical consultation rules out the presence of known physical disease, there are still medical alternatives. Although most people will never go to a physician for generalized anxiety, drug treatment is possible if they do. The original first line of drug treatment, the antianxiety drugs, are still the most popular. However, my impression is that they are massively overprescribed, can have deleterious side effects, and are not any more effective in helping anxious persons than is neighborly reassurance.

When the bodily experience of anxiety is overwhelming, however, antianxiety drugs can provide *short-term* relief. Other promising classes of drugs are the antidepressants and beta-blockers (such as Inderal, usually used with cardiac symptoms).

A fifty-five-year-old father of two had all but renounced his faith a decade ago when he was led to believe that his anxiety was incompatible with faith. His conclusion at that time was that since he had anxiety, he must not have faith. Although spiritual issues were clearly present, it was possible that the physical feelings of anxiety were stumbling blocks that seemed insurmountable. Therefore, since he had a recent physical that indicated no organic problems, it was suggested that he consult with a psychiatrist about medications. An antidepressant was prescribed, and he has since had some relief from his anxiety symptoms and has been attending church again.

Panic

Unprovoked experiences of panic are very common in Western cultures. They seem to be appropriate experiences for those living in societies that are increasingly fast-paced, time-conscious, and success-oriented. In a typical panic attack, people are usually involved in very ordinary activities—reading, eating dinner, driving a car—when suddenly their heart begins to pound, they cannot catch their breath, they

Figure 8.5. Possible Contributions of Heart
and Body in Panic Attacks

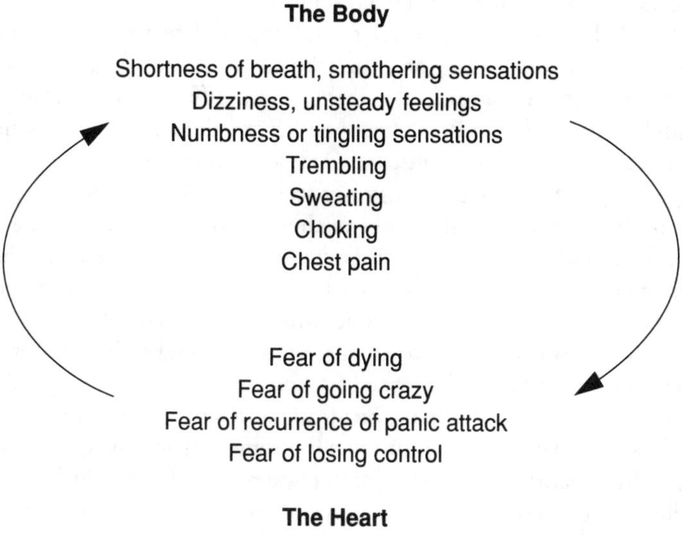

The Body

Shortness of breath, smothering sensations
Dizziness, unsteady feelings
Numbness or tingling sensations
Trembling
Sweating
Choking
Chest pain

Fear of dying
Fear of going crazy
Fear of recurrence of panic attack
Fear of losing control

The Heart

feel dizzy, lightheaded, and faint, and they might feel as if they are about to die. The attacks can last from two to twenty minutes.

They are distinct from generalized anxiety in that whereas generalized anxiety is more persistent, panic attacks are discrete and intense episodes.

As you may have guessed, a biblical approach to panic attacks takes into account both the physical and spiritual components (Figure 8.5). Both aspects are clearly present in panic attacks. However, issues of the heart tend to be the most common initial cause.

There is fairly broad agreement that most panic attacks have a non-physical origin. Even though they generally strike during routine activities, most people indicate that the first episode was a response to circumstances such as an illness or accident, loss of a close relationship, or separation from family (such as starting college). Also, the first attack may occur in a situation that was reminiscent of an earlier experience that was frightening or traumatic. For example, an experience of being trapped may induce a panic attack because of its similarities to a much earlier incestuous experience when a person was forcibly molested. Therefore, counseling should include a history of the episodes, a review of earlier experiences that were emotionally similar to panic attacks, and a biblical perspective on the inciting circumstances.

A slight variation is when panic attacks date back to an initial attack that was induced by an otherwise silent medical problem such as hyperthyroidism. Diagnostically, this is more difficult to determine but counselors can still minister effectively. Even though counselors might not know what initially caused the attacks, they can offer a biblical perspective that, although it may not stop the panic, can promote faith and spiritual maturity in the midst of these frightening events. They can remind affected persons that their bodies of clay can experience problems for many different reasons, but their hearts can be renewed. Some of the potential medical culprits for panic will be discussed later.

In the absence of underlying disease, there tend to be two forms of medical intervention. Perhaps the best-known treatment is the paper bag. Although low tech (but cheap), breathing into a paper bag during a panic attack is often very effective in relieving some physical symptoms. Most people hyperventilate during panic episodes, and hyperventilation can produce or exacerbate the bodily symptoms of panic. Therefore, one "treatment" is to teach people not to hyperventilate but to breathe into a paper bag during panic attacks.

The other treatment for panic attacks is antidepressant drugs or the heart medication Propranolol (Inderal). There have been numerous studies that demonstrate the effectiveness of the antidepressant drugs in panic attacks (Grunhaus, Gloger & Weisstub, 1981; Hollander, Liebowitz & Gorman, 1988). At first glance, it seems odd that a drug that might help those who are depressed would also help those who experience distressing anxiety. But it is really not that peculiar. First, remember that there are no clear dividing lines between psychiatric diagnoses. Also, realize that it is not uncommon for people who are depressed to also experience occasional panic attacks.

Phobias

Phobias often go hand-in-hand with panic attacks. That is, persons avoid or are phobic of places where they had panic attacks or fear they might have attacks. Phobias are surprisingly common, but they tend to be invisible even to close friends. For example, friends may think that someone who avoids bridges is a little eccentric, or someone who avoids elevators at all cost is an exercise fanatic. They may be unaware that phobias secretly dominate the lives of those who experience them.

Phobias are characterized by irrational fears that are recognized as being excessive or unreasonable in proportion to the actual danger involved. The most common is agoraphobia (*agora* is Greek for marketplace). Agoraphobia has three main themes: fear of being alone, fear of leaving home, and fear of being in situations where one cannot quickly leave or find help. Within this range are dozens of common fears, such as using public transportation, being in theaters, elevators, restaurants, or supermarkets, and waiting in lines. Agoraphobia is more than simply not liking these situations. Rather, people actively seek to avoid them, to the point where they may become completely housebound or enslaved by the fear.

The symptoms of panic attacks (Figure 8.5) can be divided into those experienced by the body and heart. As such, the bodily symptoms of phobias are treated like those of panic attacks, with antidepressants and paper bags.

Obsessive-Compulsive Disorder

A forty-nine-year-old housewife is tortured by a fear of germs (the same phobia that characterized the late billionaire Howard Hughes). In a fanatic pursuit of cleanliness, she can use more than 225 bars of soap on herself every month, wears rubber gloves even to switch on a light, and makes her husband sleep alone so she won't be contaminated by him. (Goodwin, 1986)

Obsessions are irrational, intrusive, sometime repugnant thoughts, images, or impulses. Compulsive rituals are meaningless, unwanted, repetitive acts that result from the thoughts and impulses. In minor forms they are very common—sudden intrusive thoughts, not stepping on cracks, checking to see if a door has been locked or an oven turned off. In more severe cases, they are life-dominating.

The intrusive thoughts that are characteristic of obsessions are characteristically vivid, and they are often aggressive, sexual, magical, or religious (and often, blasphemous). Persons may have obsessional thoughts of injuring a child, leaping from a window, or shouting obscenities during a sermon. Persistent doubts are commonplace: "Am I forgiven?" "Did I lock the door?" "Did I catch a disease from the person on the train?" Magical, obsessional formulas often follow the equation, *thoughts equals acts*. Therefore, "thinking bad thoughts about my husband

Figure 8.6. The Possible Cycle
in Obsessive-Compulsive Disorder

Body/Demonic/Testings/World

Recurrent and persistent ideas,
impulses, or images

Dealing with obsessions by works
rather than grace
Legalism
Guilt

The Heart

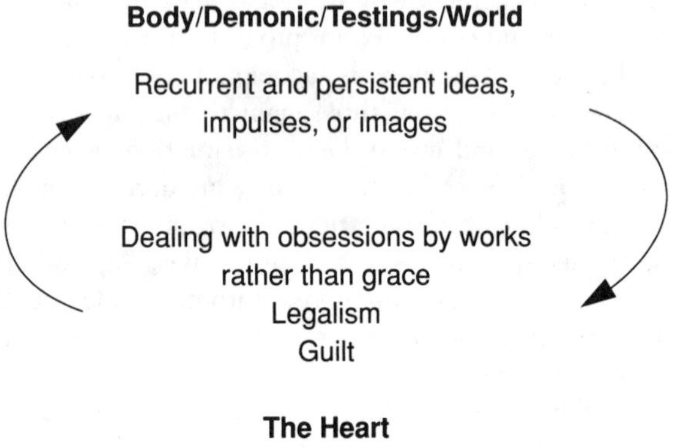

will cause him to die." Persons then spend their days consumed with what they caused, or what they might have caused, and they try to undo the damage. At other times, the obsessional thought may be more innocuous—a word, phrase, song, or rhyme that interferes with the normal train of thought.

The compulsive rituals become legalistic means of neutralizing or atoning for the obsession. Afraid, unwilling, or untaught—those who persistently obsess don't go to God for forgiveness and the assurance of "no condemnation." Instead, they use their rituals to appease God or assuage his perceived wrath.

Intrusive, obsessive thoughts can come from a variety of sources (Figure 8.6). They can begin in the heart as a ploy to appease God's perceived wrath, or they may be unrelated to issues of the heart. As such, they could have their origin in the demonic or "human tradition and the basic principles of the world" (Col. 2:8)—two sources which affect the person in the same way as the body. Some people will then allow their hearts to succumb to these temptations and an obsessive-compulsive pattern emerges. Whatever their source, it is safe to say that those who experience obsessive symptoms need assistance in applying the biblical material about the death and resurrection of Jesus to their experiences and their sense of guilt and lack of control.

The physical contribution to obsessive-compulsive disorder is uncertain. Presently, there are vague hints of physical differences between those with symptoms and those without, but the data are still difficult to interpret. The most promising area of research uses PET scans. With this technique, preliminary evidence suggests that those who exhibit obsessive-compulsive problems may have significantly increased brain activity in the basal ganglia area of the brain (Schmeck, 1988). This is the same area that is involved with movement disorders such as Parkinson's disease. But again, even if these data were conclusive (which they are not) the remaining question would be, "Are the physical differences causes or consequences?"

Regardless of the contribution of the body to these symptoms, it is biblically permissible to take advantage of helpful medical treatments. That is not to say that medicine will put an end to legalism or works righteousness. Medicine cannot change the heart. Medicine can, however, suppress some of the bothersome thoughts which make people more susceptible to sin.

Antidepressant drugs are being widely used with some success in suppressing these troublesome thoughts and behaviors. The most effective is chlorimipramine (Anafranil).

A somewhat unusual report on alleged physical underpinnings to obsessive-compulsive symptoms received some publicity. It involved a nineteen-year-old male whose symptoms abated after he survived a self-inflicted gunshot wound to the head! The pinnacle of the "don't try this at home" remedies, this did not provide evidence for an organic origin to his symptoms. It is probable that after the suicide attempt, the underlying spiritual problems were simply expressed in other ways. The original report indicated that while the young man's obsessions were less severe, "he remained intolerant of disorder and demanded that the kitchen and bathroom be kept spotless" (Solyom, Turnbull & Wilensky, 1987).

Post-Traumatic Stress

Post-traumatic stress disorder (PTSD) is an elaborate way of saying that a person had a horrible experience in the past and is having a difficult time dealing with it now. A descendant of the World War I "diagnosis" of shell shock, PTSD was revived after the Vietnam war and soon became a disease that was compensable by the Veterans Administration. Later, it was elevated to disease status by the American Psychiatric Association, and it was enlarged to include any past traumatic event (rape, abortion, child abuse.)

Characterized by a host of symptoms, including intrusive remembrances and detachment from others, PTSD has no known organic base whatsoever. That is not to say that being sinned against or witnessing the effects of a fallen world is anything less than horrible and traumatic. Indeed, God has special compassion for those who have been victimized. PTSD, however, is an example of how renaming a problem which the Bible addresses comprehensively can take it away from biblical counselors and put it into the exclusive realm of medicine.

Medical Diseases That Mimic Anxiety

In the same way that diseases can cause the physical aspects of depression, so there are diseases that can cause the bodily experiences of anxiety. In fact, up to 50 percent of those who have a diagnosis of anxiety or one of its subcategories may have a physical illness directly related to their symptoms (Torem, Saravay & Steinberg, 1979). The spectrum of possible underlying physical problems is very similar to that of depression. However, the most common mimickers are endocrine disorders, drugs, and heart disease.

Endocrine disorders. Endocrine disorders and their resulting hormonal imbalances can exert powerful emotional and behavioral effects. Since hormones travel throughout the body and are not highly specific, when out of synch they tend to affect both brain and body. Therefore, endocrine disorders are prime candidates for causing the cognitive, emotional, and other bodily problems associated with anxiety.

Hyperthyroidism. The thyroid consists of two walnut-sized glands that are in the neck below the Adam's apple. Their two principal hormones, triodothyronine (T_3) and thyroxine (T_4), regulate the speed of bodily processes. Therefore, hyperthyroid counselees are typically nervous and exhibit tremors, rapid or irregular heartbeats, intolerance to heat, sweating, weakness ("energized fatigue" [Taylor, 1982]), hair loss, and the enviable symptom of weight loss—in spite of a good appetite. Menstrual irregularities in women and impotence in men are also common. Perhaps the most dramatic or at least most obvious symptom that often occurs in hyperthyroidism is something called exophthalmos. This condition is characterized by an unusual bulging of the eyes.[6]

Without warning, the wife of a resident physician began to feel extreme anxiety accompanied by difficulty sleeping, tremulousness, and heavy perspiration. Her husband interpreted these changes as manifestations of the stress of being the wife of a resident. So he started her on a minor tranquilizer.

The symptoms, however, did not improve; in fact, the woman became more agitated, anxious, and eventually obsessed with the thought that she was probably mentally ill. Finally, she was admitted to a psychiatric hospital. During the hospitalization, she was found to have an unexplained elevation in her heart rate and significant weight loss. Laboratory studies confirmed a diagnosis of hyperthyroidism. She was treated with radioactive iodine, after which her "anxiety" subsided. (Martin, 1979)

Hyperthyroidism is usually a result of thyroid tumors that can be either relatively benign or fast-growing and malignant. Diagnosis is usually made on the basis of a physical exam and blood studies (T_3, T_4, TSH, TRH), and treatment consists of surgery, antithyroid drugs, or radioactive iodine. The effectiveness of radioactive iodine is a result of the thyroid's penchant for absorbing much of the body's available iodine. When it absorbs the radioactive variety, diseased thyroid tissue will die.

Pheochromocytoma. Pheochromocytoma is a tumor in the adrenal gland, specifically the adrenal medulla. Although rare, it causes classic physical symptoms of anxiety—and it provides an opportunity to remember some basic anatomy and physiology. The adrenal gland secretes adrenaline and noradrenaline, substances that mimic sympathetic nervous system arousal. Attacks are characterized by intense fear and a feeling of impending death, sweating, dizziness, rapid heart rate, high blood pressure, and headache.

Hypoglycemia (low blood sugar). Hypoglycemia means there are inadequate levels of the sugar glucose in the blood. It can have different organic causes, such as pancreatic overproduction of insulin, inadequate storage of glycogen in the liver, or overdoses of insulin (making diabetics or hyperglycemics prime candidates for hypoglycemia). The most well-known (and debated) type of hypoglycemia, however, is called functional or reactive hypoglycemia.

Suspicion abounds regarding the reality of reactive hypoglycemia because it is associated with a plethora of symptoms and unreliable blood tests. Yet, although some physicians still doubt the diagnosis (suggesting it is a convenience for the hypochondriac more than a real disease), most physicians accept that reactive hypoglycemia is real, but overdiagnosed.

Cognitive and emotional symptoms range from irritability and despondency to panic, confusion, and psychosis. Physical symptoms are most often characterized by lack of energy as well as sleep difficulties,

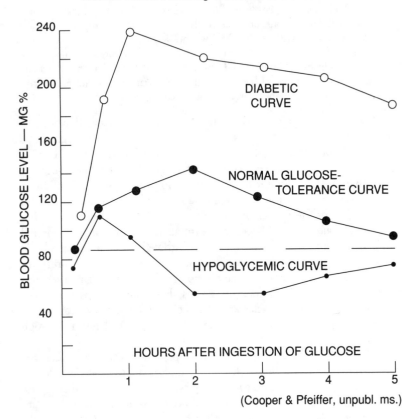

Figure 8.7. Diabetic, Normal, and Hypoglycemic Blood
Glucose Levels Following a Glucose-tolerance Test

(Cooper & Pfeiffer, unpubl. ms.)

headaches, and chest and abdominal pains. If some of these symptoms are
present, especially if accompanied by a "sweet tooth," heavy drinking of
alcohol, or unusual dietary patterns, and neither the situation nor the
spiritual life of the person warrants such a response, then reactive
hypoglycemia should be considered.

The specific test for hypoglycemia is the glucose-tolerance test,
preferably the five- or six-hour tests. These are usually preceded by a
three-day, high-calorie carbohydrate diet. Then, before breakfast, individuals go to a medical laboratory for fasting glucose levels. Next, they

are given a drink containing a specific amount of glucose and the blood sugars are tested at one-half hour, one hour, and then hourly intervals. Normal glucose levels hover around 80-100 milligrams per 100 cubic centimeters of blood. If the fasting level is 60, or one of the samples falls below 50, then reactive hypoglycemia is possible. Yet some investigators point out that some symptoms of hypoglycemia may emerge at much higher rates. These suggest that a diagnosis of "relative hypoglycemia" be made if any specimen falls twenty below the fasting level or falls more than fifty points in one hour (Ross, 1975)—(Figure 8.7).

The treatment is fairly simple but demands a certain amount of self-discipline. It consists of a low-carbohydrate, high-protein diet that avoids sugar, white flour, and caffeine (maybe more, depending on the book or physician). Food is usually eaten in smaller quantities but more frequently.

Estrogen. Estrogen is commonly prescribed after hysterectomies or for menopausal symptoms and the prevention of osteoporosis. It is reported to have the potential to induce panic attacks.

> A fifty-eight-year-old woman began having panic attacks two to three times a day. Each attack consisted of overwhelming fear, rapid heartbeats, shortness of breath, and sweaty palms. She had never experienced these until the last four months—one month after she started taking estrogen to prevent osteoporosis [weakening of the bones]. After unsuccessful treatment with the antianxiety drug Xanax, her physician noted the close relationship between her symptoms and the beginning of estrogen treatment. The estrogen was discontinued. Within a week all panic symptoms were gone. (Price & Heil, 1988)
>
> A thirty-five-year-old woman was treated with estrogen after a hysterectomy. She immediately began to have panic attacks five to six times a week. These consisted of a sense of impending doom, immobilizing fear, heart palpitations, and shortness of breath. Her physician increased the estrogen, and her symptoms became worse. Finally, the woman noticed that the estrogen made her intolerant of coffee or any caffeinated beverage, that is, caffeine would precipitate a panic attack. After this, estrogen was discontinued. Within two weeks her panic attacks and anxiety had ceased. (Price & Heil, 1988)

Drugs and Other Medical Causes

The list of drugs and diseases that can cause physical symptoms of anxiety is very similar to those that cause depression (see Tables 8.1 and

8.2). One disease worth noting, however, is mitral valve prolapse. This common heart condition is present in at least one-third of people with panic disorder. The symptoms are identical: chest pain, shortness of breath, dizziness, numbness and tingling, skipped heartbeats and feelings of anxiety. The cause of mitral valve prolapse is not known, there is no definitive treatment, and its symptoms, while bothersome, are rarely life-threatening. But for those whose panic attacks are related to this disorder, it might be reassuring to know the physical origin of the symptoms.

Schizophrenia

As for me, you must know that I shouldn't precisely have chosen madness
if there had been a choice.

—Vincent Van Gogh (1889)

Albeit the heartland of psychiatry, schizophrenia remains a will o' the wisp, full of shadows and chimera. Explorers here have laboured hard to define the territory, establish landmarks, and to discover the cause and meaning underlying what they have seen. Alas, this journey of discovery has been painstakingly slow. (Bebbington & McGuffin, 1988, p. 1)

A chimera without doubt, schizophrenia remains a mystery to modern psychiatry and medical research. Its symptoms can often be suppressed by medication, but its causes are hidden.[7] A biblical approach, however, offers clarity to this otherwise murky terrain. Essentially, this approach is no different than the approach established with the previous symptoms: it recognizes contributions and interactions of the body and the heart. But before developing the biblical model, first consider the medical background and popular opinions on schizophrenia. As you do, try to reinterpret the data according to a biblical framework.

Terms and Definitions

The term *schizophrenia* (literally "split mind") was coined in the early 1900s by the Swiss physician Eugen Bleuler (1857-1939). He called it schizophrenia because "the 'splitting' of the different psychic functions is one of its most important characteristics" (Bleuler, 1911). This splitting, however, was not of the personality. Rather, it was the splitting of psychic functions—emotions and thoughts. Bleuler hypothesized that these functions, which work in concert in most people, seemed to operate autonomously in schizophrenia. That is, distressing thoughts might be accompanied by no emotion, or emotions may be apparently unrelated to thoughts.

At the time, Bleuler was careful to surround his theory with caution. He emphasized that the term *schizophrenia*, while singular, actually represented a group that included several "diseases." Also, he stated that there was no known underlying pathology, no known treatment, no known cause. In sum, he stated, "We do not know what the schizophrenic process actually is" (p.466). Yet he was certain that it was a disease.

To be brief and simplistic, things have not changed much. The only significant change has been the serendipitous development of antipsychotic medication. Otherwise, the area is fairly chaotic. Some have suggested that the only way to proceed is to drop the "semantic titanic" of *schizophrenia*, and redefine the entire area of madness—an interesting suggestion but one unlikely to be implemented.

The present boundaries for the term *schizophrenia* are established by *DSM-III-R*. It tends to focus on *disordered and confused thinking* such as incoherent, illogical, or disorganized thinking and speech; delusions; hallucinations; and highly inappropriate emotional responses.[8] A popular distinction is between positive (active) symptoms and negative (passive) symptoms. Those with positive symptoms are conspicuous and unsettling to others. They often report or exhibit delusions of persecution, insulting hallucinations, inappropriate laughter or tears, sudden unprovoked rages, and obviously disconnected speech. Those with negative symptoms have toneless voices and expressionless faces. They avoid eye contact, speak infrequently—perhaps never completing a sentence—and seem to be unaware of the feelings of others. If these positive or negative symptoms persist for six months, they are called schizophrenic. If they are more transient, they are called schizophreniform.

Medical Perspective

Millions of dollars and the most sophisticated technology have gone into the search for an organic cause to schizophrenia. But like depression and anxiety, researchers have not uncovered a brain abnormality that is unique to those with schizophrenic symptoms. What they have found are as follows: (1) the syndrome is universal, it is apparent in all known cultures; (2) it seems to have a genetic component; and (3) it responds favorably to drugs that interfere with the neurotransmitter dopamine (Jablensky, 1988). Also, although not popularized by medical researchers, most all investigators acknowledge the presence of personal, familial, and societal causes in schizophrenia.

Genetics. There is evidence for a genetic contribution to schizophrenia that is difficult to dispute. The average incidence of schizophrenia in the general population is about 0.5 percent to 1 percent; that is, 1 in every 100 to 200 people will demonstrate schizophrenic symptoms. In siblings of those with schizophrenic symptoms, the rate is much higher, about 10 percent. Twins have an even higher rate. With fraternal twins (from different eggs), when one twin has schizophrenic symptoms, 14 percent of the others exhibit similar symptoms. With identical twins (from the same fertilized egg), when one twin exhibits schizophrenic-like symptoms, 46 percent of the other twins do also. Even more persuasive are adoption studies. The evidence suggests that of adoptees with biological schizophrenic mothers and adopted nonschizophrenic mothers, 16 percent develop schizophrenic symptoms (Black, Yates & Andreasen, 1988; McGuffin, 1988). This is far more than would be expected if there was no genetic component.

This genetic evidence suggests that schizophrenia has some hereditary contribution, but at this point, further interpretation is difficult. The precise means of transmission remains a mystery. Also, since the agreement between identical twins is less than 100 percent—which it would be if schizophrenia was strictly inherited—biology is certainly not the only explanation. Therefore, although the evidence proves that there is a genetic component, it also proves that there are nongenetic factors.

Medicine recognizes these nonorganic biochemical influences. For example, there is evidence that social and cultural factors are important in schizophrenia. Persons from non-Western (Third-World) cultures are associated with a better prognosis (Jablensky, 1988), as are those from families that are characterized by peacefulness. Also, there is some evidence that schizophrenia is related to economic indicators: people exhibit fewer symptoms during times of full employment (Warner, 1985).

Brain studies. Claims of brain abnormalities can also be overstated. When evaluating the brain studies in schizophrenia, it is interesting to note that researchers from the United States tend to be more certain of biological causes than researchers from the United Kingdom. In the United States, if you deny the evidence for schizophrenia as a brain disease, you are accused of having been "on an extended trip to Nepal" (Torrey, 1988, p. 133). In the United Kingdom, however, the same evidence is classified as "unrewarding" or "mixed and somewhat contradictory" (Lantos, 1988, p. 84). Without going into detail, it is safe to say that studies have shown some differences between the brains of those with and without schizophrenic symptoms. However, there are no consistent differences, and there is no evidence that the differences have anything to do with schizophrenic symptoms. Yet we should recognize that Christians have no ax to grind with a biased interpretation of the data. We recognize that evidence of subtle physical differences in those with schizophrenic symptoms as compared to those without will probably emerge. If, over the next decade, there is medical research that demonstrates unmistakable differences between brains of schizophrenics and nonschizophrenics, these data should be heralded as potentially valuable and consistent with a theory of schizophrenia that is biblically permissible. The present criticism is not intended to deny possible physical causes. Indeed, one goal is to show how physical causes can sit comfortably in the biblical data. Instead, the criticism is intended to underline the medical model's exaggeration and misinterpretation of some scientific research.

Drug treatment. Although there are no readily apparent medical causes of schizophrenia, drug treatment is very effective in subduing some of the symptoms. Skeptics, and some patients, suggest that drug treatment is only a form of chemical control that limits all thinking in general, but most people—professionals, families, and patients—are satisfied with the short-term usefulness of the antipsychotic drugs (Carpenter & Heinrichs, 1983). Counselors must be aware of this option, and be willing to obtain psychiatric consultation.

There are three significant issues in drug treatment: the decision to take medication, compliance, and how much and how long. Most people do not want to take medication. The side effects are irritating and the perceived cognitive slowing is undesirable. Therefore, if medication sounds like a reasonable option, and a person is unwilling to take it, what do you do? There are different approaches to this, from hiding it in food or mandating periodic injections to following the affected person's desire to avoid medication. A middle ground is to establish behavioral guidelines: for example, respect to family members and staying in bed at night. If the person does not abide by basic, biblically guided rules, then medication should be a possible consequence. Usually, however, if you have a good relationship with a person, and a trial of medication could be potentially helpful, you can probably persuade him or her to agree to a trial prescription.

But agreement does not mean compliance. Recognize that many persons who take medication will only pretend to, or keep it under their tongue until you leave.

Another concern with medication is whether it should be given continuously or as needed. Because of the incidence of extrapyramidal side effects, some psychiatrists are experimenting with short-term drug use in place of a lifetime drug commitment. Also, although there is evidence that medications may suppress symptoms over the short haul, over longer periods of time they may not be very helpful (Warner, 1985).

Nutrition. As with depression and anxiety, there are quite a few nutritional approaches to schizophrenia. These have not been subjected to rigorous tests, but many of them seem to have promise and appear to help some people. Families and affected persons should read some of the available literature and perhaps consult with a physician who specializes in orthomolecular medicine.[9]

Diseases that mimic schizophrenia. As with the other common psychiatric diagnoses, schizophrenic symptoms can be imitated by organic disease. Most of these diseases are mentioned in the lists associated with depression and anxiety. There is one, however, that should be underlined. With the increase of stimulants such as cocaine, amphetamines, and caffeine, there are more cases of "amphetamine psychosis." Nearly indistinguishable from schizophrenia, this may occur with either long-term abuse of stimulants or short-term abuse at toxic doses. It is most readily diagnosed when the following are observed: there is a history of stimulant drug use, the psychotic episode emerges abruptly, emotions are high (e.g., elation), and there is increased activity.

The following guidelines can help differentiate other organic psychoses from those that have no clear physical cause (functional).

1. Organic psychosis is characterized by cognitive impairment such as decreased attention, poor memory, sluggish thinking, and even altered consciousness. At times, schizophrenic symptoms can look like cognitive impairment, but they are characterized by *confusion* more than slowness.

2. Organic psychosis is usually accompanied by other signs of disease: fever, weakness, physical changes. If a person with schizophrenic symptoms has any sign of disease or seems to be in generally poor health, refer to a physician, preferably a good family physician or internist.

3. Organic psychosis, if it includes hallucinations, is characterized more by visual, tactile, smell, or taste hallucinations (see section on

hallucinations). With schizophrenia, auditory hallucinations are most common. Visual hallucinations may occur but they are less frequent. Hallucinations in other senses are rare.

4. Organic psychosis tends to have a more rapid onset with no previous history of problems. Schizophrenia often has a more gradual onset.

5. Organic hallucinations are usually vague, impersonal, or stereotypic (Currey, 1982). For example, an organic hallucination may consist of money floating through the air (impersonal) or the repetition of a musical tune (stereotypic). Schizophrenic hallucinations tend to be specific and personal. For example, hallucinatory voices may accuse, condemn, or command.

Biblical Perspective

The Bible takes a radical view of schizophrenia. But it does not simply say that it is a myth or that it is just sin. Instead, the Bible offers a powerful model that can incorporate the best of medical research.

Irrationality redefined. The heart of schizophrenia is irrationality—an inability to decipher the nature of what is real. Affected people seem to be in an illogical, private world of espionage, persecution, or fantasy. Without question, this is the most startling and perplexing aspect of schizophrenia.

The Bible's overview of irrationality begins by immediately departing from traditional perspectives. It does not exalt rationality, IQ, or logical reasoning. Rather, its emphasis is on faith. True knowledge comes from looking at ourselves and others through the lens of faith. Anything that is not interpreted through the filter of the triune God as Creator, Sustainer, Redeemer and King—the Alpha and Omega—is insanity.

With this faith-oriented view of rationality, it is not surprising that Scripture says irrationality is quite common. In fact, it says everyone is irrational or mad (Eccl. 9:3). None of us, apart from God's grace, can reason accurately. In ourselves, we are blinded, in darkness, unaware of the true reality of God and the ever-present spiritual battle. In other words, our sin has rendered us mad. As Berkouwer (1971) said, sin is "unreasonable, idiotic, and incomprehensible in light of God's love now revealed" (p.144). Having rebelled against a holy and loving God, we are frighteningly self-deceived, under a delusion or lie—not living in the real world. And no amount of medication will grant us truth. Only grace through faith is sufficient to break through the delusion.

The immediate practical advantage of this position is that it avoids an us/them distinction between those with schizophrenic symptoms and professionals. From a biblical perspective, there is no clear dividing line between rational and irrational. The only clear line is between faith and unbelief. Therefore, biblical counselors can truly say that there is no difference between themselves and the more patently insane. We are as needy as they.

Insanity as covenantal disobedience. Within this all-inclusive category of madness, the Bible mentions narrower accounts of insanity that come surprisingly close to *DSM-III-R* guidelines. One of the best examples is Deuteronomy 28:27–28:

> The LORD will afflict you with the boils of Egypt and with tumors, festering sores and the itch, from which you cannot be cured. The LORD will afflict you with madness, blindness and confusion of mind.

Deuteronomy 28 reviews some of the curses that can overtake those who disobey God's laws. In verse 27, the curses are clearly physical: tumors, festering sores, and the itch. Curiously, in the same context as these physical curses are curses that affect cognitive processes: madness, blindness, and confusion of mind. There are no apparent categorical distinctions between the two.

In Hebrew, the three psychological curses are rhyming nouns— probably suggesting that the symptoms tend to go together. The word *madness (shiggaon)* emphasizes the illogical, strange, and bizarre. Included would be symptoms such as delusions, hallucinations, and bizarre speech.

> Interviewer: "What did you think of the whole Watergate affair?"
> Patient: "You know I didn't tune in on that, I felt so bad about it. I said, boy, I'm not going to know what's going on in this. But it seemed to get so murky, and everybody's reports were so negative. Huh, I thought, I don't want any part of this, and I was I don't care who was in on it, and all I could figure out was Artie had something to do with it. Artie was trying to flush the bathroom toilet of the White House or something. . . . So I came downstairs and 'cause I pretended like I didn't know what was going on, I slipped on the floor of the kitchen, cracking my toe, when I was teaching some kids how to do some double dives." (Andreasen, 1979, p. 1319)

The second word of the triad, *blindness (iwwaron)*, points to the lonely, fearful world of the insane.

> All of a sudden things began to feel out of control. I couldn't concentrate, I couldn't sleep, and I imagined that people were talking about me. The voices [hallucinations] didn't help. They persuaded me even more that I was being persecuted. It was horrible. I couldn't trust anyone. I was desperately alone.

The third part of the triad, *confusion of mind* (*timmahon*), may describe the perceptual distortions that accompany present-day schizophrenic symptoms.

> During the last while back I have noticed that noises all seem to be louder to me than they were before. It is as if someone has turned up the volume. . . . (Torrey, 1988, p. 19)
> Colours seem to be brighter now, almost as if they are luminous painting. I'm not sure if things are solid until I touch them. (Torrey, 1988, p. 19)

Therefore, Scripture *does* specifically mention symptoms that are similar to those presently called schizophrenia. Furthermore, it indicates that these symptoms are not sinful themselves, but they are the *result* of covenant curses and therefore *consequences* of sin. In a sense, they are natural consequences of the madness of sin. It is as if the Lord, at times, simply allows the folly and madness in our hearts to be exposed for what they really are—insanity.

But we have to be very careful with this point; otherwise, there will be hazardous misunderstandings. *To say that insanity is a consequence of sin does not mean that the more obviously insane are bigger sinners.* Indeed, *all* of us, right now, are covenant-breakers. Although we might uphold the Ten Commandments with our overt behavior, our hearts constantly fall short of the law of love. Therefore, we all deserve madness, believers included. Yet because of God's restraining grace, only a very few people experience it in its more obvious forms.

Also, the covenantal curses are not reserved just for the disobedient. When reviewing Deuteronomy 28, it becomes obvious that these "curses" extend to include maladies that affect us all. As such, although they are curses for the unbeliever, they can be forms of training and discipline for the maturing believer. In such cases, the experience of schizophrenic symptoms becomes an effective way to remember that everything we have belongs to God, including our rationality. From this perspective, it is similar to Paul saying, "When I am weak, then I am strong" (2 Co 12:10). As the Lord can use physical sickness to mature his people and

Figure 8.8. Possible Contributions of Heart
and body in Schizophrenia

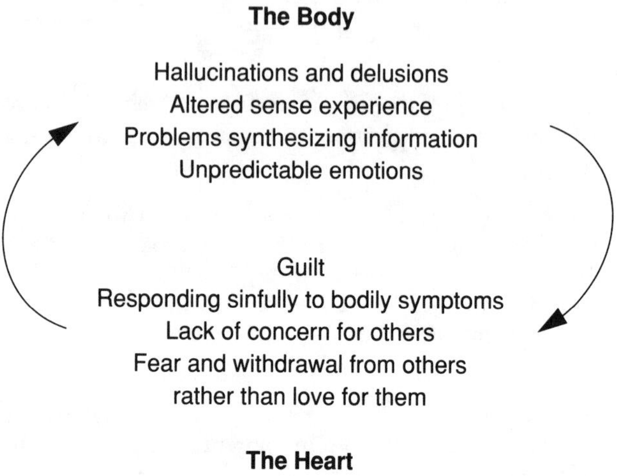

The Body

Hallucinations and delusions
Altered sense experience
Problems synthesizing information
Unpredictable emotions

Guilt
Responding sinfully to bodily symptoms
Lack of concern for others
Fear and withdrawal from others
rather than love for them

The Heart

bring glory to himself, he can also use cognitive changes and insanity to make us more dependent on him.

The question then becomes, "Why do some people become insane?" We could beg the question and emphasize the "party line"—that although madness affects fallen creation, madness cannot keep us from knowing God or living for him. And if obvious madness does emerge, we are empowered and commanded to walk humbly before the Lord. But eventually the answer to this question is "I don't know." The question is basically "Why is there suffering?" And although the Bible certainly has answers to this question, they are not as comprehensive as some might like. The better question is, "How can I live by faith even when my thinking processes are being assaulted?" As in any suffering, we live by placing our faith in the Savior who died for sins and rose from the dead.

Body and heart in insanity. To summarize a biblical perspective, schizophrenia, like the other psychiatric disorders, has aspects that emerge out of both the body and the heart (Figure 8.8).

When the symptoms have their cause in the heart, they can be traced to sinful patterns of life. These issues of the heart then trigger the covenantal curses of Deuteronomy 28.

Madness can also be caused by brain dysfunction (genetics, brain abnormalities) in which case affected persons certainly appear insane, but the heart does not have to respond sinfully. Therefore, it is possible to have schizophrenic symptoms but have neither a specific, sinful origin to them nor a sinful response. It is as if the Bible says, "In your madness, sin not."

Most common, however, are interactions between bodily symptoms and sinful responses. In these cases, heart and body provoke each other. For example, guilt (heart) leads to mild delusions that people are talking about you; these lead to fear and withdrawal (heart). In susceptible people, delusions then become more persecutory and include hallucinations (body); the heart, in turn, reacts and refuses to know complete forgiveness or express love to others.

As you can see, pastors and biblical counselors are indispensable to those with schizophrenic symptoms and their families. Without their input, issues of the heart are never addressed, and the cycle of insanity might needlessly persist. Biblical counselors are the only ones who are in a position to understand both body and heart. They recognize that the bodily symptoms and the ensuing confusion associated with schizophrenia are powerful assaults on the heart. Therefore, with love and patience, they call hearts to faith and obedience. Also, biblical counselors do everything they can to roll back the effects of the curse. To this end, if there are organic indicators, counselors refer people for medical consultation. In the absence of clear organic signs, counselors, together with affected persons and psychiatrists, weigh the potential benefits of antipsychotic medication.

This perspective, rather than being threatened by medical developments, actually anticipates them. The Bible welcomes effective medical treatments for the bodily changes associated with schizophrenia. These treatments represent small pictures of how God will some day remove the curse from his creation. Therefore, when effective, medical therapy can be used with thankfulness.[10]

Although there are many other counseling issues, there is one final problem that should be emphasized. Families of those with schizophrenic symptoms also have pastoral and counseling needs. They are usually perplexed, guilty, and angry when faced with schizophrenic symptoms in the home. Therefore, counselors are indispensable in offering biblical guidelines for communication and expectations.

Mania and Bipolar Disorder

Mania is the opposite of depression. Thoughts come *quickly*, intensity and passion are *greater*, and there is a sense of *well-being*. Although technically a problem with emotions rather than reasoning, in *DSM-III-R* it is placed along with depression under mood disorders. However, since the behaviors associated with manic episodes are so dramatic and unusual, mania actually has more similarity to schizophrenia than depression. In fact, it is frequently confused with schizophrenia.

Mania is popularly called manic-depression or, more technically, bipolar disorder. These terms are intended to describe how mania often, but not always, fluctuates with depression; people swing from one emotional pole to the other. Affected persons can have a manic episode for a few weeks and then gradually move into a depressive stage. Some people suggest that these fluctuations can even alternate hour to hour.

Most people tend to experience ups and downs, but the peaks of mania, or the peaks and valleys of manic-depression (bipolar disorder), are noticeable to even the casual observer. Mania has several key features. Mood is described as euphoric, cheerful, or high. It may seem enthusiastic to the distant observer, but it is easily recognized as excessive by friends. Thoughts race, persons feel more productive (although their activity is usually chaotic), and they seem to have an incessant desire to talk and interact with people. Speech may be patently bizarre or incoherent or may include strange associations. Plays on words or word associations by sound rather than meaning (clanging) are also common. There is a decreased need for sleep. Sometimes people will go for days with little or no sleep but still seem energetic.

Of particular importance to pastors and counselors are the religious aspects of some forms of mania. With inflated self-confidence, those with manic behaviors often feel like they have special knowledge, and they may become frustrated or even violent if their ideas aren't universally recognized. In a church context, it is not unusual for affected people to perceive themselves as especially gifted, and they may be very disruptive in services.

This grandiosity also translates into a sense that everything they do will turn out well. As a result, excesses may be apparent in reckless driving, foolish business investments, the pursuit of fleeting romantic relationships, buying sprees, or sinful sexual behavior.

I knew at a very young age that something was not right. The overt symptoms didn't start until my late teens. . . . I rode the wild roller coaster. . . . In mania, I spent a great deal of money on things I didn't need. . . . You feel euphoric. Nothing you do has any negative consequences. You can go anywhere, be anybody, marry anybody. [During depressive phases] there's no hope; I'm a terrible person; I should kill myself. . . . This sort of depression goes further [than sadness]. The support of friends is meaningless, the only answer is to kill yourself. [Having witnessed my suicide attempts] my children went through utter hell. (Patty Duke, 1989)

Mania usually appears between the ages of twenty and thirty-five. Its onset can be either rapid or fairly gradual, developing over a period of weeks. If it emerges gradually, early symptoms often begin with a decreased need for sleep; progress to increased activity, uncharacteristic excitement, and racing thoughts; and culminate in strange speech and psychotic symptoms such as persecutory delusions.

Medical Perspective

The most popular medication for mania is lithium. Like other psychoactive medications, it treats no known biological cause, but it does reduce the physical symptoms of mania in the majority of cases. Response to lithium can take a few days; therefore, it is best used when counselors or pastors detect the early warning signs of impending manic symptoms such as sleep loss and compulsive talking and make a quick referral to a psychiatrist or overseeing physician. If manic symptoms are in full bloom, then a more rapid-acting drug such as an antipsychotic is initially used.

Some psychiatrists, in keeping with an illness model, prefer to keep individuals on lithium even after symptoms subside. This, however, is a debatable practice. The rule of thumb tends to be that when mania occurs at a younger age and when there are only a few months between manic episodes, lithium is used more long term. If the occurrence of mania has been fairly solitary, or recurrences are separated by years, then lithium is often limited to the time of the episodes themselves. If persons do choose to avoid long-term lithium, then it becomes even more important for pastors, counselors, and friends to understand the way a manic episode develops. It might then be possible to identify the early signs of a possible recurrence.

Genetics. Other than medication, the active area of research in mania and manic-depression is genetic research. The most popular genetic investigations were done with the Old Order Amish of Lancaster County, Pennsylvania. Because of the closed nature of the community and the abundance of family records, investigators were able to complete a significant ten-year study among the Amish. But the results, although announced with fanfare, are not as certain as some suggest. They state that a gene, chromosome 11, is at fault in manic-depression. But studies are not unanimous and the data are still very preliminary. Perhaps the most that can be said about genetic studies is that there is a family tendency toward the physical manifestations of mania and manic-depression, but it is likely that spiritual and "environmental" factors "turn on or off" the genetic propensity (Hostetler, 1987).

Mania and genius. An interesting observation in the research on mania is the occurrence of manic symptoms in those who are well-known leaders and artists. Manic symptoms were most likely present in composers Gustav Mahler, Hector Berlioz, and Robert Schumann; poets Lord Byron and Edgar Allan Poe; statesmen Winston Churchill and Oliver Cromwell; writers such as F. Scott Fitzgerald; and actresses such as Patty Duke. Yet any conclusions from this tenuous relationship are suspect. It certainly does not mean that mania causes great accomplishments.

Organic causes of mania. Since mania and anxiety are both characterized by increased mental and physical activity, the potential organic causes of mania are very similar to those associated with anxiety. Drugs remain the number one culprit (Table 8.9, from Stasiek & Zetin, 1985).

> After being inappropriately euphoric for over five weeks, a sixty-nine-year-old man with an eight-year history of Parkinson's disease became flagrantly manic. He was described by the family as hyperactive, without his normal inhibitions, and full of exaggerated self-confidence. When the family could no longer tolerate his behavior, they brought him to the hospital. In the hospital it was noted that he had recently (five weeks prior) increased his L-Dopa. After an adjustment of his medication, the symptoms subsided and the man, to the delight of his family, returned to his normal level of functioning. (Ryback & Schwab, 1971)

Biblical Perspective

A biblical perspective on mania is very similar to what has been said about other disorders, namely, that mania has no known organic cause,

Table 8.9. Medical Causes of Mania

Drugs
  Decongestants
  Bronchodilators
  Calcium
  Antidepressants
  Phencyclidine (PCP)
  Steroids (especially for systemic lupus erythematosus)
  Tolmentin (for arthritis)
  Stimulants
  L-Dopa
Metabolic diseases
  Vitamin B_{12} deficiency
  Aftereffect of weaning
  Dialysis dementia
  Hyperthyroidism
Infection—syphilis
Central nervous system disorders
  Brain tumor
  Multiple sclerosis

medication can reduce some of the physical symptoms, and it can be divided into issues of the body and heart (Figure 8.10).

It is possible that the peculiar euphoria of mania is triggered by physical processes. If mania is caused in this way, biblical living is difficult but certainly possible.

It is also theoretically permissible that mania is a consequence of sinful issues of the heart. Not uncommonly, counselors will observe clearly sinful precursors. Or, it is common to find a history of being sinned against but without the spiritual resources or knowledge to respond to that history in a godly way.

> Bill, a thirty-five-year-old physical therapist and father of two young boys, was found walking in the snow, barefoot, singing and shouting to himself or anyone who would listen. Unwilling to go to a hospital, he was involuntarily committed by his wife and friends. His mania subsided within six hours, but he found himself shackled in a mental hospital—an experience that is still etched in his mind.
>
> Later, he reviewed the manic episode. "I was mad at my wife. I wanted to get her attention and 'punish' her for what she did. I knew that what I was doing was wrong, but it didn't matter to me. After about an hour, something strange happened. I felt like I was no longer in control. I felt like

Figure 8.10. Possible Contributions of Heart
and Body in Mania

The Body

Decreased sleep
Increased physical energy
Racing thoughts
Misperceptions and delusional thinking
Distractibility

Unwillingness to hear counsel from others
Lack of submission to authority (church or state)
Insensitivity to the perspective of others
Pride

The Heart

I was taken captive by this out-of-control excitement. At the time, it was
scary but OK. Now, it seems like it was hell."

Either way mania develops, counseling addresses issues of the heart
as well as the body. The heart is approached through "normal" biblical
counseling; counselors seek to know counselees and interpret their lives
and circumstances through a biblical grid. The body can be examined for
organic causes, or lithium might be used to restrain some of the physical
symptoms.

Notes

1. The closest things available to diagnostic tests are the Dexamethasone
Suppression Test (DST), the thyroid-releasing hormone (TRH) stimulation test,
and the stimulant challenge test. But the DST and TRH stimulation tests are
rarely sensitive in more than 50 percent of cases, and the stimulant challenge test
tends to be very subjective because of unclear laboratory guidelines (Carroll,
1985; Fawcett & Kravitz, 1985). Also, none of these tests demonstrate that a
physical problem *caused* depression.

2. There are certainly other drugs that have been used for depression, such
as the anti-anxiety drug Xanax, amphetamines, thyroid hormones, and even
anticonvulsants. But these drugs are rarely used initially.

3. ECT was outlawed by voters in Berkeley, California. But the law has been overturned.

4. A helpful resource is The Huxley Institute for Biosocial Research, 900 North Federal Highway, Boca Raton, FL 33432.

5. Hypothyroidism is first suspected by these signs and symptoms, and then by an analysis of the thyroid hormones T_3 and T_4, and TSH. Another test, the thyroid-releasing hormone (TRH) test, is reported to be the best screening device. In one study, the TRH test identified 100 percent of those with thyroid failure, whereas the TSH test identified 50 percent, and the T_3 and T_4 assays identified only 10 percent (Sternberg, 1976). These tests can be performed by most physicians.

6. The late actor-comedian Marty Feldman is a memorable example of exophthalmos.

7. I will only discuss insanity that is experienced as real. No doubt there are many who can feign insanity for profit, but my position is that insanity, as commonly understood, is a real phenomenon.

8. Schizophrenia is defined as follows *(DSM-III-R)*:

A. Presence of (1), (2), or (3) for at least one week
  (1) Two of the following:
    (a) delusions
    (b) prominent hallucinations
    (c) incoherence
    (d) catatonic behavior
    (e) flat or grossly inappropriate affect
  (2) Bizarre delusions, such as delusions of being controlled, thought broadcasting, or thought insertion,
  (3) Prominent hallucinations such as a voice keeping up a running commentary on the individual's behavior or thoughts, or two or more voices conversing with each other.
B. Functioning in work, relationships, and self-care are far below previous levels.

9. The Huxley Institute (previously cited under depression) is a useful resource. Along with literature, staffers have lists of orthomolecular physicians. Also literature is available through The Schizophrenia Association of Greater Washington Inc., Wheaton Plaza Office Building North, Suite 404, Wheaton, MD, 20902.

10. There are many books that offer helpful, practical suggestions for families that live with a person with schizophrenic symptoms. Unfortunately, they all have a medical model bias and they are unaware of moral issues. But with some biblical "recasting" they can be useful. Some of the popular ones are as follows:

E. Fuller Torrey, *Surviving Schizophrenia: A Family Manual* (New York: Harper & Row, 1988).

Kayla Burnheim, Richard Lewine, and Caroline Beale, *The Caring Family: Living with Chronic Mental Illness* (New York: Random House, 1982).

Mona Wasow, *Coping with Schizophrenia: A Survival Manual for Parents, Relatives and Friends* (Palo Alto, Calif.: Science and Behavior Books, 1982).

9
Other "Masquerading" Symptoms

Along with the more common counseling problems such as depression and anxiety, counselors often hear of or observe other symptoms that may be warning signs of organic disease. These problems are rarely the main focus of counseling, but they are often part of a cluster of complaints that accompany the presenting problem.

Headaches

One of humanity's most universal complaints are headaches. Each year in the United States up to 85 percent of the population will have a headache, and 5 to 7 percent will seek medical aid. Most headaches are benign; that is, they are not lethal and do not indicate the presence of a dangerous disease, yet almost 10 percent have a serious underlying cause. Because of the sheer number of persons affected, counselors should understand certain aspects of headaches, and because of the potentially life-threatening nature of some headaches, counselors should know which accompanying symptoms suggest dangerous head pain.

The following section reviews the three major categories of head pain: migraines, muscle tension headaches, and organic headaches.

Migraine

The migraine family includes common, classic, and cluster migraines. Popularly called "sick headaches, " they are typically on one side of the head (unilateral) and are usually associated with nausea. However, they shun stereotypes: they are exceedingly variable and occur with a dazzling array of other symptoms as well. In fact, headache is *never* the sole symptom of a migraine, and there are actually times when migraines occur in the absence of a headache.

Common migraine. Common migraine, as the name indicates, is the most prevalent type of migraine, occurring in over 80 percent of migraine attacks. Vague premonitory signs, or prodromes, may occur a few hours or days before the headache, consisting of changes including decreased or increased energy level, food cravings, and gastrointestinal discomfort. The headache itself usually begins on one side of the head and gradually, as the aching or throbbing continues, becomes more diffuse. It may last a matter of minutes, but it typically lasts from eight to twenty-four hours, and sometimes even days or a week. Nausea, both literally and figuratively, is invariable. Affected persons turn away from food, light, sound, and, indeed, from everything. It is almost as if life itself makes them sick as they withdraw from all outside stimulation.

Of particular interest to counselors are the possible migrainous mood changes. These mood changes seem to be more than the extreme emotions that may have caused the migraine, and they are not just responses to pain. They might begin, prior to the headache, with irritable or anxious hyperactivity and proceed to an intense experience of depression that can be either active or passive. In its more energetic form it can be expressed by anger and loathing that are intolerable for families. Expressed passively, it looks like a dutiful but hopeless acceptance of suffering and thoughts of suicide.

Classic migraine. Classic migraines occur in about 10 percent of migraine sufferers. They are distinguished from common migraines in that classic migraines rarely last longer than three to four hours, and they are usually accompanied by more specific early warning signs, called auras, that may occur up to thirty minutes before the actual headache.

These auras can be fascinating. Symptoms run the gamut from visual hallucinations to changes in emotions, thinking, memory, and speech. The best-known and probably most common of the auras are visual, including brilliant dancing stars, visual radar "blips," distortions of size ("Alice in Wonderland syndrome"), transient, shimmering colors, geometric objects, and kaleidoscopic transformations. It is likely that some people have mistaken these experiences as mystical communications from God (Sacks, 1985). Also reported are negative visual symptoms that are experienced like the initial stages of blindness.

A forty-six-year-old man was admitted to the hospital for observation after a mild heart attack. After waking early in the morning with spots in front of his eyes, he was bewildered by their persistence. However, when the areas seemed to grow and become darker, panic overwhelmed him—he was certain he was going blind. Immediately, he was surrounded by physicians and nurses who labored for an accurate diagnosis: stroke, hysteria, seizure, or tumor. During questioning, one physician asked about a history of migraine. Indeed, the man had experienced occasional migraines since his teen years, and he often had visual auras, although never negative ones. Within forty-five minutes, when his vision returned to normal, the medical team realized it was a migrainous episode.

Even more dramatic, however, are the mood changes that may precede migraine attacks. They tend to appear suddenly, with no apparent provocation, and they are usually marked by their intensity. They range from the terrifying, such as a sense of imminent danger or even death, to the pleasurable, laughable, and near mystical.

Auras that affect cognitive functions are also characteristic of migraines. Difficulty reading, unusual writing mistakes, language problems that mimic aphasia, déjà vu experiences, and dreamlike states are just some of the unusual symptoms. Furthermore, to make them even more unusual and prone to misdiagnosis, these and all other auras can periodically emerge *without any accompanying headache*. In such cases they are called migraine equivalents. I suspect they are fairly common but unrecognized as fleeting migranous symptoms.

A forty-four-year-old man suffered very occasional attacks of migraine from adolescence. In one attack, he experienced a profound dream-like state followed by visual phenomena. While at work on a New York winter day, he suddenly couldn't remember where he was. He actually thought he was in California, on a hot summer day. And he thought his secretary was his wife, moving about on a verandah. Only when she said, "Are you sick or something?" did he wake up and recognize the perplexed face of his secretary. (Sacks, 1970)

For forty-five minutes [a normally self-possessed girl of fifteen] experienced an aura during which she giggled without intermission. . . . When she recovered from this state, she apologized in these terms: "I don't know what I was laughing at—I just couldn't help it—everything seemed so funny, like laughing gas." (Sacks, 1985, p. 97)

Table 9.1. Foods Known to Precipitate Migraines

Chocolate	Caffeine	Alcohol, especially red
Citrus fruits	Herring	wine
Bananas	Avocado	Large amounts of MSG
Chicken livers	Fresh breads	Pork
Nuts, peanut butter	Dairy products	Doughnuts
Ripened cheeses	Fermented, pickled, or	Onions
	marinated foods	

These auras are detected by way of their sudden, episodic nature; their unreal or overwhelming quality, their brief duration, and their typically ineffable quality.

When the auras are followed by headache, the head pain in classic migraine is initially one-sided and throbbing, and it often spreads to the entire head. It may occur with other symptoms such as nausea, vomiting, and avoidance of light (photophobia). At times, the migraine may be relieved by vomiting.

Cluster migraine. Not always included in the migraine category, the cluster headache has a particular penchant for men in their thirties and forties. The headache usually occurs in a series of closely spaced attacks or "clusters." Average durations are six to eight weeks, and they can then be silent for months or even years.

The headache often wakes the person out of sleep and is described as an intense, deep, boring pain behind the eyes. (It is not uncommon for migraine sufferers to have a thesaurus full of different descriptions of their pain.) Attacks occur about one to three times a day, each lasting, on the average, forty-five minutes. Associated symptoms include runny nose, tearing, pacing, walking, and rocking.[1]

Treatment of migraine. Treatment of migraine tends to be a lesson in medical overkill. Medications are usually prescribed quickly without full regard given to other possible causes. Known culprits include irregular sleep hours, sleeping late, alcohol and drugs, hypoglycemia, stress, and certain foods (Table 9.1). Hormonal changes, and oral contraceptives in particular, are notorious causes. In fact, up to 70 percent of women improve when they withdraw from their oral contraceptives (Friedman, 1982). Also, many women improve during the hormonal changes of pregnancy.

A cause that waxes and wanes in popularity among physicians is "stress," the secular equivalent to issues of the heart. There is no question that many migraines are intimately related to problems in living.

A forty-three-year-old woman had incessant migraines but reported a near idyllic home life. She indicated that her marriage was strong and her children were doing well; she seemed to be very content. After a few weeks, however, some chinks were observed in her armor. Closer inspection revealed financial bankruptcy, a very uncomfortable and distant marital relationship, a teen who was abusing drugs, and worry about middle age.

In these cases, it is almost as if migrainous symptoms act like a physical release valve. Internal chaos is released in a storm of physical symptoms. Interestingly, some people report that migraines actually make them feel better when they are over, but the same problems gradually mount until the next episode. Therefore, although clear biblical issues are not always burrowed under migraine symptoms, they must always be considered in chronic sufferers.

If there is no change in the head pain after considering these causes, other treatments are available. There is a plethora of medications that have demonstrated some usefulness with migraines, but none of them are universally effective, and all of them have potential side effects and complications. Treatment begins with over-the-counter analgesics, yet even these can have troublesome side effects if taken in large quantities. Persons consuming large amounts of aspirin or acetaminophen (more than 100 tablets per month) may develop "rebound" headaches from the medication. That is, there can be a worsening of the headache three to four hours after taking analgesics, and when the analgesic is stopped, headaches may be worse than ever. If analgesics fail, physicians may try the aspirin-containing mild tranquilizer, Fiorinal. The problem with any tranquilizers, however, even those that are relatively mild, is that they are easily abused and can be addictive.

Ergotamine tartrate and its derivatives (e.g., Cafergot, D.H.E.) and methysergide (e.g., Sansert) are the old standbys in migraine treatment. (Ergotamine has also demonstrated the "rebound" phenomenon.) Newer medical treatments include nonsteroidal anti-inflammatory drugs, Inderal, Catapres, and antidepressant drugs such as Elavil and Nardil.

Remember, no drug is perfect. You should be alert to any new symptoms that developed after the drug trial was initiated.

Muscle Tension Headaches

Muscle tension headaches, also called muscle contraction headaches, are the most common headaches. Those affected rarely seek
medical advice but treat themselves with over-the-counter analgesics such
as acetaminophen, aspirin, and ibuprofen. Muscle tension headaches
have no prodromes, are usually on both sides of the head, and can last for
hours to days and, in some cases, never go away. They are described as
continuous, deep pressure; or tightness—"a flaming belt"—following a
hatband pattern around the head.

A fifty-nine-year-old man complained of headaches for over twenty
years. They occurred almost daily, were not clearly localized, and were often
described as a band of pain around his forehead. A chronic pill-popper, he
would follow whatever pain relief remedies were in vogue. He had been to
many physicians, and was subjected to numerous tests, but no cause was
found. Finally, after he struggled with many of the physical features of
depression (problems sleeping, fatigue, and some emotional lability) he
reluctantly went for biblical counseling.

During counseling he soon revealed bitterness and anger that were
directed toward his employers, spouse, parents (who were deceased), and
whoever crossed him that day. As he began to deal biblically with these
issues in his life, his headaches gradually diminished in intensity and
frequency.

Treatment for these headaches is similar to that for migraine. In
fact, some researchers suggest that muscle tension headaches are very
similar to migraines. Perhaps the major difference in treatment is that
physicians are quicker to point to a functional cause for muscle tension
headaches, and counseling is often the first line of treatment.

Organic Headaches

The remaining 10 percent of headaches are induced by physical
problems that are often treatable but potentially lethal if left unexamined.
These causes range from high blood pressure to brain tumors.[2] Here are
some guidelines to keep in mind.

First, when in doubt, refer to a physician. Don't play diagnostician.
Be especially alert for the following signs:

1. Headaches that are accompanied by physical abnormalities such
as fever, stiff neck, high blood pressure, sweating, visual problems,
flushing, and hoarse voice.

2. Headaches that are accompanied by cognitive or personality changes.

3. Headaches that develop for the first time after age fifty or are different in quality or location from previous headaches (Currey, 1982).

Counseling

Although this is not a comprehensive picture of headaches and their treatment, it familiarizes you with the basic categories and reminds you that some headaches may signal serious physical problems. And since most headaches have a nonorganic component, be aware that counseling may be a very important part of treatment.

When treatable organic causes of headaches have been ruled out, the task of counseling those with headaches is no different than any other counseling: you understand the person, his or her circumstances, and the appropriate application of God's Word. In the case of headaches, this means that you should understand when and, if possible, why the headaches began, and the circumstances around their fluctuations. Then you proceed with "normal" biblical counseling. There are, however, certain unique problems for which you should be prepared.

People with chronic head pain may complain of side effects of headaches such as loss of sleep, fatigue, and irritability. Also, up to half of those with chronic head pain report some sort of depression, either in the form of a depressed mood or as a preoccupation with the headache and a lack of initiative (Sternbach, 1986).

Sometimes headaches become the central preoccupation in life and those affected miss work, quit jobs, disrupt the home, and eventually find meaning in being defined as invalids. If this is the case, you as the counselor must help them realize that there is a powerful "payoff" to adopting a sick role—it can offer control, power, and freedom from daily duties.

Another problem unique to those with head pain is that they may be constantly looking for the elusive cure. Doctor-shopping and fad remedies, often at great expense to families, are commonplace. Also, although some refuse prescription medication, most will have tried a few. And, as mentioned before, the majority of medicines that are used to treat headaches can be associated with addiction. Be alert to this, especially in the chronic patient. Know what medications counselees are taking, and ask specifically when they take them and how much. People addicted to medication probably have headaches that are a result of their withdrawal symptoms.

Finally, people who have headaches are suffering with sometimes excruciating physical pain. Perhaps the most challenging part of counseling is to offer a meaningful and biblical understanding of suffering.

[Told by a pastor] Mary, fifty-five-years-old, had been married for thirty years when her husband died. He was very concerned about his wife up to the last few minutes of his life, and, almost just before he died, he asked me to read a manuscript which he had prepared (he had planned for me to have it after his death). The manuscript told the story of his wife's pain over the years. It was entitled "PAIN—TO WHOM CAN WE TURN?"

I'd known the couple for a number of years and was aware that she suffered from chronic head pain. What I didn't know was the story behind the pain—the anguish, bitterness, and addiction to drugs. They were keeping all these to themselves, partly because of shame, partly because of despondency and hopelessness.

The manuscript revealed the woman's ordeal. She had chronic, severe headaches, usually experienced behind her eyes. After a number of different treatments, in desperation she had an operation which severed the trigeminal nerve (a nerve controlling parts of the face). Unfortunately, the operation was not only unsuccessful in relieving the pain, it also made her eyes begin to bulge out. Nothing could stop this side effect and it left her almost housebound because of her embarrassment.

Her husband's letter indicated that his wife was angry toward the medical community, struggling with her faith, addicted to painkillers, and feeling guilty about all these. He asked for help.

Hallucinations

Most people know exactly what to do when a friend or counselee has hallucinations—they refer them to someone else! Yet I appeal to the scientist-investigator in you to consider these most unusual symptoms. Afterward, you will, at least, not be so alarmed by them, and you will probably find them very interesting. The following overview will introduce you to the fascinating subject of hallucinations and give you some guidelines as to when to expect the presence of treatable, physical disease.

Hallucinations are sensory deceptions. They are sensory experiences, in any of the five senses, that do not correspond to any external, real, tangible objects or events. For example, hallucinators hear voices, even though no one is actually talking, or they see things when the objects are not physically present. To take a more popular illustration, heavy drinkers might see the famous pink elephants prancing on the walls, when in fact there are none. Hallucinations are distinct in that delusions are cognitive misinterpretations rather than sensory deceptions. Delusions are cognitive because they are in the realm of thought and ideas, not sensory experience. People with delusions see and hear accurately, but they misinterpret the information. For example, a delusional man may actually see a policeman, but he misinterprets the data and believes that the policeman is a secret agent with the KGB. Or he might actually hear a noise in his car but misinterpret it as a person hiding in the trunk who wants revenge.

Frequently, these delusions go hand-in-hand with hallucinations. The hallucinator, surprised and perplexed by the hallucinations, constructs a delusional world in an attempt to understand the sensory data. For example, a woman may experience hallucinatory voices that command certain behaviors, but she may misinterpret these hallucinations as part of a global conspiracy that is backed by an ex-husband. I have heard of a comic-tragic delusion where a school teacher began hearing voices and made sense out of them by believing they were coming from a transmitter—implanted, one night, in his nose. Sadly, he pleaded with surgeon after surgeon to remove the horrid microscopic receiver. One doctor actually gave him an X-ray which was, of course, normal. But the man happened to see the X-ray and, noticing a white spot in the nasal area, was even more convinced that the radio was real. The man constructed a delusion to account for the hallucinatory voices.

Hallucinations are also distinguishable from illusions or sensory *distortions*. Illusions are a restructuring of real events and usually have an organic origin. For example, sounds may seem louder, fainter, and more or less distant. Visual objects may appear stretched, inverted, changed in color, or bent, and they may reappear or not fade away (Hacaen & Albert, 1978; Currey, 1982). Also, illusions can be cognitive rather than sensory. For example, the unfamiliar may seem strangely familiar (déjà vu), or the familiar may appear unfamiliar, unreal, or dreamlike (jamais vu). Even distorted emotions can fit into this category when they are organically distorted beyond what the context suggests (Kolb & Whishaw, 1985).[3]

Hallucinations tend to have one of three causes: they may be part of a package of symptoms called schizophrenia, they may be a danger sign indicating the presence of organic brain or eye disease, or they may simply be normal, in which case you alleviate patients' fears and tell them to enjoy the show!

Schizophrenic Hallucinations

Schizophrenic hallucinations, the best-known, are considered to be nonorganic. As you know, that does not mean that medical treatment is irrelevant. There are medications that suppress the majority of schizophrenic hallucinations; yet schizophrenic hallucinations do not indicate the presence of life-threatening disease.[4]

These hallucinations may occur in any of the senses, but they are most frequently auditory, occasionally visual, and rarely involve taste, smell, or touch. The rule of thumb is that if a person with schizophrenic symptoms mentions hallucinations that are neither visual nor auditory, consider them as part of an underlying disease that is separate from the schizophrenic symptoms. In schizophrenia, auditory hallucinations are present in 35 to 94 percent of diagnosed individuals, and visual hallucinations are present in 5 to 72 percent (Currey, 1982). The published percentages are probably underestimates because hallucinations usually carry a stigma in Western culture and may be denied by active hallucinators. This means that if someone demonstrates the bizarre communication and delusions of schizophrenia, it is likely that he or she is also hearing hallucinatory "voices."

Schizophrenic hallucinations are intriguing and mysterious to researchers, and they tend to be absolutely horrible to the victims. They typically emerge between the late teens and late twenties (first-time hallucinations after age thirty should be considered organic), and they are part of a schizophrenic package. This means that the hallucinations are often accompanied by other symptoms such as delusions, incoherent speech, and a significant decline in the person's social and occupational function. In up to 40 percent of affected persons, these symptoms remit and residual symptoms may be negligible. In some, however, the symptoms tend to persist and recur.

In order to understand the typical profile of these hallucinations, consider the following examples. Notice how the auditory hallucinations can sound like one voice or many, and they can talk to the person or about the person. Also, notice that the hallucinatory message tends to be negative, critical, directive, compelling, and part of a delusional system.

She has been hearing voices for the past several years . . . men . . . and women constantly threatening her, calling her the most horrible names such as whore, prostitute. (Linn, 1977)

. . . they said "get lost" . . . also made sexual accusations against him . . . frequently tell him not to eat and that he is not worthy of the food. (Linn, 1977)

. . . [The voices were] calling him all kinds of names . . . [he was] hearing these for about eighteen months "night and day" . . . voices predict things, mostly bad things that are going to happen to him and they do happen. (Linn, 1977)

They tell me what colors to wear . . . and they tell me the sexual significance of peoples' clothes. They tell me that people know my sins. They tell me how the minister is really giving me secret messages. They get really bad at night.

The voice has been tormenting me, trying to frighten me to death, telling me that I am going to be killed in the road, spending a lot of time trying to talk me into killing my son out of love so he won't be left without me [when I die], telling me the house is going to catch on fire in the middle of the night. It has filled my mind with so much filth that I can't stand it.

Several key questions emerge from these examples. One is, Can a person with schizophrenic symptoms tell the difference between real and hallucinatory voices? Interestingly, although hallucinators find their voices to be quite compelling, they know the difference between an external voice and their internal voice. Sometimes they will refer to the hallucination as the "voice in my head."

Another important question is, "How much control does a schizophrenic have over hallucinations?" My observation is that although some people may encourage and even follow their hallucinations, hallucinations are sensed as separate from the person and perceived to be outside the person's control. As such, you rarely can simply tell a person, "Stop hallucinating." Yet even though the actual experience of hallucinations is difficult to control, hallucinators usually realize that they are not at the mercy of the voices (Larkin, 1979). They realize that a hallucinatory command that violates their conscience can be resisted. So, although counselors can't say, "Stop hallucinating," they can say, "Stop sinfully acting on your voices." The operating principle is that even though hallucinations may be extremely difficult and distracting, the heart is not forced to respond sinfully to the "commands" of the voices.

Rather, the heart can choose to have faith and do right even when deluged with hallucinations that accuse.

A third question is related to the negative and critical nature of most schizophrenic hallucinations: "These voices sound like demonic accusations. Are these people demonized/possessed/oppressed?" There are a few ways to answer this, One answer is, "Yes, they may be demonic voices." Anyone who has spent much time with people who demonstrate schizophrenic symptoms will at some point be frightened by the patent evil in the hallucinatory commands, accusations, or visions. The question then becomes, "What is the most powerful way to combat the work of Satan?" There are various perspectives on this one. My own experience and understanding of Scripture affirm that the most powerful way to combat Satan is with powerful warfare implements: faith, repentance, love, and obedience. These are necessary and sufficient for the battle.

Another related interpretation of the hallucinatory voices is that the voices' accusations are the same as hallucinators' self-assessment or their perception of society's or God's assessment. From this perspective, hallucinations represent real feelings that people have about themselves. This does not rule out any demonic influence. Rather, Satan can use these feelings as an opportunity to distract people from daily trust in God. Therefore, whatever their interpretation, schizophrenic hallucinations are part of an intense spiritual battle, and the ultimate treatment is a response of faith to a clear proclamation of God's forgiving love.

The following suggestions are not intended to be exhaustive, but they offer an outline of counseling suggestions for schizophrenic hallucinations.

1. Since the word *hallucinations* can be frightening, derogatory, or unclear, be aware of other ways to get data on hallucinations. For example, "Have you ever heard (seen, smelled, tasted, or felt) something which was only sensed by you and not by others who were there or might have been there?" Or, "Do you ever hear 'voices'?"

2. Nonauditory hallucinations should be considered to be organic until medically investigated. Refer people who have visual, sense, taste, or smell hallucinations to their GP, internist, or neurologist.

3. Don't be sidetracked by hallucinations. If hallucinations are apparently nonorganic, be careful about trying to fully understand them or their accompanying delusions. Certainly, an attempt to understand people will include trying to understand their world of hallucinations, but too much emphasis on hallucinations and delusions may detract from

---

more important and basic biblical guidelines and teaching. Also, my experience is that you can actually encourage hallucinations by discussing them too often.

4. Schizophrenic hallucinations can sometimes be suppressed by antipsychotic medication. Counselors should be aware of that resource and, if warranted, refer affected persons to psychiatrists.

Organic Hallucinations

A second category of hallucinations consists of those that have an organic cause that is often treatable. To give you an idea of how many medical problems can potentially result in hallucinations, Tables 9.2 and 9.3 list *some* of the known causes.

Drugs remain the number one culprit. When taken in excess, any drug, prescription or otherwise, can produce toxic states and associated hallucinations in any of the five senses. Perhaps the best-known of these hallucinations are formication hallucinations in which there is a feeling that insects are crawling on (or inside) the skin.[5] These are most likely to occur in alcoholics, the elderly, those who attempt suicide, those with physical illness, and those taking high doses of medication. Usually, toxic hallucinations occur along with other cognitive changes such as impaired intellectual abilities, disorientation, or inability to recognize others.

You are already familiar with some of the other causes of organic hallucinations. But one that you might find surprising is migraines. About half of all patients with migraines experience visual hallucinations. The most prevalent hallucination is called a fortification spectrum—a shimmering zig-zag spectrum in the peripheral visual fields—but fully formed hallucinations are also reported. These may occur even when there is no headache, in which case they are called migraine equivalents. Very curious phenomena associated with the migraine aura, or premigrainous symptoms, are macropsia and micropsia. Also called the "Alice in Wonderland syndrome," these strange hallucinations are characterized by everything looking either large or small. Apparently, Lewis Carroll, a migraine sufferer who wrote *Alice in Wonderland*, used his experience with size distortion as part of his famous story.

An interesting aspect of nearly all organic hallucinations is that they are usually qualitatively different from the schizophrenic variety; therefore, they can be very helpful in distinguishing organic from nonorganic problems. They do not have the same accusational, compelling quality. Even psychotic patients can differentiate between their schizophrenic

Table 9.2. Medical Problems Associated with Hallucinations

Central nervous system disorders
  Brain tumors
  Head trauma
  Insufficient blood flow in the brain (stroke, ischemia)
  Migraine
  Seizures—especially those originating in the temporal lobe
General medical
  Dehydration
  High fever
  Liver or kidney failure
  Nutritional deprivation
Eye or optic nerve disease
Toxic states
  Alcohol or drug withdrawal
  Hallucinogenic drugs
  Drug intoxication—with almost any drug

Table 9.3. Drugs Associated with Hallucinations
(from Cummings, 1985)

Hallucinogens	Antidepressants
LSD	Imipramine
Psilocybin	Maprotiline
Mescaline	Anti-Parkinson agents
Amphetamines	Anticholinergic drugs
Cocaine	Levodopa
PCP	Hormones
Nitrous oxide	Steroids
Drugs associated with withdrawal	Thyroxin
Alcohol	Bromide
Barbiturates	Digoxin
Opiates	Cimetidine
Meprobamate	Propanolol
Sympathomimetics	

hallucinations and those that are drug induced (West, 1975). For example, LSD or mescaline hallucinations are often unformed visual sensations, simple geometric forms, small animals, friendly human figures or caricatures, religious imagery or alterations of color, size, shape, and number (illusions and hallucinations). These hallucinations are usually independent of a person's emotional state. Also, they are readily seen in the dark or with eyes closed.

Although there are exceptions to any rule in diagnosis, the following guidelines can alert you to hallucinations that have been misdiagnosed as schizophrenic or "functional." Organic hallucinations tend to have the following characteristics:

1. They are not incorporated into a delusional system. People usually have insight into their unreality.

2. They are usually nonauditory. Visual hallucinations are most frequent.

3. They tend to be impersonal, nondirective, noncompelling, mundane, or emotionally neutral. For example, if they are auditory, mechanical and musical sounds are more frequent than voices. Sometimes they are repetitive sounds or images that have no apparent meaning to the person, such as dollar bills floating through the air and strange "thuds."

4. Affected persons may find their experiences perplexing, or they may fear "going crazy." Schizophrenics rarely have that concern.

5. They serve no apparent purpose. Schizophrenic hallucinations sometimes act as an agent of the conscience, pronouncing judgment. Organic hallucinations have no context.

6. They are usually of recent onset. There is not a long history of unusual behavior or hallucinations (Currey, 1982).

"Normal" Hallucinations

The third category of hallucinations consists of those that are unrelated to psychosis and have no apparent medical underpinnings. They are simply innocuous experiences that, although occasionally startling, are not cause for concern.

The most common normal hallucinations are called hypnogogic hallucinations. These occur in the drowsy interval between waking and sleep. To be more specific, hypnapompic hallucinations occur while waking and hypnogogic hallucinations occur before falling asleep. They are usually visual, although they may also be tactile or auditory, and they are usually well-formed objects that appear to be coming toward the person.

> When I woke up there were elephants dancing on the walls. I watched them for a few minutes—they were pretty interesting—then they faded away.
>
> There was a red fluorescent glow hovering around the room. I woke and saw it was a frog—suspended in the air. At the moment, it seemed perfectly normal. I woke up my wife, who is getting used to these nighttime

incidents, got up, found something to hit it with, but it started going out the door and disappeared. After a few seconds I realized it wasn't real.

They may initially be frightening, but they do not indicate a serious physical problem. In fact, some investigators (who probably experience them) suggest that they are common and related to good mental health! There are, however, some physical problems which can produce these hallucinations. Hypnogogic hallucinations may suggest narcolepsy, in which case they are accompanied by sleep attacks, sleep paralysis, and cataplexy (see Sleep Disorders), yet narcolepsy is treated more by common sense than by medical intervention. Also, some drugs have been implicated in hypnopompic hallucinations. Schlauch (1979) reports on a sixty-one-year-old woman who developed hallucinations after taking imipramine, an antidepressant, and the hallucinations stopped immediately after discontinuing the medication.

> She began to waken about once a night, between 2 and 4 A.M. Initially, she saw her bedroom bathed in a red glow, although she knew it should be dark. She saw one to three people around the room, dressed in white. Some were strangers and others were known to her.
>
> She became quite frightened when these figures came toward her, and she would close her eyes. . . . Once, she spoke to her husband in Polish "so that they wouldn't understand me."

Other causes for hallucinations in normal individuals include sensory deprivation, intense emotional experiences, and sleep loss. Sleep loss has long been associated with hallucinations. Transient hallucinations may appear after two to three days of sleep deprivation, and prolonged episodes may occur after five to ten days. These hallucinations, however, are clearly distinguishable from the schizophrenic variety as they are usually meaningless, visual, transient images.

Intense emotion is a less known cause of hallucinations, but they are not unusual in counseling. I have seen three girls, who had no acquaintance with each other, who experienced hallucinations soon after being sexually mistreated by a relative. Curiously, two of the girls saw "shadows" in the form of a male adult. These shadows would watch them do their homework from a corner of a room; they would be just over the girls' shoulders—barely in view—when they walked home from school. With all three girls, the hallucinations subsided. With one, however, they persisted for over a year.

Another example of hallucinations that are neither schizophrenic nor organic is a report on a thirty-one-year-old woman who, after her father died when she was fourteen, had been promiscuous, had two illegitimate babies, and had been a vagabond for several years. You might find it interesting that her husband indicated that she was psychic.

> She had begun "to see a woman carrying two babies" who was bothering her. . . . "I heard something scratch on the screen on the window, and I looked over that way, and here comes this lady with two children . . . and I said 'Oh Lord, I must be dreaming,' so I slapped myself on the face, you know, and she said, 'No, you are not dreaming . . . I've come after you. . . .'"
>
> "[The woman] she's got a v-shaped face and almond eyes, and she's got two sharp teeth and just a little bit of hair and sharp pointed ears." The lady held two babies, and when one of the babies opened his mouth, "out of his mouth came another head like his. Out of that head came little snake-like things with little heads like the big ones." The lady's name was Lucicer— "not Lucifer because I called her Lucifer and she told me never to confuse her name like that again." (Fitzgerald & Wells, 1977, p. 382)

For the inexperienced, hallucinations in any sensory modality mean you should get consultation. If, however, you have opportunities to see many persons with schizophrenic symptoms, you will recognize the distinctive nature of psychotic hallucinations, and you may refer these hallucinators only to be evaluated for psychiatric medication. But play it safe. Hallucinations should first indicate to you an organic and not psychological problem.

Impotence, Frigidity, and Other Sexual Disorders

Open discussion of sexual problems continues to be a counseling taboo. Counselors are reluctant to ask questions, and counselees are usually hesitant to raise the subject—especially if they see the counselor outside the counseling office. Many Christian counselors prefer to play it safe and discuss only the standard marital problems packet: communication principles, marital roles, and finances. Sexual dysfunctions, however, are surprisingly common.

Most sexual dysfunctions are nonorganic, and they are treated with accurate data on sexuality and relationships in an explicitly biblical framework. Yet up to 20 percent of sexual dysfunctions may be solely a result of treatable physical problems (Kaplan, 1974). It is these physical problems that are our focus of interest.[6]

To most people, sexual dysfunction is synonymous with frigidity in women and impotence in men, but the words frigidity and impotence tell us very little. Both words, in popular as well as professional usage, are used erratically. For example, most people agree that impotence is an impairment of penile erection, but the exact nature of the impairment is unspecified. Impotence may refer to any of these conditions:

—Loss of sexual interest
—Inability to achieve an erection whenever the spouse is sexually interested
—Premature ejaculation
—Retarded ejaculation
—Erection but no ejaculation
—Ejaculation but no erection
—Inability to obtain or maintain a firm erection

Likewise, frigidity is also unclear. Among husbands, it often means that the sexual desire of their wives does not match their own (a definition of selfishness or *machismo*, not frigidity). But it also refers to any of the following:

—No sexual desire
—Muscle spasms around the vagina that may prevent intercourse (vaginismus)
—No orgasms
—Orgasms only in certain situations or after very lengthy stimulation

In order to have more concise distinctions among these symptoms, think in terms of two overlapping systems of nomenclature for sexual dysfunctions: (1) disorders of desire, excitement, and orgasm, and (2) functional/organic. That is, each phase of a sexual relationship—desire, excitement, and orgasm—can be disrupted by problems that range from functional to organic. Most of these problems will fall within the functional end of the continuum, some will be organic and others will be both.

Male Sexual Dysfunction

From the chronological perspective of desire, excitement, and orgasm, the most common male sexual dysfunctions are as follows:

Changes in sexual desire. The key to detecting organic problems is whether or not there has been an uncharacteristic or unwarranted change from a previous level of functioning. Therefore, if a man has always been uninterested in sex or chronically had a low level of desire, there is no reason for alarm if his wife mentions his low sexual interest. Certainly, there may be significant counseling issues, but they are unlikely to be organic. Those who had an active sexual interest and suddenly, for no apparent reason, have little or no interest are the ones who have possible organic problems. This does not mean definite organic problems, but it does mean that these men should consult their GP or internist. Drugs, temporal lobe dysfunction, and head injuries are some of the known causes of changes in sexual desire (see Table 9.4).

Desire	Excitement	Orgasm
No or decreased sexual interest	Erectile dysfunction	Premature ejaculation, retarded ejaculation, or no ejaculation

Changes in erection. Impotence, or problems with erection, tends to be the most common male sexual concern. In this culture, masculinity is still tied to sexual "performance." Therefore, affected men are usually very concerned with anything that hints of impotence.

Impotence can refer to a variety of different symptoms. Some men believe that they are impotent when they can have good erections, but the erections are inconsistent or occur at times other than during sexual intimacy. This is not organic impotence. The best question to ask these men is, "Do you *ever* have an erection?" Or, more specifically, "Do you ever have an erection when you wake up?" If the answer is "yes, " the man is most likely experiencing a problem that is functional rather than organic. If there is actual organic impotence, you will find that the person has probably functioned well in the past but is presently having either a less firm or no erection. Furthermore, there are *never* any times when he sustains a full erection. This condition can be referred to a urologist.

Both organic and functional impotence can have a variety of causes. Some of the organic causes are summarized in Table 9.4. The list of possible functional causes is even longer. To discover them, you simply have to gather specific data in different areas: the quality of the relationship, "performance" pressures (which are increasingly common in our society which emphasizes sexual performance), historical baggage in the form of sexual attitudes and experiences, and biblical understanding

Table 9.4. Medical Conditions That Can Affect Sexual Desire
or Response in Males and Females

Drugs	Alcohol, barbiturates, sedatives, anti-anxiety drugs, antipsychotics such as Haldol and Mellaril, narcotics, antihypertensives, anticholinergics such as Cogentin.
Liver disease	Cirrhosis, hepatitis, mononucleosis
Endocrine disorder	Diabetes, hypothyroid, acromegaly, Cushing's disease, hypopituitary, any disease that affects testosterone levels (e.g., Kleinfelder's Syndrome)
Neurological disease	ALS, nerve damage viasurgery, multiple sclerosis, temporal or frontal lobe dysfunction, epilepsy
Surgical conditions (female)	Poor episiotomy, poor hysterectomy, obstetrical trauma, removal of ovaries and adrenals
Conditions that cause pain on intercourse (Female)	Imperforate hymen, infection, herpes, allergy to spermacides or vaginal deodorants, endometreosis, ovarian tumor or cyst, prolapsed uterus, tender surgical scars, and insufficient lubrication
(Male)	Herpes, prostatitis, genital spasms that cause pain after ejaculation, inflammation of the testicles, and post-ejaculatory headache

of sexuality. As the nonorganic cause becomes apparent, biblical counselors should be able to handle these problems.

Changes in orgasm. Men can have normal desire and erection but have changes in their orgasms. The most common culprits here are drugs and older age. Drugs such as the antipsychotics can affect the nervous system in such a way that, of the different parts of the sexual response, only orgasm is affected. Age is not a treatable medical problem but it does have an effect on orgasm. Although older men can certainly be sexually active, even men in their late thirties will probably notice that they need longer time between orgasms and have decreased ejaculate volume.

Female Sexual Dysfunction

Females tend to have fewer organic sexual dysfunctions than males. The male sexual response is physiologically more complex—there are more places where something can go wrong—and it is therefore more susceptible to physical problems. The female sexual response, on the other hand, is surprisingly tolerant of physical problems that affect men.

For example, diabetes, a notorious culprit in male sexual dysfunction, rarely affects the female response. Likewise, age, which affects the ejaculatory power and period between ejaculations in men (refractory period), again seems to have little effect on female sexual functioning. Yet, whereas males tend to be more frequently affected by physical problems, females are more susceptible to functional causes. Female sexual function is more fragile in the face of a poor marital relationship, a difficult sexual history, or guilt. Unlike males, who are notorious for being sexually excited with little provocation, healthy females usually need, at least, a satisfactory relationship and a longer "warm-up" period to respond sexually.

Changes in desire. With females, the chronological distinctions of desire, excitement, and orgasm are very useful. In disorders of desire, often called frigidity, women simply have little or no interest in sexual intimacy, and they may actually work diligently to avoid it. Other women with little or no desire may quietly endure a sexual relationship out of duty or in order to preserve the marriage. Although there are some medical illnesses and drugs that can affect sexual desire, the predominant causes are functional; for example, fears of losing control, of intimacy, failing to perform, pain, rejection, and childbirth; anger and power struggles; embarrassment; and guilt from previous sexual relationships.

Changes in excitement. The excitement phase, analogous to erection in males, physiologically consists of clitoral and vaginal vasodilation (engorgement with blood), and vaginal lubrication. Unlike males and their more physiologically complex excitement phase, females rarely have dysfunction in this phase. More likely, disorders of excitement or arousal are related to problems of sexual desire.

Changes in orgasm. Orgastic dysfunction is easily separated from disorders of desire and excitement. Whereas the excitement phase consists of vasodilation, orgasm is a genital reflex that leads to a contraction of the genital muscles. Also, women can be sexually unresponsive but still experience orgasm, or they may be sexually responsive but inorgasmic. Orgastic dysfunction is a common phenomenon that has many varieties: the woman may have never experienced orgasm, she may have experienced it only in the distant past, perhaps premaritally; or she may only have orgasms under very specific conditions and not during coitus. There are some medical problems that raise the threshold for the orgastic reflex. For example, antidepressants, anti-anxiety drugs, and antipsychotics are known offenders (Segraves, 1988). However, the problem is infrequently organic and is very amenable to change.

Vaginismus. One category that does not fit neatly into those described is vaginismus. Vaginismus is an involuntary spasm of the muscles surrounding the vaginal entrance, thus making intercourse impossible. Even medical examinations of the vagina are difficult, and some women must be anesthetized prior to a gynecological exam. Not surprisingly, these women avoid coitus. But they do not necessarily avoid intercourse because of lack of desire, excitement, or ability to have orgasm. Indeed, most women with vaginismus are sexually responsive and can have orgasms, as long as sexual activity excludes coitus. The difficulty is that intercourse is painful for these women.

Although vaginismus is clearly a very distressing problem for both spouses, it is also very treatable. Most approaches are twofold: biblically address any underlying problems, and, with the advice of a gynecologist, suggest that the vaginal opening needs to become accustomed to penetration. This can be accomplished in the privacy of their home, as either husband or wife gently inserts catheters of gradually increasing size into the vagina.

Sleep Disorders

Sleep has been an object of speculation and interest throughout recorded history. It is a time of rest and peace, a time of potential danger, a time that can be abused by either ignoring it or loving it (Pr 20:13), and a euphemism for death.[7] The Roman poet Ovid called sleep the "counterfeit of death" (Borbely, 1986). During sleep, however, there is a lot happening: hallucinations, dreams, sleepwalking, and constant brain activity. Futhermore, since the discovery of the electroencephalograph (EEG) by the German neurologist Hans Berger in the 1920s, sleep has been a burgeoning area of research.

Normal Sleep

Sleep is part of the cyclical rhythms found throughout creation. Years, months, seasons, days and nights—these are the created world's analogs to our daily biological rhythms.

The major breakthrough in sleep research was the realization, by way of EEG monitoring, that there were two distinct types of sleep, quiet and active. Active sleep is called REM, because of its characteristic rapid eye movements. Quiet sleep, called non-REM (NREM), consists of four stages that are thought to be restful with slow and regular brain waves and no rapid eye movements.

Sleep normally begins with stage 1 NREM. This stage may include slowly rolling eyes, dreamlike hallucinations, and occasionally a sudden, muscular jerk. Stage 2, sometimes considered the first real sleep stage, is only distinct from stage 1 because of increased voltage activity on the EEG. About fifteen to thirty minutes later, stages 3 and 4 begin. These stages, characterized by slower and larger brain waves, together last about an hour; then the sleeper moves back into stage 2 and almost immediately into REM. The REM stage lasts for about ten to fifteen minutes during which time dreaming takes place. (Dreaming may occur in other stages, but it is most characteristic of REM.) After the short REM period, the ninety-minute NREM/REM cycle is repeated. Therefore, a person will usually go through four or five cycles each night.

This pattern varies with age. The younger adult tends to sleep, on the average, seven to nine hours each night and can manage to fall asleep within five to twenty minutes. This norm, however, does not fit everyone, especially those at the ends of the age spectrum. The newborn and young child sleep much longer and spend proportionately more time in REM sleep. The older adult sleeps less, has more frequent awakenings, and has proportionately less REM sleep. Some older persons can be very upset about insomnia when they simply need to be reassured that they have a decreased need for sleep.

Seven to nine hours is only the average, and there are many exceptions to the rule. Twenty percent of the population sleep less than six hours per night, 10 percent sleep more than nine hours, 4 percent sleep less than five or more than ten. An Australian study found a seventy-year-old nurse who claimed to sleep about an hour a night. In a sleep laboratory, she averaged sixty-seven minutes per night over five nights with no naps or significant tiredness during the day (Meddis, Pearson & Langford, 1973). Not surprisingly, this woman, and others who have shorter sleep rhythms, tend to view the rest of us as lazy. They may be right, but laziness cannot be determined simply by the amount of time spent in sleep.

Sleep's innate biological rhythm can be stretched but not significantly changed. Also, it is fairly sensitive. It does not like shift work, changes in time zones, or irregular hours. There are reports of some persons who have learned, in laboratory settings, to reduce their sleep by one to two hours, but most of us, once we hit our biological pace, remain within narrow parameters.

To help answer the question "Are you getting enough (or too much) sleep?" the American Medical Association asks these additional questions:

—Do you need an alarm clock to waken you? Do you have a hard time getting up? Do you drop off easily in front of the television, at concerts, or at meetings? Do you habitually sleep in during weekends? If so, you may be getting too little sleep.

—Do you lie in bed long after the lights are out? There are many reasons for this, but it is possible that you simply don't need as much sleep as you think. (Dement, Frazier & Weitzman, 1984)[8]

Insomnia

Insomniacs are people who experience poor sleep at night with unpleasant consequences during the day. They may chronically report, "I didn't sleep a wink last night." This is technically inaccurate because no sleep, even for a few nights, is very rare. Yet there is no denying that difficulties sleeping color the entire lives of insomniacs, and their complaints are not to be overlooked.

Some insomnia is normal. Stress, shift changes, naps—many events can lead to transient insomnia. And some persons will just have to accept that they are not champion sleepers. Yet when there is a chronic problem getting to sleep, waking often throughout the night, and awakening very early, there are causes that can often be identified and corrected.

Some of these causes can be combatted by increasingly sophisticated medical treatments for insomnia, but the first line of attack consists of practical advice that comes out of recent sleep research (Dement, Frazier & Weitzman, 1984).

Keep a regular schedule. Try to go to bed and get up around the same time each day. And, as a rule, avoid sporadic napping. The best way to anchor your sleeping schedule is to get up at the same time every day, regardless of when you go to bed. For retired persons or those with few responsibilities, it means they must find something that is worth getting up for!

Deal biblically with worry or an overloaded schedule. Worry is certainly a key issue in insomnia. When the lights go out our minds can race, trying to solve the problems of the day. Or we can obsess over the tasks that are undone. Often these issues can be whittled down to unbelief in God's love and sovereignty, fear of failure, or simply being over-scheduled.

One of the better-known insomniacs was Martin Luther. When he began his lengthy controversy with the Roman church, he was still a monk and obligated to perform all daily monastery duties as well as prepare for university lectures, debate with the church's best, and live with the realization that he was going against the church. This proved to be too much. He gradually got behind in saying the required prayers from the prayer book, and, in an attempt to get "caught up," went three days without food or drink. This was followed by five painful, sleepless nights. After a sedative and a period of recovery, he fell behind in his prayers over three months. Then he took his first step away from the traditions of the church. He gave up the prayer book. As such, it might be argued, somewhat tongue-in-cheek, that insomnia was a significant cause of the Protestant Reformation.

But Luther didn't learn from his temporary reprieve from insomnia. After leaving the church, he continued with the same breakneck pace, and was an insomniac throughout his life. (See Bainton, 1950, p. 152)

Pay attention to what, and when, you eat. Avoid coffee, tea, colas, and other caffeinated drinks. They have their peak effectiveness within two hours but they may have a continued effect for up to seven hours. Also, avoid large dinners right before bed. A full, uncomfortable stomach may make sleeping difficult.

Exercise regularly, preferably in the late afternoon. Vigorous exercise before bed tends to be arousing and should be avoided. By contrast, if there is no exercise during the day, sleep is less sound.

Create a bedtime ritual. This is especially useful for children. A warm bath, a good book, reviewing the day—anything that will allow you to wind down an hour or so before bedtime can be helpful. Be careful about books, however. A thriller or thought-provoking book may be too stimulating.

Use your bedroom for sleep (and sex). If your bedroom is the place you argue, do your taxes, or watch exciting TV, it may become a stressful place and not conducive to rapid onset of sleep.

Avoid drugs and alcohol. These are the most typical culprits in disturbed sleep. Alcohol may help you relax and fall asleep more quickly, but the price will be paid in early awakenings and more shallow sleep.

Smoking continues to be high on the taboo list: it is a stimulant, and smokers run the risk of falling asleep with a cigarette still lit. Street drugs such as amphetamines, cocaine, and LSD are notorious offenders. If a teen has a recent unexplainable insomnia, street drugs must be considered.

Prescription and over-the-counter drugs, even when used as directed, are often singled out as the cause of disrupted sleep. If your insomnia coincided with starting a new medicine, then you should check with your physician.[9] Paradoxically, the class of drugs most commonly implicated in disturbed sleep are sleeping pills! Prescription sleeping pills include the benzodiazepines (Dalmane, Restoril, Halcion, Valium, Ativan) and the infrequently used barbiturates (Amytal, Nembutal). In some circumstances, they may be useful for short periods of time. But people usually develop tolerance to their effectiveness, and they gradually increase the dose, many times developing a physical dependence. Also, sleeping pills tend to disrupt the deep stage 3 and 4 sleep, and they often lead to daytime tiredness.

If you have been taking sleep medication for over a month and your sleep is disrupted or you are taking a high dose, you should consult with your physician. Your physician may supervise a gradual withdrawal from the pills in order to minimize withdrawal symptoms. Don't be surprised if sleep may initially get worse. Some people experience "rebound insomnia," but over the course of a week or two it will improve.

Over-the-counter sleep aids such as Nytol, Sleep-Eze, Sominex, and Compoz are no better than the prescription pills. There is evidence that they are ineffective in inducing sleep, and they can have potentially deleterious side effects.

Keep your room dark, well ventilated, and at a comfortable temperature.

Block out noise, especially noise that is sporadic or unpredictable. Soundproofing with heavy curtains, rugs, insulated windows and doors is often helpful. If you still can't dampen the noise from your neighbor's stereo, consider "masking" the noise with continuous, personally meaningless sound such as air conditioners, fans, or "mood" music such as gentle breezes and waves lapping on the shore.

Don't worry about it. At the risk of sounding glib, no one ever died from lack of sleep. In fact, some depressed persons actually benefit from sleep deprivation (Gillin, 1983). At worst, the effect is similar to missing a meal or two—it is uncomfortable but not life threatening. If your body really must have sleep, you will sleep.

The horror stories associated with lack of sleep tend to be sensationalized. It is true that some people can have unusual experiences with sleep loss. For example, Charles Lindbergh reportedly conversed with "ghosts" on his transatlantic flight. But hallucinatory or psychotic experiences are very rare. Tyler (1955) found such changes in only seven of 350 persons who were kept awake for 112 hours, and these changes were temporary and did not interfere with most everyday activities. Also, these persons, as well as those in similar reports, were sleep-deprived individuals and not insomniacs.

Certainly, changes in mood occur fairly consistently with sleep loss. Fatigue, irritability, and poor concentration are frequent complaints. But these complaints are neither life-threatening nor significant detriments to work and social functioning.

Insomnia and Depression

Sleep and depression are intimately related. Up to 90 percent of depressed persons report decreased sleep (Nelson & Charney, 1980). This connection led some physicians in the early 1900s to induce continuous sleep with barbiturates for two to four weeks (Mendelson, 1987). The treatment was not effective, but it did pave the way for the very active area of modern sleep research in depression.

The current research, however, is taking an opposite approach. Instead of artificially inducing sleep, experimenters are prolonging wakefulness. This can take different forms such as skipping a night's sleep, waking earlier, or going to bed later. At this point it is clear that some people have a significant positive change in their experience of depression after these treatments, but the changes may be brief, lasting only twenty-four hours.

Other treatments for depression-related sleep problems include standard fare such as counseling and antidepressant medication.

If sleep problems persist when depression does not appear to be a significant factor, and the guidelines above have been followed, there are possible physical problems to consider.

Excessive Daytime Sleepiness (EDS)

The most common treatable cause of excessive sleepiness (the result of insomnia) is called sleep apnea. It simply means "no breath" and is characterized by snoring, restlessness during sleep, daytime tiredness, and a host of other symptoms such as difficulty concentrating, personality changes, headaches, and even impotence.

Sleep apnea has two different forms. Upper airway or obstructive apnea is a result of airway blockage and is distinguished by almost violent snoring. Central apnea occurs when the airway remains open but the diaphragm and chest muscles stop working. It can occur even when snoring is absent.

> Don is thirty-two years old and has snored loudly since he was four. Recently, the snoring has become much more persistent. Don's wife relates that he must make a supreme effort to breathe. He perspires so heavily that he drenches the sheets. In the morning, she often finds him sitting or kneeling on the side of the bed. Don falls asleep while visiting friends and even at work. His personality has changed, too. Previously, his wife notes, "He had a wide range of interests; he could converse intelligently on a myriad of topics and had a quick wit and a good sense of humor. Now his interests have greatly diminished; he no longer converses easily. He often simply does not think about anything and seems actually depressed much of the time." (Dement, Frazier, & Weitzman, 1984, p. 159)

In the more common obstructive apnea, snoring is usually the first apparent symptom and can date back to early childhood. It is loud, suddenly interrupted by silence, then followed by gasping until normal breathing begins. This pattern may recur hundreds of times throughout the night, but the episodes are rarely remembered. People just feel like they had a bad night's sleep.

The snoring may precede psychological symptoms by as much as twenty years. These new symptoms are usually the result of sustained low levels of oxygen in the brain and the resultant global deterioration. Personality changes, intellectual decline, hallucinations, and decreased interest in sex are the most notable counseling-related symptoms. Other symptoms include morning headaches, bedwetting (especially if a person has been a non-bedwetter for years), sleepwalking, and poor memory for certain events.

The treatment for sleep apnea runs the gamut from changes in diet to surgery, so consultation with a good neurologist is necessary. Non-invasive treatments include the following: avoid depressants such as alcohol and tranquilizers, don't smoke, elevate the head during sleep, and lose weight. More technical interventions include medication, corrective surgery to enlarge an upper airway tract, and, in extreme, intractable cases, permanent tracheostomy. For central sleep apnea there are also a host of possible treatments. Weight loss, avoiding respiratory suppressants such as alcohol and tranquilizers, and sleeping on one's side rather than one's back are the nonmedical treatments. Medication and a pacemaker-like device for the diaphragm are also available.

The other relatively common cause of excessive sleepiness is narcolepsy. Characterized by unpredictable sleep "attacks," lasting usually fifteen minutes or less, narcolepsy is as common as multiple sclerosis. (I have often been amazed at the unusually high percentage of narcoleptics in my classes!) It is easily mistaken for laziness, but the sleep attacks of narcolepsy tend to be unavoidable and unresponsive to cold showers, keen interest, or exercise.

Frequently, especially in the later stages, narcoleptic sleep attacks occur with a triad of other symptoms. Cataplexy is diagnostically the most significant. Cataplexy has been called the "marionette syndrome" because it results in sudden muscle weakness that is akin to a marionette with its strings cut. It is usually triggered by strong emotions, from elation to anger, and it can result in a range of muscular responses from complete collapse to subtle muscle weakness or twitching.

Other components of narcolepsy include hypnagogic hallucinations (see section on hallucinations) and sleep paralysis. Sleep paralysis is simply the sense that, upon waking, you cannot move. You are immobile—completely paralyzed. This frightening experience usually lasts only a few seconds, but it may continue for up to twenty minutes. When it lasts longer, it has a Sleeping Beauty look to it—the affected person can be aroused by touching or speaking.

> During the intensely hot summer of 1825, I experienced an attack of this affection. Immediately after dining, I threw myself on my back upon a sofa, and, before I was aware, was seized with difficult respiration, extreme dread, and utter incapability of motion or speech. I could neither move nor cry, while breath came from my chest with suffocating paroxysms. During all this time I was perfectly awake . . . judgment was never for a moment suspended. . . . The fit did not continue above minutes: by degrees I recovered the use of sense and motion; and, as soon as they were sofar restored as to enable me to call out and move my limbs, it wore insensibly away. (Mendelson, 1987, p. 223)

Although hypnagogic hallucinations and sleep paralysis are occasionally found in people without narcolepsy, excessive tiredness, sleeping at inappropriate times, and cataplexy must alert you to the probability of narcolepsy. More definitive diagnosis can be made by the growing number of sleep centers that exist at many major hospitals.

Narcolepsy is caused by an apparent reversal of the NREM/REM cycle. Instead of going first to NREM stages and then to REM, narcoleptics tend to go immediately into REM sleep. Hence, their occasional hallucinations are closely related to REM dreams.

Treatment consists of good sleep habits, regular naps, and in more extreme cases, stimulant drugs. Counseling is also a necessary "treatment" in some cases. Job-related problems are commonplace, as are automobile accidents. Some states place driving restrictions on those who have lapses of consciousness, and employers may be intolerant of a worker's need for multiple naps. These and other issues related to the narcolepsy are important areas for discussion.

Other Disorders Related to Sleep

There are other interesting sleep problems that have little or no medical significance, but they may emerge in counseling situations.

Sleepwalking occurs fairly often in children, less often in adults. The basic treatment is to steer the person back to bed (if he or she has gotten up) and create an environment that would protect the sleepwalker from injury.

Bed-wetting is the most common of childhood sleep problems. At age four, up to 40 percent of children still wet their beds; at age nine, 7 percent; at age 12, 3 percent. Even in adulthood it is not terribly uncommon. The disorder usually runs in families and improves with age. The course may be expedited by taking the child to the bathroom before going to bed, allowing the child to clean up after himself or herself, and having night lights. Some people suggest bladder-stretching exercises or "wetness alarms" that are available in larger stores. In some instances, there is a treatable medical dysfunction that underlies the bedwetting. Therefore, when in doubt, check with your physician.

Tremors, Tics, and Other Changes in Body Movement

Although people do not come to counselors for problems with bodily movements, uncharacteristic involuntary movements can be early symptoms of brain diseases that underlie depression, anxiety, or other counseling problems. As noted in chapters 3 and 4, apart from simple reflexes, bodily movements start in the brain, not the muscles. The frontal lobes, subcortical areas, and cerebellum are particularly influential. When these areas are subtly disrupted, changes in body movement can be a useful warning sign.

An obvious example of the diagnostic usefulness of movement disorders is alcohol intoxication. Long before one is close enough to smell someone's breath, the casual observer, even a child, can spot those who are inebriated. Their staggering gait gives them away. Movement disorders are so helpful in detecting drunkenness that before the advent of the breath-a-lyzer, police identified drunk drivers by having them walk in a straight line. The implicit assumption was that toxic substances that alter brain activity also affect movement. Counselors can make use of the same principles.

It is unfortunate that people who have spastic cerebral palsy sometimes suffer harassment and misunderstanding when police officers mistake their awkward gait as an indication of inebriation.

Tremors

Tremors are usually classified as action tremors or resting tremors. Action tremors, also called intention tremors, are rhythmic, involuntary movements that are apparent during purposeful action and typically cease during rest. They usually affect the hands, sometimes the feet, occasionally the limbs. As such, they might be evident when reaching out to shake hands or signing a name to a check.

There are quite a few medical problems that produce action tremors. Of particular importance to counselors are tremors associated with psychoactive drugs and alcohol abuse. With psychoactive drugs such as lithium or tricyclic antidepressants, action tremors mean that affected persons must be medically reevaluated. The medications may be toxic or cause unwanted side effects. With alcohol, action tremors mean that there has been a long history of abuse that is affecting overall health.

Other medical problems that have been known to produce action tremors include hyperthyroidism, cerebellar tumors or strokes, syphilis, multiple sclerosis, and Wilson's disease. All these diseases can affect intellect and mood.

Wilson's disease is probably the only new disease on this list. It is a rare, inherited disorder of copper metabolism that is characterized by resting tremors, action tremors, poor coordination, intellectual changes, writhing movements, and other unusual movements. At times the tremor is so dramatic that it is called a *flapping tremor* because it looks as if people are "beating their wings." It is noteworthy to counselors because the majority of cases begin as personality or intellectual decline.

The onset of the disease is usually in childhood or adolescence, but it may be delayed even until the fifties. If left untreated the disease cripples, produces dementia, and ends in death.

Action tremors are not always indicators of medical disease. They may be present with excessive fear or worry, or they may be unrelated to counseling or medical problems. In these cases they are called benign, familial, hereditary, essential, or senile tremors. Medically they are insignificant. However, they may be a source of embarrassment, and people with benign tremors have been known to drink alcohol in order to suppress them.

Resting tremors, as their name indicates, appear when the limbs are at rest, and they sometimes disappear during intended movement. These tremors are best known as a symptom of Parkinson's disease and a side effect of antipsychotic medication. They can also occur with old age and Alzheimer's disease.

Although resting and action tremors may be medically insignificant, unless they are experienced only for a short time and are obviously related to fear or anxiety, they should be medically evaluated.

Tics: Tourette Syndrome

Children usually demonstrate occasional, odd bodily movements, habits, spasms, or tics during their preteen years. These spasms might consist of brief acts that once served some purpose. Perhaps a grimace or unusual body movement coincided with parental attention. If so, children can subtly relate the two events as cause and effect; that is, the grimace causes attention, and the movement can become an ongoing habit. These are best handled by either ignoring the behavior or noticing when the habit was initially paired with a particular circumstance and offering the child another perspective of the event. Whatever the case, these tics are common and of little concern.

When these habit spasms continue for over a year, however, they may indicate the emergence of a group of symptoms that together are called Tourette syndrome (TS).

When Robert was twelve, his mother noticed that he started shaking his hair out of his eyes repeatedly. She took him for a haircut, but he didn't stop shaking his head. Then Robert's mother noticed that when he was reading he rested his chin on his chest or shoulder oddly. A physician suggested that he was suffering from stress from a recent automobile accident. Then he started blinking and rolling his eyes frequently. An ophthalmologist said his eyes were fine. He began sniffing and clearing his throat, even though it wasn't the right time of year for his allergies. "Suddenly I realized that I saw Robert doing things my father and uncle had done, and I felt something just wasn't right," said Robert's mother.

After being alerted to Tourette's by a television program, she took her son to two physicians. Both proclaimed him fit and without Tourette's. The diagnosis was finally established by a pediatric neurologist.

Thinking back, Robert's mother realized that Robert was a perfectionist (compulsive) even at age one and a half, when he lined up teddy bears in his crib—just so—before sleeping. In school, this translated into constant erasing, rewriting, and ripping up imperfect papers. (Dyan, 1988)

First described by the French physician Gilles de Tourette in 1885, the syndrome is a movement disorder that begins between the ages of two and sixteen and lasts throughout life. It is characterized by distinctive body tics, but it might also include noises and vocalizations. Body tics usually appear first and include rapid eye-blinking, facial twitches, or other movements of the face, torso, or limbs. Noises and inarticulate sounds often follow. They include repeated sniffing, throat-clearing, coughing, grunting, and imitating the movements of others. Curiously, some of these behaviors are only apparent when they are forbidden!

People with TS rarely demonstrate all these symptoms. Most will exhibit symptoms that wax and wane with varying degrees of intensity. Also, with practice, some of the symptoms can be postponed, substituted, or controlled. At work or in important social situations, the more severe symptoms are subject to some control. Most people, however, indicate that control takes considerable energy and concentration, and it comes with the sense of increased inner tension. Subsequently, symptoms may emerge even more explosively in a friendly setting where control is not as important.

The cause of TS is unknown. No clear biological markers have been found. Most people, however, presume that it is a neurological condition. To support this, researchers cite both evidence that it runs in families and PET scans that suggest abnormalities in the basal ganglia, the general area that is affected in Parkinson's disease. Yet, at present a cure is nowhere in sight.

But like the medical approaches to psychiatric problems such as schizophrenia or depression, lack of a cure does not mean that the unwanted symptoms are unresponsive to medication. There are medications that suppress TS. Interestingly, the most common drug is Haldol, a popular antipsychotic.[10] Yet people with TS are split as to whether this is actually a treatment or not. Many persons refuse the medication because of the unwanted side effects, especially mental and physical sluggishness. These people prefer the tics and the enhanced energy levels to feeling doped. Others find a middle ground. They use drugs during times when tics are socially undesirable and they "let fly" and avoid medication during vacations and weekends.

From a biblical perspective, the vocalizations of TS are cause for reflection. If Tourette's is a neurological problem, as some people suggest, can a bodily problem lead to "involuntary" profanity? This is complicated by differences in a biblical perspective on profanity. Some Bible students suggest that much of modern profanity is not forbidden by the third commandment, "You shall not misuse the name of the LORD your God." However, it is safe to say that profanity is rarely encouraging or edifying. It usually points to a heart that is angry or impatient. Therefore, it seems to be more related to the heart than the body and can be controlled. And with this, the secular research agrees (at least in the case studies). Everyone agrees that "stress, " at least, aggravates Tourette symptoms. Obscenities and other behaviors usually occur in social situations; they are less frequent when affected persons are resting and alone. For example, Creak and Guttman (1935) described a boy whose obscenities were apparent only when he was teased in school. In another case, they describe a girl whose symptoms were only grunts and sniffs. After two illegitimate pregnancies, however, she peppered her Tourette's vocalizations with obscene sexual language. Likewise, Kurland (1965), another investigator, described two girls whose obscene language was apparently related to their poor relationships with their mothers.

Tourette syndrome is not a life-threatening problem. It does not affect life span or overall physical health. But it certainly raises counseling issues. Foremost is the embarrassment caused by some symptoms. Persons unaware of the involuntary nature of the problems can be quite cruel, especially in school. Affected persons can respond by lashing out, withdrawing, or finding personal meaning in their symptoms.

These responses are certainly amenable to biblical refining. The other symptoms, the occasional profanity or disruptive noises in church, must be handled wisely. Counselors and pastors must be careful when they draw lines between sin and sickness.[11]

Abnormal Gait

Ordinary walking is no easy task. It demands coordination of a number of body movements and balance. Consequently, it can be disrupted by quite a few different brain problems.

Rather than memorizing a long series of diseases associated with abnormal gait, an easier method would be to recognize normal walking. Notice the size of steps, speed, how far apart the feet are, and arm swing. If you notice peculiarities in a person's gait, ask him or her about it. Is it different from a previous level of performance? If so, encourage the person to have a medical examination.

One disease which is rare but worth noting is called normal pressure hydrocephalus. As its name suggests, this disorder is characterized by normal pressure within the cerebrospinal fluid of the brain, but the ventricles are enlarged. Therefore, there is probably too much water ("hydro") in the brain ("cephalus"). Normal pressure hydrocephalus appears around age fifty and is characterize by three different symptoms: depression or intellectual decline, loss of bladder control, and difficulties walking.

Notes

Headaches

1. Cluster headache is usually fairly easy to diagnose, but it can be confused with trigeminal neuralgia, temporal arteritis, pheochromocytoma, and Raeder's paratrigeminal syndrome (Kudrow, 1983).

2. Other potential physical causes of headaches include meningitis or another central nervous system infection, angioma, aneurysm, subdural hematoma, temporal arteritis, trauma, and mitral valve prolaspe (Amat et al., 1982).

Hallucinations

3. Illusions are usually visual and organically based. Some physical causes for illusions include drugs, delirium, visual problems, vascular disease, epilepsy, and brain tumors.

4. Nonorganic hallucinations are also common in severe depression and mania. Up to 80 percent of people with a depressive psychosis experience auditory

hallucinations (Lowe, 1973). Also, in depression there may be mood-congruent hallucinations of death, decay, and personal filth. I recall one article that mentions a peculiar taste hallucination that can occur after the death of a loved one.

5. Some of the typical offenders of toxic hallucinosis include alcohol, atropine derivatives, phenothiazines, digoxin, sodium bromides, quinine, and corticosteroids.

Sexual Disorders

6. Many of the comments in this section are from Helen Kaplan's two books *The New Sex Therapy* (1974) and *Disorders of Sexual Desire* (1979). These books have a psychoanalytic orientation yet their discussions of treatment techniques are especially valuable. If marital counseling is going to be the bulk of your counseling work, these books would be worthwhile to read and have as a reference.

Sleep and Sleep Disorders

7. English words pertaining to sleep are derived from the Latin, *somnus* and *soper*, from which we get words such as somnolent, somnambulist (sleepwalker), and soporific. The Greek god of sleep, Hypnos, has also contributed words, such as hypnosis, hypnotic, and hypnagogic.

8. *The American Medical Association Guide to Better Sleep* is a very interesting and thorough treatment of sleep disorders. It discusses much of the material in this section and goes into greater depth.

9. Insomnia may be caused by medications for asthma, thyroid disorders, and weight reduction. Also, it can result from any irritating medical condition including headaches, lung disease, chest pain, heart failure, and ulcers.

Tremors and Tics

10. Other medications used include Catapres (clonidine), Orap (pimozide), Prolixin (fluphenazine), and Clonopin (clonazepam).

11. The Tourette Syndrome Association is a very helpful resource. The address is 41-02 Bell Blvd., Bayside, NY 11361.

10
Avoiding Misdiagnosis

Part III has been a call to counselors to make distinctions between spiritual and organic problems. Without doubt, this is no easy task. Since the heart and body are one, parceling out the unique contributions of each to cognition, emotions, and behavior is rarely straightforward. The task, however, is important. At stake is a biblical understanding of people and effective ministry, not to mention potential suffering, financial expense, and even life or death.

The process of differentiating between the moral and the physical begins by simply realizing that just about any counseling symptoms can have organic links or causes. To maintain this "organic consciousness," pastors and counselors need to first develop a basic practical theology of the person: heart and body. There is nothing more practical than good theology, and biblical counselors must have a theology that explains the impact of physical problems. Armed with this very basic theology, along with its practical implications, pastors and counselors can remain appropriately alert to potential organic problems.

The other fundamental ingredient to accurate diagnosis is humility. Pastors and counselors must be aware of their diagnostic limitations. One book does not make an expert. When in doubt as to possible organicity, rely on others who are more knowledgeable than yourself. Refer counselees to *medically astute* psychiatrists,[1] internists, or general practitioners. You will never harm someone by referring him or her for medical consultation.

Clues for Avoiding Misdiagnosis
Change from a previous level
No readily identifiable cause
Symptoms appear after age forty
Presence of chronic or recent disease
Use of drugs: licit or illicit

Diagnostic Clues

In order to make informed judgments on the presence of possible organic causes, there are only a few alerting clues and signs with which you should be aware. You don't need to be a walking compendium of diseases and their associated signs and symptoms. The first series of clues act as a general screening device or net. Used properly, these clues should catch about 90 percent of organic causes. By themselves, they do not prove an organic cause. But, at least, they mean that organic problems are possible. Perhaps a rule of thumb can be that any combination of two diagnostic clues is sufficient reason for medical consultation.

Change from a previous level. The most important clue is whether or not there has been a *change* from a previous level. Does a wife say, "He is just not himself any more"? What was the person like before the problems arose? How is he or she different now? Has the person always been this way, or is there no apparent history of similar symptoms? Have you been alert to changes in all areas: social, emotional, thinking, memory, work, energy level, and appearance?

> A previously successful diplomat was returned home because of loss of interest in his work and declining performance. He was sent for psychiatric help, but he became increasingly apathetic and was dismissed. He took various less attractive jobs, without any success, and was finally employed keeping pigs. Finally, after a bout of severe headaches, he was found to have a large frontal lobe tumor. (Geschwind, 1975)

To answer these questions, counselors must get reliable information about present and past functioning. This is especially important because organic diseases can cause *fluctuating* psychological changes. For example, hypoglycemia is notorious for having different symptoms at different times. Affected persons are fine one minute, but the next minute they are confused and irrational. Also, some people with subtle organic problems may demonstrate blatant intellectual changes in an unstructured situation at work or home, but they may be relatively lucid during a counselor's structured interview. Therefore, it is critical to establish a clear history of the problem. Occasionally, a counselee will offer a history that is unclear or unreliable. In such a case, ask if you can speak with other sources: family, friends, previous pastors, relatives, ex-spouses, or employers.

One of the more important changes is in memory function. Although complaints of poor memory are not uncommon in depression and other nonorganic experiences, memory decline is a red light that cannot be ignored. The problems for counselors is, again, obtaining reliable information. Does the person only perceive memory changes or are they real? To get this information, counselors cannot simply ask, "How is your memory?" If this is the only screening question, those with good memories will say they are bad, and those with bad memories will say they are good. Instead, questions must be much more specific. Ask about the person's job. Has he or she been uncharacteristically forgetting appointments or deadlines? What about changes in relationships? Have there been changes in remembering conversations, telephone numbers, counseling appointments, sermons, or birthdays?

Corroboration of memory problems by family is critical. Don't just ask, "Is your spouse's (or parent's) memory worse than before?" Get specific examples of memory changes. If there are definite changes from a previous level, medical consultation is warranted.

No readily identifiable cause. A second clue to detecting organic problems is that there is no readily identifiable cause for the changes. That is, problems are not easily explained by circumstances or spiritual commitments. This is a tricky clue and easily missed, because most counselors have no problems finding putative causes. In fact, a significant problem that I observe among inexperienced counselors is that they have theories for everything! Every act can be explained in detail without resorting to any organic explanations. Experienced counselors are also persistent theory-builders. But they usually hold their theories more tentatively and are careful to corroborate them with counselees.

When this clue is coupled with the previous one, it may be a more powerful screen. For example, perhaps there are many difficult circumstances in a person's life that are germane to the counseling issue, but if a person has typically faced these difficulties in the past without any significant problems, then there is reason to "think organic."

Symptoms appear after age forty. A third clue is the age of the person. If changes in psychological and emotional functioning appear for the first time after age forty, then an organic cause must be considered. Prior to age forty, some emotional turbulence is common. Also, the major (functional) psychiatric symptoms—mood disorders, anxiety, schizophrenia, and mania—characteristically have their first appearance by no later than the mid-thirties. By forty, most people have settled into a certain style that is adaptable and flexible but still retains the same basic shape. Deviance from that general pattern, with no apparent cause, might indicate an organic problem.

If there is a change from a previous level of functioning, no readily apparent causative circumstances, and the person is over forty, then physician referral is definitely warranted. Have the counselee see his or her family physician or internist, and, if you as the counselor will not be speaking with the physician, make sure that the counselee knows the purpose of the consultation.

Presence of chronic or recent disease. A fourth clue is the presence of known disease. Chronic diseases that mimic counseling problems run the gamut from allergies to multiple sclerosis. Likewise, more acute or recent sicknesses (e.g., pneumonia, seizures) also have potential counseling-related symptoms. This text either discusses or lists the best-known culprits, but when in doubt, confer with a knowledgeable physician.

> A seventy-two-year-old man went into the hospital for a diabetes check-up and reported to the nursing staff that he had been hallucinating the last several days. He was being treated for pneumonia at the time and had never had any previous history of hallucinations or psychiatric diagnoses, but he was immediately moved to the psychiatric ward.
>
> The hallucinations were very interesting. They consisted of old songs that were popular when he was younger, often sung with a large, intrapsychic chorus. In fact, many times the gentleman would sing along with gusto, and he would ask his wife to do the same. The suspicion among the psychiatric staff was a diagnosis of schizophrenia. However, within two days, after the pneumonia improved, he was symptom-free. He was eventually moved back to the general medical ward after his psychiatrists realized that the isolated symptoms were a consequence of the acute pneumonia.

Use of drugs: Licit or illicit. A final alerting clue is the presence of drugs, the most common cause of organic psychological changes.

Remember, although drugs do not always have psychoactive effects, almost any drug, even at prescribed doses, can affect intellect, behavior, or mood. Drugs taken at high doses are almost bound to affect cognitive and emotional function.

A sixty-five-year-old pastor's wife asked for an immediate counseling appointment because of a family crisis. When she came for counseling she tearfully recounted her story. She described her marriage as fairly good in the past, but said that it took a recent turn for the worse when her husband—officially retired—continued an active ministry even though his wife expected more time together. When asked if her husband's time for ministry bothered her, surprisingly, she tearfully exclaimed, "No, not really." But she did say she was feeling very depressed.

Her depression seemed to emerge over the previous week to ten days. She had no history of previous depression, and there were no major changes in her life. She did indicate that two months earlier she had started taking sleeping pills at the prescribed dose. It was suggested that she confer with her physician and consider stopping the sleeping pills. She stopped the medication and two days later her depression was totally gone.

A simple rule is that you should be familiar with *all* the drugs your counselees are taking: licit or illicit. This takes very little time, and you will quickly find yourself aware of the purposes and side effects of many drugs without having to always look them up in the *Physician's Desk Reference*. The benefits of this approach are greater than simply detecting organic problems. Drugs can reveal the presence of chronic diseases that may cause a great deal of personal suffering and change of life style. They may also reveal habitual or recreational use of illicit drugs and alcohol, even though those problems were not previously revealed because counselees considered them to be irrelevant to the counseling.

The most obvious indicator of a drug-related cause to counseling problems is when cognitive or emotional changes follow on the heels of the introduction of a drug. But realize that the association may not be chronologically intimate. Some drugs may take years before they gradually become toxic. Also, some drugs may suddenly have a more profound effect after major surgery or other significant illness.

Diagnostic Signs

Clues are thought-provoking suggestions. They are very helpful, but in themselves, they do not provide definitive answers. They must be accompanied by further sleuthing and clinical judgment. Signs, however, are easy. Like roadmarks on a highway, they tell you what to do. There is very little room left for guesswork or judgment. In distinguishing organic from functional, there are a few such signs. When any one of these signs are apparent, there should be medical consultation.

Signs That Warrant Immediate Medical Referral

Changes in consciousness
  Disorientation
  Occasional lapses of consciousness
  Unconsciousness
Change in vital signs
Recent head injury
Visual disturbances
Changes in headaches
Changes in body movement

Changes in consciousness. "Consciousness" is a common medical term that can refer to a spectrum of different signs. These signs are similar in that they all refer to a person's level of alertness and awareness. It includes experiences that go from a momentary blank stare to unconsciousness or coma.

Disorientation. Physicians commonly talk about disorientation to person, place, or time. That is, someone may not know who they are, where they are, or the time, date, or year. Disorientation to person is very unusual and only characteristic of severe dementias or delirium (confusion, poor awareness, and inattention—typically associated with drugs). Disorientation to place and time, however, are much more common and may be present in persons who seem very normal. In my own counseling I have had delightful and seemingly profitable conversations with people, only to notice that on their information forms they were ten years off on the date! Likewise, I have been surprised when apparently lucid counselees mention in passing that they are in a place other than my office.

Remember that physical disease and delirium can wax and wane. Not all disoriented persons remain so minute to minute. Therefore, be particularly alert to comments by the family such as "sometimes he acts real confused," "she is just out of it every evening." Persons may be relatively lucid for the few minutes that you speak with them, but they may be quite confused at other times. Refer these people immediately.

Occasional lapses of consciousness. Lapses of consciousness are associated with a few different organic problems. They are especially characteristic of partial complex seizures. As you recall, these seizures can last from seconds to minutes. Affected persons are conscious but unresponsive, and there is little or no memory of the incident. Does a counselee report memory lapses? Do family members ever observe times when the counselee is peculiarly unresponsive—even for very brief periods? They may be signs of treatable but potentially dangerous seizures, and they warrant immediate referral to a primary physician or neurologist.

Lapses of consciousness are also reported in nonorganic problems. The most well known examples are psychogenic fugues. No doubt you have heard of people who wandered for miles or days with apparent amnesia for the experience. These can have organic bases, but they usually are surrounded by difficult life circumstances and a desire to avoid certain painful situations. But play it safe. When there is a history of lapses of consciousness, get medical consultation.

Unconsciousness. Any history of unconsciousness that has not been medically investigated and diagnosed is immediate cause for medical consultation. Seizures, severe head injuries, alcoholic blackouts—there are quite a few possible causes. All of them can be potentially life threatening and all of them can affect intellect or mood.

Change in vital signs. Counselors don't check anyone's heart rate, blood pressure, or temperature before counseling sessions. But if you ask counselees to complete some sort of fact sheet prior to counseling, worthwhile screening questions would be these (see appendix C for a comprehensive health questionnaire for counseling):

Have you had recent fevers or elevated temperature?

Does your heart ever race or beat irregularly?

Do you know your blood pressure? Is it normal?

If you hear that there are any abnormalities in someone's vital signs (especially if they have not been explained by a primary physician), refer them for medical consultation.

Recent head injury. Head injuries can cause a host of counseling related problems. These are most apparent when there has been a four- to seven-day post-traumatic amnesia (PTA), but psychological changes might also be apparent with a much shorter or no PTA. Cognitive, emotional, or personality changes that emerge after a head injury must be evaluated medically.

Head injuries are even more significant in the elderly. "Bumps on the head" that hurt only for a moment, when followed by psychological changes, might mean subdural hematoma. These small bleeds between the skull and the brain can emerge very gradually with seemingly innocuous changes, but they can develop into dramatic intellectual and physical deficits that lead to death.

> Former President Reagan underwent surgery on September 8, 1989 to remove a subdural hematoma that his doctors attributed to a fall from a horse July 4, two months before. The subdural fluid was discovered during a routine examination at the Mayo Clinic in Rochester, Minnesota. The former President was without symptoms, but physicians advised him to have the fluid removed in a routine procedure.
>
> "In severe cases, subdural hematomas can kill within a few hours or days, or they can cause symptoms that develop weeks or months later. They can cause paralysis, memory loss and other problems.
>
> "But often, as seems to be the case in Friday's statement about Reagan, they can be present without causing any symptoms." (Altman, 1989, A26)

Another group that is particularly prone to head injury is heavy drinkers. People who frequently consume large amounts of alcohol are more prone to experience serious falls or get in fights or car accidents. To complicate the diagnostic process, these people may have no recollection of a head injury. Therefore, with known heavy drinkers who demonstrate psychological changes, counselors must be alert to abrasions on the head or face, complaints about scalp tenderness after a bout of heavy drinking, or reports from friends about a significant blow to the head.

Visual disturbances. The eyes are quite sensitive to brain changes. Their optic tracts run from the front of the brain to the back (the occipital area). As a result they are affected by tumors, strokes, multiple sclerosis, and many other neurological diseases. They are also easily affected by drugs and other disorders that change blood chemistry.

Counselors must respond to symptoms such as double vision, unusual episodes of blurry vision, distorted vision, or visual hallucinations.

Change in headaches. Ten percent of headaches are caused by underlying disease. As mentioned in the section on headaches, be especially alert to *changes* in a headache pattern. Is a headache in a different place? Described differently? More painful? Accompanied by a stiff neck, fever, nausea, or vomiting? Headache changes should be explained. They warrant immediate referral.

Changes in body movement. Counselors rarely think of body movements as a potential indicator of brain dysfunction, but all movements have their initial impetus in the brain. Muscles are responding to brain impulses. Therefore, movement disorders are another sign of organicity.

Counselors should be sensitive to changes in walking (gait), tremors in the hands or head, and unusual jerks or twitches.

Notes

1. I emphasize "medically astute" because many psychiatrists are not. One study indicated that fewer than 35 percent of practicing psychiatrists surveyed ever perform physical exams. Thirty-two percent admitted they felt incompetent to perform even a rudimentary physical (Sternberg, 1986).

11
Conclusion:
Sin or Sickness?

Before I came here I was confused about the subject.
Having listened to your lecture I am still confused.
But on a higher level.

—Enrico Fermi

Distinguishing issues of the body and heart has been a central theme of this book. However, it has not been the only theme. The book actually has set out to intertwine apologetic, ministerial, and devotional strands.

The Apologetic Goal

The apologetic goal has been to defend Christianity from being blindsided by the medical model. With its dazzling array of technology and its private vocabulary, the medical model has left the Christian community starstruck, unable to respond to its claims. Left unopposed, this secular revolution has begun to reduce everything to biological roots. In the process, it has relabeled many spiritual issues as diseases and disseminated a false gospel that is only going to grow. As are result, there has been a gradual erosion of biblical authority.

In order to "take every thought captive"—that is, to think biblically about the issues around us and reclaim biblical territory—I have presented a very basic biblical model. This model only includes elementary theological data, but that does not make it simplistic or naive. Indeed, basic truths of Scripture are really all we need to address the biological revolution or any other assault on the Bible. Our task is the new application of old truths rather than developing new theological systems. The biblical position is this: the ravages of brain injury, disease, or dysfunction cannot rob us of spiritual vitality. At the core of our being we are moral creatures, image-bearers of the Most High. Certainly, this center can be defaced and suppressed, but the culprit is sin, not sickness. This position is dismissed by secular, biological perspectives, but interestingly, in actual practice, secular positions acknowledge that there is an initiating, moral center of persons. For example, a group that has been at the forefront of biological approaches to schizophrenia indicated that schizophrenia is never an excuse for "ugly behavior" (Pfeiffer et al., 1970). "Ugly behavior" is not the same as acknowledging that we live our lives before God, but it is an admission that even in the face of biological abnormalities, something in the person is spared. As Christians, we have the privilege of knowing what that something is.

Heresy can either destroy or have a refining effect. It can destroy by subtly eroding our biblical positions and leaving us without confidence in God's Word. But there is a silver lining to the medical model attacks. Heresy has an ability to refine theology and biblical practice. It forces the Christian community to evaluate current theological formulations as well as develop a position that will both defend a Christian approach and, in a winsome way, persuade others of the strength of the biblical position. From this perspective, the biological model has been most helpful. It has forced us to reexamine the biblical data on moral responsibility as well as make more precise delineations between heart and body. Without its prodding, new applications of biblical material would remain untapped, and our faith would not be reminded of the comprehensive nature of the simple truths of Scripture.

The Ministerial Goal

The book then took this theoretical information to the streets. With the biblical and biological foundations covered, the goal was to improve the practice of ministry. To this end, common organic problems and some of their neglected counseling implications were reviewed. Guidelines were also established to distinguish problems of the heart from disorders of the body. But perhaps the most important practical application of the material was in its development of the category of *asthenia* or weakness. That is, in what ways do brain changes manifest themselves in emotions, thinking, or behavior; and how can we understand these unique weaknesses?

In one sense, this particular emphasis is no different from that of a book on missions or cross-cultural ministry. In cross-cultural ministry, the goal is to understand people who are very different from ourselves. They have a different language, culture, and style of thought. Indeed, there are always spiritual commonalities, but the differences sometimes seem insurmountable and render ministry particularly difficult. We need to understand how others think so that we may minister effectively.

Analogously, when confronted with brain dysfunctions (i.e., anyone!), counselors must enter a world that is foreign to their own. Emotions can fluctuate without provocation, sensory data can be a mosaic of perceptions that have no unifying pattern, and self-awareness can also have a fragmented or distorted quality. To those counselors who are unfamiliar with the cognitive and emotional variations imposed by brain changes (*asthenia*), the ministry experience is no different than trying to dialogue with an Islamic nomad. I hope that you now have several mental pegs on which to place previously unrecognized behavioral data.

The Devotional Goal

There is one final, and perhaps most important, strand that needs to be highlighted. That is, "How has my faith been edified? How have I come to know Christ better?" Admittedly, the information in this text is more technical than devotional, but spiritual encouragement can be found in many arenas.

There are at least two points that might aid personal growth in faith. One is that "nothing can separate us from the love of Christ." Many people already know this, but now "nothing" is enlarged to include physical disorders. By faith, we can anticipate an unimpaired, growing relationship with Jesus Christ. Neither the ravages of time nor disease can impair spiritual eyesight. Truly, a real comfort and joy!

The corollary to this is that we should expect that those who have disease—even disease that affects the brain—to be powerful ministers of the gospel. There has been a subtle prejudice in the church. Ministry is done by the healthy and intellectually competent; others are ministered to. But if it is true that spiritual vitality is largely unimpeded by disease or poor brain functioning, then we should expect to be edified by a whole new group of people. In fact, since they are in a position to develop a more refined faith through the fire of disability, their impact in the kingdom might have special prominence.

A final faith-builder is this. We should be encouraged to be people who hope. Of the triad of faith, hope, and love, perhaps the most neglected of these is hope. We are often too satisfied with what we have now to yearn for the consummation of all things when Jesus returns. But all this talk about disease should remind us that all is not well. It should cause us to meditate on the time when there willbe no disease. It should remind us that Jesus is the resurrected Savior who conquered death, and we, as his siblings, now look forward to the final application of that event.

> The body that is sown is perishable, it is raised imperishable; it is sown in dishonor, it is raised in glory; it is sown in weakness, it is raised in power; it is sown a natural body, it is raised a spiritual body. (1 Cor. 15:42–44)

Appendix A
Two Brains?

As we move into neuropsychology, I would like to do a little debunking of both the scientific mystique and some popular notions of brain functioning. Recognize that the brain sciences are data-rich but theory-poor. Although neuroscientists know a great deal about individual neurons, they become more speculative when it comes to an overall theory of brain functioning. Don't let the veil of science fool you. Brain research simply has no dominant theory on how to correlate the workings of neurons with the activity of the mind (heart). And nowhere is this more apparent than in the currently popular discussion about right brain and left brain.

According to the theory, the right hemisphere of the brain is purportedly the creative, emotional, and intuitive brain while the left hemisphere is the coolly calculating, rational brain. Yet this modern formulation, like previous theories, is naive and more a barometer of cultural issues than biological ones.

This is fairly typical of brain research. Since its beginning, it has always embodied a wide variety of social, personal, and religious concerns, reflecting the dominant cultural metaphors of the day. In the early 1800s, it was explicitly a religious battleground, and brain scientists were part theologian and part physician. The religious theory was that the brain was indivisible. Physicians and theologians speculated that if you broke the brain into different functional components, then you would lose the soul (spirit).

This inadequate religious theory continued until it was opposed by a French medical society that "since its inception, . . . had become notorious as a focus for left wing, anticlerical activity in French science" (Harrington, 1987, p. 40). Out of this background Paul Broca made the then-heretical suggestion that language was located in the left hemisphere of the brain. This may not sound so radical now, but at the time it was equivalent to saying that a person is not created in the image of God. The thinking was that language was a spiritual function, not a biological one.

During the remainder of the 1800s and into the early1900s, theories about brain function proliferated, and they continued to reflect the dominant themes in the culture. Their standard approach was to put all the bad or mysterious in the right and all the good in the left. For example, the right hemisphere was associated with "inferior" nonwhite races, madness, social undesirables, and women! The left was the province of the white race, intelligence, and men. You might find it interesting to know that during this time there were elaborate educational programs to train the "right brain."

For various social and political reasons, these early right brain-left brain theories were dormant during the next fifty years. Finally, in the early 1960s, the time was right again. The sixties were marked by growing social and ideological divisions. There was an undercurrent of antagonism toward science, technology, and their companion—rational, analytic thinking. And, as an alternative, mysticism and "consciousness-raising" activities emerged. The inevitable brain theory was provided in 1970 by Robert Ornstein's book, *The Psychology of Consciousness*, which argued that our Western left brain had victimized our neglected, mystical right brain. Subsequently, civil rights issues were appended and the left hemisphere became synonymous with an evil technological society, while the right hemisphere was the underdog, the victim of "heartless discrimination and oppression" (Harrington, 1987; Calvin, 1983).

That there are differences between the left and right hemispheres is beyond question. Yet the differences are less clear than the popular literature might indicate (e.g., Betty Edwards', *Drawing on the Right Side of the Brain*). What was once the only definitive difference between the hemispheres—language function—is even being reevaluated. The left hemisphere does have greater language competence, but that may be a result of the left hemisphere's more general function as manipulating or generating sequentially organized actions, especially those, like language, that occur in rapid succession. The right hemisphere, by default, has a slight advantage in elementary nonverbal functions (Corballis, 1980, 1983; Currey, 1982).

At this time, there is no firm evidence that there are different processing styles between the two hemispheres. But this evidence will be slow to move into popular thinking. Any broad, popular changes in a theory of brain function await not future scientific progress but changes in religious, cultural, and political metaphors. Indeed, brain sciences do not rest on a solid rock.

Appendix B
Guide to Psychotherapeutic Drugs

All drugs are listed by trade (brand) names, followed by normal adult dose range and generic name. Side effects are listed in order of frequency.

qd = each day
bid = twice daily
tid = three times daily
qid = four times daily

I. Antianxiety drugs (tranquilizers, anxiolytics) — used with symptoms associated with anxiety such as muscular tension, insomnia, and excessive fears.

A. Benzodiazepines — side effects include drowsiness, ataxia, and confusion. Withdrawal symptoms have occurred on abrupt discontinuance.

Ativan	1–10 mg qd	Lorazepam
Centrax	20–60 mg qd	Prazepam
Klonopin	.5–20 mg qd	Clonazepam
Librium	5–25 mg tid to qid	Chlordiazepoxide
Paxipam	20–40 mg qd	Halazepam
Serax	10–30 mg tid to qid	Oxazepam
Tranxene	15–30 mg qd	Clorazepate dipotassium
Valium	2–10 mg bid to qid	Diazepam
Verstran	20–60 mg qd	Prazepam
Xanax	1–4 mg qd	Alprazolam

B. Meprobamate — side effects include drowsiness, ataxia, and confusion. Dependence has occurred.

Equanil	1200–1600 mg qd	Meprobamate
Meprospan	1200–1600 mg qd	Meprobamate
Miltown	1200–1600 mg qd	Meprobamate

C. Buspirone HCl—unrelated to other antianxiety drugs, there is currently no evidence that it can lead to dependence. Side effects include dizziness, insomnia, nervousness, and GI disturbances.

| Buspar | 1–5 mg tid | Buspirone |

D. Miscellaneous
  1. Antihistamines—side effects are usually mild and transitory. They include drowsiness, hangover, anticholinergic effects.

| Atarax | 25–100 mg tid to qid | Hydroxyzine |
| Vistaril | 25–100 mg tid to qid | Hydroxyzine |

  2. Chlormezanone—side effects include drowsiness, rash, dizziness, and depression.

| Trancopal | 200 mg tid to qid | Chlormezanone |

  3. Combination drugs

Deprol	Meprobamate and an antidepressant
Librax	Librium and Quarzan (an anticholinergic for peptic ulcer)
Limbitrol	Librium and Elavil (an antidepressant)
Menrium	Librium and Estrogen (for menopausal symptoms)
Pathibate	Meprobamate and Pathilon (for GI spasms)

II. Antidepressants—used with persistent depression as well as panic, phobias, and obsessional thoughts and compulsive behaviors.

   A. Tricyclics—response in one to four weeks. Side effects include anticholinergic effects, orthostatic hypotension, drowsiness, and weight gain.

Adapin	75–300 mg qd	Doxepin
Amitril	75–300 mg qd	Amitriptyline
Anafranil	75–225 mg qd	Clomipramine
Asendin	200–300 mg qd	Amoxapine
Aventyl	40–200 mg qd	Nortriptyline
Elavil	75–300 mg qd	Amitriptyline
Endep	75–300 mg qd	Amitriptyline
Ludiomil	75–225 mg qd	Maprotiline
Norpramin	75–300 mg qd	Desipramine
Pertrofrane	75–300 mg qd	Desipramine
S-K Pramine	75–300 mg qd	Imipramine
Sinequan	75–300 mg qd	Doxepin
Surmontil	75–300 mg qd	Trimipramine
Tofranil	75–300 mg qd	Imipramine
Vivactil	30–60 mg qd	Protriptyline

   B. Triazolopyridine—similar to tricyclic except faster acting.

| Desyrel | 150–400 mg qd | Trazodone |

   C. Fluoxetine—side effects include nausea, anxiety, nervousness, insomnia, and drowsiness.

Prozac   20–80 mg qd   Fluoxetine
D. Bupropion—side effects include restlessness, agitation, anxiety, and insomnia.

Wellbutrin   225–450 mg qd   Bupropion

E. Monoamine Oxidase Inhibitors—usually used when tricyclics fail or anxiety is prominent. Must be accompanied by restriction in foods, beverages, and drugs with high amine content. Response in one to four weeks. Side effects include hypertension, restlessness, insomnia, dizziness, and anticholinergic effects.

Marplan   30–50 mg qd   Isocarboxazid
Nardil   45–90 mg qd   Phenelzine
Parnate   20–60 mg qd   Tranylcypromine

F. Combination drug

Triavil   Elavil and Trilafon (an antipsychotic)
Etrafon   Elavil and Trilafon

III. Antipsychotics (major tranquilizers, neuroleptics)—used with delusions, hallucinations, and illogical thinking associated with schizophrenia, mania, and other psychotic problems. Side effects include drowsiness (especially in the first week), orthostatic hypotension, anticholinergic effects, extrapyramidal effects, tardive dyskinesia, akathisia, dystonia, inhibition of ejaculation, and weight gain. They may be accompanied by Cogentin or Benadryl to alleviate some side effects.

A. Phenothiazines—(A) Aliphatic, (B) Piperazine, (C) Piperdine

Compazine   15–150 mg qd   Prochlorperazine (B)
Mellaril   150–800 mg qd   Thioridazine (C)
Proketazine   5–400 mg qd   Carphenazine (B)
Prolixin   2.5–10 mg qd   Fluphenazine (B)
Quide   20–160 mg qd   Piperacetazine (C)
Serentil   30–400 mg qd   Mesoridazine (C)
Sparine   50–1000 mg qd   Promazine (A)
Stelazine   2–40 mg qd   Trifluoperazine (B)
Thorazine   50–2000 mg qd   Chlorpromazine (A)
Tindal   60–120 mg qd   Acetophenazine (B)
Trilafon   4–8 mg tid   Perphenazine (B)
Vesprin   60–150 mg qd   Triflupromazine (A)

B. Butyrophenone

Haldol   1–15 mg qd   Haloperidol
Inapsine   Injection only   Droperidol

C. Thiozanthenes

Navane   6–60 mg qd   Thithixene
Taractan   30–600 mg qd   Chlorprothixine

D. Dibenzoxazeapine

Loxitane   20–250 mg qd   Loxapine

E. Dihydroindolone

| Moban | 15–225 mg qd | Molindone |
| Lidone | 15–225 mg qd | Molindone |

IV. Antimanic—used witn manic episodes and bipolar symptoms.

Lithium—side effects include nausea and fatigue (especially in the first week), tremor, thirst, edema, and weight gain. Mental confusion is a common sign of toxicity.

Eskalith	300 mg tid or qid	Lithium
Lithane	300 mg tid or qid	Lithium
Lithonate	300 mg tid or qid	Lithium

V. Sedatives—all drugs used for insomnia are potentially harmful if used for over six months.

A. Benzodiazepines (see antianxiety drugs)

Dalmane	30 mg qd	Flurazepam
Halcion	.25–.50 mg qd	Triazolam
Restoril	15–30 mg qd	Temazepam

B. Antihistamines—side effects include drowsiness, hangover, and anticholinergic effects. Effectiveness is questionable.

Compoz	Over-the-counter	Pyrilamine
Cope	Over-the-counter	Pyrilamine
Nervine	Over-the-counter	Pyrilamine
Sominex	Over-the-counter	Pyrilamine

C. Miscellaneous

Doriden	500 mg qd	Glutethimide
Noctec	500–2000 mg qd	Chloral Hydrate
Noludar	300–400 mg qd	Methyprylon
Phenergan	12.5–20 mg qd	Promethazine
Placidyl	500–1000 mg qd	Ethchlorvynol

Appendix C
Health History Questionnaire

Name ———————————————— Age ——————————

Address ———————————————— Sex ——————————

Date of birth ———————————————— Phone ——————————

Occupation ———————————————— Today's date ——————————

Education ————————————————

List all current medications and daily dosage. Please include all medicines: prescription and over-the-counter (e.g., laxatives, birth control, aspirin, cold or allergy sprays, diet pills, etc.).

————————————————————————
————————————————————————
————————————————————————

How much of the following do you consume on an average day?

Coffee ———————— Tea ———————— Soft drinks ————————

	Yes	No
1. Have you ever had surgery that required anesthesia?	☐	☐

Please list them and include dates: ————————————

————————————————————————
————————————————————————

	Yes	No
2. Are you currently being treated by a physician?	☐	☐

For what medical problem(s)? ————————————

————————————————————————
————————————————————————
————————————————————————

	Yes	No
3. Have you had any of the following?		
Nausea or vomiting (recently)	☐	☐
High temperature/fever (recently)	☐	☐
High blood pressure	☐	☐
Diabetes	☐	☐
Cancer (what type?) _____	☐	☐
Epilepsy or seizures	☐	☐
Concussion or other head injury	☐	☐
Stroke	☐	☐
Multiple sclerosis	☐	☐
Parkinson's disease	☐	☐
4. Have you had any recent weight or appetite changes?	☐	☐
5. Do you have any problems with your heart?	☐	☐
Mitral valve prolapse ☐ Open heart surgery ☐ Congestive heart failure ☐ Palpitations ☐ Angina ☐		
6. Have you ever been treated for liver or kidney problems?	☐	☐
Hepatitis ☐ Cirrhosis ☐ Dialysis ☐		
7. Do you have respiratory or breathing difficulties?	☐	☐
Asthma ☐ Emphysema ☐ Pneumonia ☐		
8. Have you ever lost control of your bowels or bladder?	☐	☐
9. Have you had any recent sexual problems?	☐	☐
[Men] problems having or maintaining an erection ☐ [Men] problems with ejaculation ☐ [Men and women] recent difficulties achieving orgasm ☐		
10. [Women] Have you had any recent menstrual changes?	☐	☐
Do you menstruate regularly?	☐	☐
11. Have you had any problems with speech?	☐	☐
Slurring words ☐ Difficulty remembering the names of common things ☐		
12. Have you had any changes in your vision?	☐	☐
Double vision ☐ Blurry vision ☐ Temporary blindness ☐ Tunnel vision ☐ Visual hallucinations or distortions ☐		
13. Have you ever blacked out or had no recollection of recent events?	☐	☐
14. Do you experience headaches?	☐	☐
Please describe them. _____		
_____		
_____		
_____		
Are they new or different from previous headaches?	☐	☐
15. Have you hit your head recently?	☐	☐
16. Is there a spot on your head that is sensitive to touch?	☐	☐

	Yes	No
17. Do you have pain or stiffness in your neck?	☐	☐
18. Have you noticed any changes in your walking?	☐	☐
19. Do you get dizzy or lose your balance easily?	☐	☐
20. Have you had difficulties with your coordination?	☐	☐
21. Do your hands tremble sometimes?	☐	☐
22. Has your handwriting changed?	☐	☐
23. Are you unusually sensitive to heat or cold?	☐	☐
24. Do you have any allergies?	☐	☐

To what are you allergic? _____

_____

	Yes	No
25. Do you have strong cravings for particular foods?	☐	☐
26. Do you often feel fatigued, lethargic, or ill between meals?	☐	☐
27. Have you had any persistent rashes?	☐	☐
28. Have you recently had any unusual hair loss?	☐	☐
29. Have there been any changes in your sleep pattern?	☐	☐

Early morning wakenings ☐ Excessive tiredness ☐ Difficulty falling asleep (insomnia) ☐

30. Have you or others noticed any change in any of the following?

Personality or emotions	☐	☐
Memory (amnesia)	☐	☐
Work performance	☐	☐

	Yes	No
31. Do you sometimes find yourself laughing or crying for no apparent reason?	☐	☐
32. Have your sensory responses (sight, touch, taste, hearing, smelling) ever been distorted, exaggerated, or diminished?	☐	☐
33. Have you ever sensed (seen, heard, felt, tasted, smelled) something that you think only you sensed and not others who were around you?	☐	☐
34. Have you recently had a feeling that you had experienced a situation or had been someplace before, although you were actually experiencing it for the first time (déjà vu)?	☐	☐
35. Have you had any thoughts that just seemed to go on and on and you couldn't stop?	☐	☐
36. Has drinking alcohol ever interfered with your job or personal relationships?	☐	☐

What is your alcohol consumption per week? _____

	Yes	No
37. In the past six months have you used street drugs or other drugs for nonmedical reasons (e.g., narcotics, cocaine, barbiturates, marijuana)?	☐	☐

Manual for the Health History Questionnaire

This questionnaire, if answered accurately, is designed to screen for the majority of physical problems that can mimic psychological problems. It is most useful when given to persons who exhibit any one of the diagnostic clues; i.e., change from a previous level, symptoms first appear after age forty, presence of a recent or chronic disease, use of licit or illicit drungs.

Since these data are an important part of understanding the whole person— heart and body—ask the client to read every question carefully. If you are uncertain about reading or comprehension levels, ask a family member or someone who knows the counselee to help complete the information.

The questionnaire is designed for rapid evaluation. After reviewing the demographic data and the questions on medication and caffeine consumption, you are only concerned about "yes" answers. If a counselee checks "yes," investigate the answer more fully using the information in this manual.

Demographic Data

Age. Be alert to the age of the person. Some diseases and symptoms emerge in a specific age range (e.g., multiple sclerosis can appear in the twenties, though the average age of onset is thirty-three). Persons fifty and older are especially prone to having cognitive or intellectual changes that are induced by physical problems. The most important question is "Do the symptoms represent a change from a previous level of functioning?" If the symptoms are new and the person is over forty, recommend a medical consultation.

Occupation. Be familiar with the chemicals and pollutants to which the person is exposed. Did the problems begin with a change in job or exposure to new chemicals? There are quite a few neurotoxins in the work place such as the solvent methylene chloride (delusions and hallucinations), pesticides (tremors, nervousness, and neurological changes), toluene—a chemical used in paints and explosives (bizarre behavior), mercury—found in vacuum pumps, fungicide, and mirror manufacturing (personality changes, memory problems), and and manganese—found in steel foundries and the manufacturing of linoleum. Here is a list of *some of* the jobs, places, or objects associated with neurotoxins:

Airplane hangers	Furs
Antifreeze	Gardening
Artificial flowers	Insulators
Auto mechanics	Mining
Auto painting	Paper working
Bookbinding	Photographic equipment
Brass and bronze	Plumbing
Cosmetics	Refrigeration repair
Dentistry	Shoe working
Dry cleaning	Soaps
Paints and enamels	Storage batteries
Etching	Waterproofing
Explosives	Welding
Exterminating	

Medications

Medications are the number one cause of physically based psychological problems. Do you know all the medications a person is taking? Do you know the potential side effects (consult a recent edition of *Physician's Desk Reference*)? Does the person taking the medication know its purpose and the prescribed dosage? Are different physicians prescribing different medications? If so, make sure at least one physician knows about *all* the medicines.

Did psychological problems occur soon after the person began or changed medication? Refer the person back to a physician.

Medication may also be the cause when intellectual or emotional symptoms are not clearly tied to the beginning of medication. Some medications can become toxic after weeks or months of steady ingestion.

Caffeine

Caffeine can lead to a host of physical and psychological symptoms in sensitive persons. The symptoms will usually look like anxiety: restlessness, insomnia, flushed face, GI complaints, muscle twitching, or irregular heartbeats. Physician referral is not necessary if caffeine is involved, but recognize that it will be difficult for anyone to stop or decrease caffeine consumption.

Medical History

For the following questions, look for "yes" responses. If the responses are all "no" and they are accurate, it is unlikely that physical disease is involved in the presenting problem.

1. *Have you ever had surgery that required anesthesia?* Sometimes people will not remember their health history, but they will remember their surgeries. Therefore, this question is a way to reveal a history of diseases that can affect intellect or mood (thyroid surgery, brain surgery). Also, any surgery that uses general anesthesia can lead to short-term depression, tearfulness, and even subtle cognitive changes.

2. *Are you currently being treated by a physician?* If the person is being treated, know the medical problem and the medications. If you are unfamiliar with the diagnosis or unsure whether the medical problem affects brain functioning, obtain permission to talk with the physician.

3. *Have you had any of the following medical problems?* Nausea and vomiting can be inconsequential, but they can also be indicators of brain tumor or other problems that potentially affect intellect and mood. If present, the underlying cause should be determined.

Fever, or any prolonged elevation of vital signs, must be checked by a physician. Fever associated with a headache and stiff neck is characteristic of meningitis or brain infection.

High blood pressure may by a symptom of pheochromocytoma, Addison's disease, or other endocrine problems that can affect psychological functioning.

Diabetes does not cause many psychological changes in itself, yet it is a very difficult disease (compliance with diet and injections, impotence, visual problems). If there are psychological changes, persons may be hypoglycemic from too much insulin. Therefore, if there is transient lethargy or confusion, refer the clients back to their physicians. An adjustment in the dosage of medication may be needed.

Cancer, even if successfully treated, can recur. It can often begin as subtle psychological symptoms (intellectual and emotional changes).

Epilepsy and seizures usually mean grand mal seizures. Clients who have had grand mal seizures should have had a medical evaluation. In adults, seizures are often a sign of brain tumors. The more subtle psychomotor seizures are covered in other questions.

Concussion or head injury, especially if accompanied by any transient loss of memory or post-traumatic amnesia (PTA), can result in subsequent behavioral changes. Some of these conditions improve over a period of a year or two, but others may persist. If there has been a head injury, make sure the person is evaluated medically. Subdural hematomas are a serious but treatable possibility.

Strokes are notorious for their effect on intellect, speech, or emotions. If there has been a stroke and you are unfamiliar with a client's associated behavioral changes, consult with the overseeing physician.

4. *Have you had any recent weight or appetite changes?* In teenagers, anorexia is an obvious possibility with weight loss. But be especially alert to changes in weight when there has been no apparent change in appetite or calorie consumption. You should ask for a medical evaluation. Appetite changes are common in many different physical problems.

5. *Do you have any problems with your heart?* Congestive heart failure, mitral valve prolapse, high blood pressure, cardiac insufficiency, atrial tachycardia (rapid heartbeat) have all been associated with emotional changes, intellectual changes, or both. Also, many endocrine problems (pheochromocytoma, thyroid dysfunction) that affect intellectual or emotional functioning can accelerate the heart rate. Most good GPs and internists can quickly diagnose and treat these problems.

6. *Have you ever been treated for liver or kidney problems?* Depression has been associated with hepatitis; liver cancer and cirrhosis (look for a history of alcoholism) often include emotional and intellectual changes. Also, liver problems can inhibit the breakdown of drugs and lead to toxicity even when only small amounts of toxins are involved.

Nephritis (kidney inflammation), kidney failure, and other kidney problems can affect thinking and emotions. Also, like the liver, kidney problems affect the rate of drug metabolism, so inadequate functioning can lead to toxicity even if the person is taking recommended dosages.

7. *Do you have any respiratory difficulties?* The respiratory problems listed have been misdiagnosed as anxiety, depression, and schizophrenia. Also, medications used to treat these problems are associated with psychological side effects.

8. *Have you ever lost control of your bowels or bladder?* This kind of problem is rare in a healthy person. If "yes," refer the person for a physical exam.

9. *Have you had any recent sexual problems?* The majority of sexual problems are more a consequence of problems in terms of relationship, guilt, or traumatic sexual histories. However, if a man is no longer having any erections—even upon awakening—then an organic problem is likely (e.g., diabetes). Women are less likely than men to have organic sexual problems, but problems with sexual desire and sexual response can be associated with treatable, physical diseases.

10. *[Women] Have you had any recent menstrual changes?* Underlying problems include thyroid dysfunction, Sheehan's syndrome (hypopituitarism), excessive exercise, anorexia, and menopause. Of course, most menstrual changes in post-menopausal women are normal.

11. *Have you had any problems with speech?* Although profound aphasias are obvious, mild aphasias can be undetected by even a trained observer (or hearer).

Subtle speech or word-finding difficulties may suggest a small stroke, atypical migraine, or early signs of dementia.

12. *Have you had any changes in your vision?* Visual disturbances include the following:

Transient blindness (MS, infection, transient ischemia, increased intracranial pressure, migraine).

Transient visual field defects (glaucoma, migraine, TIAs, tumor), double vision (MS, diabetes, drugs, thyroid, myasthenia gravis, trauma, meningitis), and visual hallucinations or distortions.

Any of these symptoms should be medically investigated.

13. *Have you ever blacked out or had no recollection of recent events?* Blackouts, "fugues," or aimless wanderings might be a convenient way to avoid difficulties, but they can also indicate alcoholic blackouts or partial-complex seizures. Try to get corroboration; obtain permission to talk with people who might have witnessed the blackouts.

14. *Do you experience headaches?* Most counselees will answer "yes" to this question, and the vast majority of their headaches will be either migraine or muscle tension headaches. Also apparent might be Chinese restaurant headahces (from MSG), hot dog headaches (from nitrites), ice cream headaches (from very cold food), withdrawal headaches (from drugs and caffeine), or morning headaches associated with sleep apnea. There are other headaches, however, that might signify life-threatening problems. If the headache is accompanied by persistent physical problems (e.g., stiff neck, fever), if it is distinctly different from previous headaches, or if it develops for the first time after age fifty, a medical evaluation is warranted.

15. *Have you hit your head lately or at all?* This question overlaps with the question on head injury. It is included because some elderly people can get subdural hematomas from seemingly insignificant bumps. If there have been personality or intellectual changes since the accident, the head injury is probably the cause.

16. *Is there a spot on your head that is sensitive to touch?* If it is new, refer to medical consultation. Older people may be suffering from temporal arteritis if the sensitivity is over the temporal lobes.

17. *Do you experience neck pain or stiffness?* This may be a symptom of meningitis, especially if it is accompanied by a fever and headache.

18. *Have you noticed any changes in your walking?* There are many different types of gait disturbances—for example, walking with a stagger, feet wide apart, loss of balance, a very slow gait, or a gait that is difficult to slow down or stop.

Some of the underlying diseases include Parkinson's disease, drug side affects or toxicity, MS, normal pressure hydrocephalus, and frontal lobe dysfunction. Any significant gait difficulty should be evaluated by a neurologist.

19. *Do you get dizzy or lose your balance easily?* Dizziness and vertigo can result from problems such as Parkinson's disease or problems of the ear or cerebellum.

20. *Have you had difficulties with your coordination?* Overshooting when reaching for an object, problems dressing, and other disorders of voluntary movement often have a neurological origin.

21. *Do your hands tremble sometimes?* Tremors may be a sign of Parkinson's disease, drug toxicity, or other medical problems that can affect intellect and mood.

22. *Has your handwriting changed?* Parkinson's disease will affect handwriting; so will diseases of the parietal lobe. Check present handwriting with past samples.

23. *Are you unusually sensitive to heat and cold?* Heat intolerance may be associated with hyperthyroidism; cold intolerance, with hypothyroidism.

24. *Do you have allergies?*
It is possible that some allergies have psychological side effects. All a person can do, however, is to gain as much control over any allergy as possible. Consultation with an allergist might be helpful.

25. *Do you have strong cravings for particular foods?* Some allergists suggest that cravings reveal food allergies. A craved substance may actually be a culprit that is affecting mood swings and level of awareness. A fast or removal of the craved substance is the usual treatment. Good books on cerebral allergies might be helpful, as would a physician with a specialty in orthomolecular psychiatry.

26. *Do you often feel fatigued, lethargic, or ill between meals?* These symptoms may indicate hypoglycemia. If there is suspicion that this is the case, consider a glucose tolerance test or try a traditional hypoglycemic diet (high protein, frequent snacks).

27. *Have you had any persistent rashes?* Rashes have a variety of causes; perhaps the most important for the counselor is lupus (SLE), which may cause psychological changes. Lupus can cause a butterfly rash across the nose and face.

28. *Have you recently had any unusual hair loss?* This symptom may indicate hyperthyroidism.

29. *Have there been any changes in your sleep pattern?* Sleep difficulties are notorious for their relation to nonorganic problems (depression, anxiety, mania), yet there are many treatable, physical causes for both hypersomnia and insomnia (endocrine problems, electrolyte disturbances, sleep apnea, or narcolepsy). If sleep problems are the only problem checked, then there is little reason to expect an organic cause. However, if there are new changes with no previous history, then medical consultation is advised. The *American Medical Association Guide to Better Sleep* is a useful book that contains good commonsense advice and reviews some of the medical culprits.

30. *Have you or others noticed any change in your personality or emotions, memory, or work?* This is an important question, so you may want to ask family members. If there has been a change from a previous level of functioning, you should always entertain the possibility of a physical cause.

31. *Do you sometimes find yourself laughing or crying for no apparent reason?* A labile, or fluctuating and uncontrolled affect, is often an early warning sign of a physical problem. If it is a new symptom, get a medical consultation.

32. *Have your sensory responses ever been distorted, exaggerated, or diminished?* This could indicate a neurological disorder (MS, tumors, migraine, seizures) or drug toxicity. If the experiences are unusual and unrelated to street drugs, get a medical consultation.

33. *Have you ever sensed something that you think only you sensed and not others who were around you?* This is a way to check for hallucinations. Some people have hallucinations but are reluctant to use the actual word. "Have you ever heard 'voices'?" is another way to ask the same question.

As a precaution, any hallucinations should be medically investigated. Some may be unrelated to medical problems; others such as schizophrenic hallucinations signify no clear organic problem but might be treated with medication (by way of a psychiatrist); and others can signify a dangerous medical problem. Condemning, critical, auditory hallucinations are typically schizophrenic. Hallucinations in any other sense (visual, taste, touch, smell) or auditory hallucinations that are impersonal noises must be investigated.

34. *Have you recently had a feeling that you had experienced a situation or had been someplace before, although you were actually experiencing it for the first time (déjà vu)?* Déjà vu is a sense of familiarity with something never seen. Episodes occur in healthy persons, but they may be a presenting symptom of temporal lobe epilepsy.

35. *Have you had any thoughts that just seemed to go on and on and you couldn't stop?* Obsessional thoughts occur in nonmedical problems (schizophrenia, obsessive-compulsive disorder), but also in seizure disorders and possibly in food allergies and vitamin deficiencies. Sometimes antidepressant medication is helpful

in limiting bothersome intrusive thoughts. If the intrusive thoughts are associated with a change in awareness (confusion, blackouts, a feeling of unreality), then psychomotor seizures are likely.

36. *Has drinking alcohol ever interfered with your job or personal relationships?* Questions about alcohol abuse are often omitted from a health interview. However, substance abuse may be the number one organic component of behavioral changes.

37. *In the past six months have you used street drugs or other drugs for nonmedical reasons?* Along with the question on alcohol abuse, this will be the most frequent organic component to behavioral changes. The obvious problem with this question is that many users will deny their substance abuse, in which case the question is more a reminder for counselors than an attempt to get information.

Health History Questions for the Counselor

Has there been a change from a previous level of functioning—intellect, relationships, job, personality? This is the first question when differentiating between physical and psychological problems. Are the answers on the questionnaire reliable? Have you confirmed the answers, if necessary, with a member of the family?

If it is difficult to get corroboration, be alert to the following clues:

General Appearance

What are the person's general appearance and personal hygiene? If these characteristics can be described as disheveled, inappropriate, or malodorous, these may be symptoms of recent intellectual decline.

Movement

Do you notice any tremors, tics, facial grimaces, or other unusual facial movements? If the person is taking antipsychotic medication, facial movements could be extrapyramidal side effects.

Are there any unusual features in the person's gait?

Face

Are there facial asymmetries such as one drooping eyelid? Consider stroke.

Are there any scars on the face? Were they from a surgery or a fight? If so, they can indicate brain injury.

Does the face seem puffy or "moon-like"? Consider hypothyroidism.

Does the nose seem especially large, or has the relative size of the nose increased over the past few years? This is common—along with enlargement of the hands—in acromegaly.

Are the eyes red? Are the pupils either very big or very small? These are characteristic symptoms of drug abuse.

Is there a difference in the size of the two pupils? This may indicate increased intracranial pressure (brain tumor).

Do you notice brown rings around the iris? This is a symptom of a rare disease that causes intellectual decline called Wilson's disease.

Are there any rashes on the person's face—especially a butterfly rash across the nose? Consider lupus.

Intellect

Is there any disorientation (to place or time)? Does the person have difficulty with attention and tracking?

How is the person's short-term memory? Does he or she recall significant moments from past and present sessions?

Appendix D
Annotated Bibliography

Andreasen, Nancy C. (1984). *The Broken Brain: The Biological Revolution in Psychiatry*. New York: Harper & Row. Written from the perspective of the medical model, this is a good overview of modern psychiatry's views on mental illness. It also contains some easy-reading sections on brain anatomy and physiology.

Bloom, Floyd E., Arlyne Lazerson, Laura Hofstadter (1985). *Brain, Mind, and Behavior*. New York: W. H. Freeman. This book is a beautifully illustrated, basic introduction to the brain. Written in part for the TV program "The Brain," its chapters include the following: rhythms of the brain, emotions, learning and memory, the malfunctioning mind, and future prospects. Worth the price for the illustrations alone.

Currey, Christine (1983). *Differential Diagnosis of Physical and Psychological Disorders*. Ann Arbor: University Microfilms International. A fairly comprehensive text on differential diagnosis. Exhaustive lists and practical guidelines. Probably most useful for an M.D.

DSM III-R(1987). *The Diagnostic and Statistical Manual of Mental Disorders*, 3d ed. —revised. Washington, D.C.: American Psychiatric Association. A useful booklet that, along with all the current diagnoses in American psychiatry, lists some differential diagnoses.

Gundry, Robert (1976). *Soma in Biblical Theology*. Cambridge: Cambridge University Press. The best theological study on the Greek word for "body." It is heavy reading but has many implications for the serious theological student.

Hill, David (1983). *The Politics of Schizophrenia: Psychiatric Oppression in the United States*. Lanham, Md.: Academic Press. A well-documented history of madness and present developments in psychiatry. It has a radical edge to it, but that makes it all the more provocative.

Isselbacher, K. J., et al. (1980). *Harrison's Principles of Internal Medicine*, 9th ed. New York: McGraw-Hill. This is the accepted summary of medical disorders.

Jones, Gareth D. (1980). *Our Fragile Brains*. Downers Grove, Ill.: Intervarsity Press. Subtitled "A Christian Perspective on Brain Research," Jones presents a summary of the more popular areas of brain research. It does not offer counseling implications, but it delivers interesting information in a nontechnical manner.

Lechtenberg, Richard (1982). *The Psychiatrist's Guide to Diseases of the Nervous System*. New York: Wiley. This text is aimed at psychiatrists and is limited to diseases of the brain. Yet it does offer practical guidelines for treatment that are relevant for counselors. Chapters include diagnostic tools, seizure disorders, speech disorders, cognitive disorders, affective disorders, sexual problems, and sleep disorders.

Lishman, Walter (1978). *Organic Psychiatry*. St. Louis: Blackwell Scientific Publications. Comprehensive and technical. It is a bit ponderous because of its many research citations, but it is well known to everyone interested in differentiating organic from psychological disorders.

Luria, A. R. (1972). *The Man with the Shattered World*. New York: Basic Books. This book is a classic. It is a first-person account of a traumatic brain wound with explanatory notes by the famous Russian neuropsychologist. Highly recommended. The only problem is that the book is hard to get.

McGovern, Constance M. (1985). *Masters of Madness: Social Origins of the American Psychiatric Profession*. Hanover, N.H.: University Press of New England. Any good history of medicine, brain sciences, or psychiatry is most valuable. This doctoral dissertation is a fine summary of the American Psychiatric Association. It traces its development from being a small group of asylum keepers to present-day biological psychiatrists and includes social, political, and economic perspectives.

McKay, Donald (1980). *Brains, Machines and Persons*. Grand Rapids: Eerdmans. This hundred-page book addresses some theological and philosophical dilemmas in brain research, and uses the computer as an analogy for understanding the brain. Somewhat helpful as an introduction.

Myers, David (1978). *The Human Puzzle*. New York: CAPS/Harper & Row. Useful for a chapter on the mind-body issue.

Penfield, Wilder (1975). *The Mystery of the Mind*. Princeton, N.J.: Princeton University Press. Penfield has made significant contributions to brain science. This particular book contains some interesting philosophical and religious musings as Penfield reviews the progress he has witnessed.

Physician's Desk Reference, 44th ed. (1990). Oradell, N.J.: Medical Economics Co. The *PDR* contains all drugs legally manufactured in the U.S. There is a brief article of each drug that includes uses and side effects. Ask an M.D. friend for an old copy.

Restak, Richard (1979). *The Brain: The Last Frontier.* New York: Doubleday. A popular book aimed at the secular layman. Some entertaining parts, but it is becoming outdated.

Sacks, Oliver (1985). *The Man Who Mistook His Wife for a Hat.* New York: Harper & Row. Anything by Sacks is great reading. This particular book is a delightful collection of case studies. His attempt to unify mind and body is fascinating and has many biblical parallels. He has followed this up with a book entitled *A Leg to Stand On* (1987).

Smith, Anthony (1984). *The Mind.* New York: Viking Press. From the author of *The Body* (1986), this text is wonderfully written, entertaining, and well researched. He seeks to attract the interest of laypeople toward the marvels of the brain.

Szasz, Thomas (1987). *Insanity: The Idea and Its Consequences.* New York: Wiley. Szasz is well known in medical circles as an iconoclast who made his mark with his first book, *The Myth of Mental Illness.* This book continues with the same theme. As with all Szasz books, it is well researched and provocative. His sections on the use of language and personal responsibility are particularly interesting. I also recommend his collection of articles called *The Therapeutic State.*

Taylor, Robert L. (1982). *Mind or Body: Distinguishing Psychological from Organic Disorders.* New York: McGraw-Hill. A very useful book aimed at the nonmedical counselor. Its strength is that it offers a general decision-making paradigm that is a fine screening procedure for a host of medical issues.

Torrey, E. Fuller (1988). *Surviving Schizophrenia.* New York: Harper & Row. A very popular book on the biological approach to schizophrenia. Its medical model biases are clear, but it gives a good summary of schizophrenia along with practical advice.

Bibliography

Adams, J. (1979). *More Than Redemption*. Phillipsburg, N.J.: Presbyterian and Reformed.

Ader, R., ed. (1981). *Psychoneuroimmunology*. New York: Academic Press.

Ajax, E. T. (1973). The aphasic patient. *Diseases of the Nervous System* 34: 135–42.

Altman, L. K. (1989, September 9). Reagan OK after brain surgery. *Orange County Register*. A1, A26.

Amat, G., et al. (1982). Migraine and the mitral valve prolapse syndrome. In M. Critchley et al., eds., *Advances in Neurology* 33: 27–29. New York: Raven.

Andreasen, N. C. (1979). Thought, language, and communication disorders. *Archives of General Psychiatry* 36: 1315–22.

————. (1984). *The Broken Brain*. New York: Harper & Row.

Anonymous. (1950). Death of a mind: A study in disintegration. *Lancet* 1: 1012–15.

Aronson, S. M., and B. E. Aronson. (1972). Clinical neuropathological conference. *Diseases of the Nervous System* 33: 481–88.

Ausman, J. I., L. A. French, and A. B. Baker. (1974). Intracranial neoplasms. In R. J. Joynt, ed. (rev. 1988), *Clinical Neurology* 2: chap. 14. Philadelphia: Lippincott.

Avery, T. L. (1971). Seven cases of frontal tumor with psychiatric presentation. *British Journal of Psychiatry* 122: 599–600.

Bainton, R. H. (1950). *Here I Stand*. New York: Abington-Cokesbury.

Barclay, W. (1962). *Flesh and Spirit*. London: SCM.

Bardach, J. L. (1969). Group sessions with wives of aphasic patients. *International Journal of Group Psychotherapy* 19: 361–465.

Bassuk, E. L., S. C. Schoonover, and A. J. Gelenberg. (1983). *The Practitioner's Guide to Psychoactive Drugs*. New York: Plenum.

Bear, D. M., and P. Fedio. (1977). Quantitative analysis of interictal behavior in temporal lobe epilepsy. *Archives of Neurology* 34: 454–67.

Bebbington, P., and P. McGuffin. (1988). Schizophrenia at the crossroads. In P. Bebbington and P. McGuffin, *Schizophrenia: The major issues:* 1–10. Oxford, U.K.: Heinemann.

Beck, A. T. (1967). *Depression: Clinical, Experimental, and Theoretical Aspects.* New York: Harper & Row.

Berg, R., M. Franzen, and D. Wedding. (1987). *Screening for Brain Impairment: A Manual for Mental Health Practice.* New York: Springer.

Berkouwer, G. C. (1971). *Sin.* P. E. Holtrope, trans. Grand Rapids: Eerdmans.

Black, D. W., W. R. Yates, and N. C. Andreasen. (1988). Schizophrenia, schizophreniform disorder, and delusional (paranoid) disorders. In J. A. Talbot, R. E. Hales, and S. C. Yudofsky, eds., *The American Psychiatric Press Textbook of Psychiatry:* 357–402. Washington, D.C.: American Psychiatric Press.

Bleuler, E. (1911). *Dementia Praecox or the Group of Schizophrenias.* J. Zinkin, trans. New York: International Universities Press.

Blumer, D., and D. F. Benson. (1975). Personality changes with frontal and temporal lobe lesions. In D. F. Benson and D. Blumer, eds. *Psychiatric Aspects of Neurological Disease:* 151–69. New York: Grune & Stratton.

Bogen, J. E. (1985). The callosal syndromes. In K. M. Heilman and E. Valenstein, eds. *Clinical Neuropsychology,* 2d ed. New York: Oxford.

Bond, M. R. (1984). The psychiatry of closed head injury. In D. N. Books, ed. *Closed Head Injury: Psychological, social, and family consequences:* 141–57. New York: Oxford.

Borbely, A. (1986). *Secrets of Sleep.* New York: Basic Books.

Bourke-White, M. (1963). *Portrait of Myself.* New York: Simon & Schuster.

Brecher, E. M. (1972). *Licit and Illicit Drugs.* Boston: Little, Brown.

Brockington, I. F., et al. (1981). Puerperal psychosis. *Archives of General Psychiatry* 38: 829–33.

Burditt, A. F., F. I. Caird, and G. J. Draper. (1968). The natural history of diabetic retinopathy. *Quarterly Journal of Medicine* 37: 303–17.

Burroughs, W. S. (1959). *Naked Lunch.* New York: Grove.

Calvin, W. (1983). *The Trowing Madonna: Essays on the Brain.* New York: McGraw-Hill.

Carpenter, W. T., and D. W. Heinrichs. (1983). Early intervention, time-limited, targeted pharmacotherapy of schizophrenia. *Schizophrenia Bulletin* 9: 533–42.

Carroll, B. J. (1985). Dexamethasone suppression test: A review of contemporary confusion. *Journal of Clinical Psychiatry* 46: 13–24.

Colby, K. M., and J. E. Sparr. (1983). *The Fundamental Crisis in Psychiatry.* Springfield, Ill.: Thomas.

Condon, J. T., and T. L. Watson. (1987). The maternity blues: Exploration of a psychological hypothesis. *Acta Psychiatrica Scandinavica* 76: 164–71.

Corballis, M. C. (1980). Laterality and myth. *American Psychologist* 35: 284–95.

————. (1983). *Human Laterality*. New York: Academic Press.

Cousins, N. (1983). *The Healing Heart*. New York: Norton.

Creak, M., and E. Guttman. (1935). Chorea, tics and compulsive utterances. *Journal of Mental Science* 81: 834–39.

Critchley, M. (1966). *The Parietal Lobes*. New York: Hafner.

Cummings, J. (1985). *Clinical Neuropsychiatry*. Orlando, Fla.: Grune & Stratton.

Currey, C. (1982). *Differential diagnosis of physical and psychological disorders*. (Ph.D. diss.) University Microfilms International.

————. (1987). Multi-infarct dementia: diagnosis and management. *Psychosomatics* 28: 117–21.

Cushing, H. (1932). *Intracranial Tumors*. Springfield, Ill.:Thomas.

Daley, R., F. Kane, and J. Ewing. (1967). Psychosis associated with the use of sequential oral contraceptives. *Lancet* 2: 444–45.

DeJong, R. (1988). Case taking and the neurological exam. In R. J. Joynt, ed. *Clinical Neurology* 1: chap. 1. Philadelphia: Lippincott.

De Lisi, L. E. and M. S. Buchsbaum. (1986). PETT of cerebral glucose use in psychiatricpatients. In M. R. Trimble, ed. *New Brain Imaging Techniques in Psychopharmacology*: 48–62. Oxford: Oxford University.

Dement, W. C., S. H. Frazier, and E. D. Weitzman, advisers. (1984). *The American Medical Association Guide to Better Sleep*. New York: Random House.

Dennerstein, L. (1988). Psychiatric aspects of the climacteric. In J. W. W. Studd and M. I. Whitehead. *The Menopause*: 43–54. London: Blackwell Scientific.

Diehl, L. (1983). Patient-family education. In M. Rosenthal, E. Griffith, M. Bond, and J.Miller (eds.). *Rehabilitation of the head injured adult*: 395–403. Philadelphia: Davis.

Dorf, A., E. J. Ballintine, and P. H. Bennett. (1976). Retinopathy in Pima Indians: Relationships to glucose level, duration of diabetes, age at diagnosis of diabetes, and age at examination in a population with a high prevalence of diabetes mellitus. *Diabetes* 25: 554–60.

Dorros, S. (1981). *Parkinson's: A Patient's view*. Cabin John, Md.: Seven Locks.

Duke, P. (1989, October 6). Interview on "20/20" about Manic Depression.

Dyan, S. (1988, September 11). Living with the vexing Tourette syndrome. *Philadelphia Inquirer*: 7–I.

Elliot, F. A. (1984). The episodic dyscontrol syndrome and aggression. *Neurologic Clinics* 2: 113–24.

Feldman, R. G., and N. L. Paul. (1976). Identity of emotional triggers in epilepsy. *Journal of Nervous and Mental Disease* 162: 345–53.

Fenwick, P. (1981). Precipitation and inhibition of seizures. In E. H. Reynolds and M. R. Trimble, eds. *Epilepsy and Psychiatry*: 242–63. Edinburgh: Churchill Livingstone.

Fitzgerald, B. A. and C. E. Wells. (1977). Hallucinations as a conversion reaction. *Diseases of the Nervous System* 38: 381–83.

Flaherty, J. A. (1979). Psychiatric complications of medical drugs. *Journal of Family Practice* 9: 243–51.

Flint, M. (1975). The menopause: Reward or punishment. *Psychosomatics* 16: 161–63.

Fowler, R. S. (1981). Stroke and cerebral trauma: Psychosocial and vocational aspects. In W. C. Stolov and M. R. Clowers, eds. *Handbook of Severe Disability*: 127–35. Washington, D.C.: U.S. Dept. of Education, Rehabilitation Services Administration.

Frances, R. J., and J. E. Franklin. (1988). Alcoholism and other substance abuse disorders. In J. A. Talbot, R. E. Hales, and S. C. Yudofsky, eds. *The American Psychiatric Press Textbook of Psychiatry*: 313–55. Washington, D.C.: American Psychiatric Press.

Frank, R. T. (1931). The hormonal causes of premenstrual tension. *Archives of Neurological Psychiatry* 26: 1053–57.

Franklin, J. (1987). *Molecules of the Mind*. New York: Atheneum.

Freeman, C. P., and R. E. Kendell. (1980). ECT: Patients' experiences and attitudes. *British Journal of Psychiatry* 137: 8–16.

Friedman, A. P. (1982). Overview of migraine. In M. Critchley et al., eds. *Advances in Neurology* 33: 1–18. New York: Raven.

Gardner, E. R., and R. W. Hall. (1982) Psychiatric symptoms produced by over-the-counter drugs. *Psychosomatics* 23: 186–91.

Gastaut, H. (1970). Clinical and electroencephalographical classification of epileptic seizures. *Epilepsia* 11: 102–13.

Geschwind, N. (1975). The borderland of neurology and psychiatry: Some common misconceptions. In D. F. Benson and D. Blumer, eds. *Psychiatric Aspects of Neurological Disease*: 1–9. New York: Grune & Stratton.

Gillin, J. C. (1983). The sleep therapies of depression. *Progress in Neuropsychopharmacology and Biological Psychiatry* 7: 351–64.

Goldberg, S. (1986). *Clinical Neuroanatomy Made Ridiculously Simple*. Miami: MedMaster.

Goodglass, H., and E. Kaplan. (1983). *Assessment of Aphasia and Related Disorders*. Philadelphia: Lea & Febiger.

Goodwin, D. W. (1986). *Anxiety*. New York: Oxford University.

Goodwin, F. V. (1971). Behavioral effects of L-Dopa in man. *Seminars in Psychiatry* 3: 477–92.

Granacher, R. P., and R. J. Baldessarini. (1975). Physostigmine: Its use in acute anticholinergic syndrome with antidepressant and antiparkinson drugs. *Archives of General Psychiatry* 32: 375–80.

Grunhaus, L., S. Gloger, and E. Weisstub. (1981). Panic attacks: A review of treatments and pathogenesis. *Journal of Nervous and Mental Disease* 169: 608–13.

Gruvstad, M., L. Kebbon, and S. Gruvstad. (1958). Social and psychiatric aspects of pre-traumatic personality and post-traumatic insufficiency reactions in traumatic head injuries. *Acta Societatis Medicorum Upsaliensis* 63: 101–13.

Gundry, Robert (1976). *Soma in Biblical Theology.* Cambridge: Cambridge University.

Hall, R. C. W., et al. (1978). Physical illness presenting as psychiatric disease. *Archives of General Psychiatry* 35: 1315–20.

_____. (1985). Psychiatric reactions produced by respiratory drugs. *Psychosomatics* 26: 605–16.

Harrington, A. (1987). *Medicine, Mind, and the Double Brain: A Study in Ninteenth-Century Thought.* Princeton, N.J.: Princeton University.

Hartlage, L. C., and M. R. Mains. (1981). *Anticonvulsant medication as a determinant of neuropsychological test profiles.* Paper presented at the annual meeting of the International Neuropsychological Society, Atlanta.

Haskett, R. F. (1987). Psychiatric effects of corticosteroids. In G. D. Burrows, T. R. Norman, and B. Davies, eds. *Drugs in Psychiatry,* vol. 4. Antimanics, anticonvulsants and other drugs in psychiatry: 237–46. Amsterdam: Elsvier.

Hecaen, H., and M. L. Albert. (1975). Disorders of mental functioning related to frontal lobe pathology. In D. F. Benson and D. Blumer, eds. *Psychiatric Aspects of Neurological Disease: 137–49.* New York: Grune & Stratton.

_____. (1978). *Human Neuropsychology.* New York: Wiley.

Hill, D. (1983). *The Politics of Schizophrenia: Psychiatric Oppression in the United States.* Lanham, Md.: Academic.

Hinkle, L. E., and S. Wolf. (1952a). Importance of life stress in the management of diabetes mellitus. *Journal of the American Medical Association* 148: 513–20.

_____. (1952b). A summary of experimental evidence relating life stress to diabetes mellitus. *Journal of the Mount Sinai Hospital* 19: 537–70.

Hoffman, B. F. (1977). Diet pill psychosis. *Canadian Medical Association Journal* 116: 351–55.

Hollander, E., M. R. Liebowitz, and J. M. Gorman. (1988). Anxiety disorders. In J. A. Talbot, R. E. Hales, and S. C. Yudofsky, eds. *The American Psychiatric Press Textbook of Psychiatry: 443–91.* Washington, D.C.: American Psychiatric Press.

Hooper, J., and D. Teresi. (1986). *The 3-Pound Universe*. New York: Dell.

Hostetler, A. J. (1987). Scientists warn role of biology miscast in wake of Amish study. *APA Monitor:* 16–17.

Jablensky, A. (1988). Epidemiology of schizophrenia. In P. Bebbington and P. McGuffin, eds. *Schizophrenia: The Major Issues:* 19–35. Oxford, U.K.: Heinemann.

Johnson, J. M., and S. Bailey. (1979). Cimetidine and psychiatric complications. *British Journal of Psychiatry* 134: 315–16.

Kahn, H. A., and R. F. Bradley. (1975). Prevalence of diabetic retinopathy: Age, sex, and duration of diabetes. *British Journal of Ophthalmology* 59: 345–49.

Kane, F. J. (1976). Evaluation of emotional reactions to oral contraceptive use. *American Journal of Obstetrics and Gynecology* 126: 968–71.

Kaplan, H. S. (1974). *The New Sex Therapy*. New York: Brunner/Mazel.

―――――. (1979). *Disorders of Sexual Desire*. New York: Brunner/Mazel.

Kendell, R. E. (1985). Emotional and physical factors in the genesis of puerperal mental disorders. *Journal of Psychosomatic Research* 29: 3–11.

Kendell, R. E., J. C. Chalmers, and C. Platz. (1987). Epidemiology of puerperal psychoses. *British Journal of Psychiatry* 150: 662–73.

Keye, W. R., Jr. (1988). PMS: The clinical approach and treatment. In W. R. Keye, Jr., ed. *The Premenstrual Syndrome: 145–53.* Philadelphia: Saunders.

Knox, D. R. (1971). *Portrait of Aphasia*. Detroit: Wayne State University.

Kolb, B., and I. Q. Whishlaw. (1985). *Fundamentals of Human Neuropsychology*. 2d ed. New York: Freeman.

Konow, A., and K. Pribram. (1970). Error recognition and utilization produced by injury to the frontal cortex in man. *Neuropsychologia* 8: 489–91.

Kozol, H. L. (1945). Pretraumatic personality and sequelae of head injury. *Archives of Neurology and Psychiatry* 53: 358–64.

Kudrow, L. (1983). Cluster headache: New concepts. *Neurology Clinics* 1: 369–83.

Kumar, R., and K. M. Robson. (1984). A prospective study of emotional disorders in childbearing women. *British Journal of Psychiatry* 144: 35–47.

Kurland, M. L. (1965). Gilles de la Tourette's syndrome: The psychotherapy of two cases. *Comprehensive Psychiatry* 6: 289–305.

Kurtzke, J. T. (1970). Studies on the natural history of multiple sclerosis. *Archives of Neurology* 22: 215–25.

Lantos, P. L. (1988). The neuropathology of schizophrenia: a critical review of recent work. In P. Bebbington and P. McGuffin, eds. *Schizophrenia: The Major Issues: 90–106.* Oxford, U.K.: Heinemann.

Larimer, T. (1989, March 19). Rebuilding a life after misdiagnosis of Alzheimer's. *Philadelphia Inquirer.*

Larkin, A. R. (1979). The form and content of schizophrenic hallucinations. *American Journal of Psychiatry* 136: 940–42.

Lavin, J. H. (1985). *Stroke: From Crisis to Victory.* New York: Franklin Watts.

Lechtenberg, R. (1982). *The Psychiatrist's Guide to Diseases of the Nervous System.* New York: Wiley.

Levy, V. (1987). The maternity blues in post-partum and post-operative women. *British Journal of Psychiatry* 151: 368–72.

Lewis, C. S. (1949). *The Weight of Glory and Other Addresses.* Grand Rapids: Eerdmans.

————. (1960). *Miracles.* New York: Macmillan.

Lewis, D. A., and G. Winokur. (1983). The familial classifications of primary unipolar depression: Biological validation of distinct subtypes. *Comprehensive Psychiatry* 24: 495–501.

Lezak, M. (1978). Living with the characterologically brain injured patient. *Journal of Clinical Psychiatry* 39: 592–98.

————. (1986). Psychological implications of traumatic brain damage for the patient's family. *Rehabilitation Psychology* 31: 241–50.

Linn, E. L. (1977). Verbal auditory hallucinations: mind, self, society. *Journal of the Nervous System and Mental Disease:* 8–17.

Lishman, W. A. (1973). The psychiatric sequelae of head injury: A review. *Psychological Medicine* 3: 304–18.

————. (1978). *Organic Psychiatry.* Oxford, U.K.: Blackwell Scientific.

Lowe, G. R. (1973). The phenomenology of hallucinations as an aid to differential diagnosis. *British Journal of Psychiatry* 123: 621–33.

Luria, A. L. (1972). *The Man with a Shattered World.* New York: Basic Books.

————. (1973). *The Working Brain.* New York: Basic Books.

Macrae, D. (1954). Isolated fear: A temporal lobe aura. *Neurology* 4: 497–505.

Mahendra, B. (1987). *Depression: The disorder and its associations.* Lancaster, U.K.: MTP.

Martin, J. J. (1979). Physical diseases manifesting as psychiatric disorders. In G. Usden and J. Lewis, eds. *Psychiatry in General Medical Practice:* 337–51. New York: McGraw-Hill.

Mavor, Huntington. (1980, March 12). Pitfalls in the diagnosis and classification of seizure disorders. Lecture at the Salt Lake City V.A. Medical Center.

McGuffin, P. (1988). Genetics of schizophrenia. In P. Bebbington and P. McGuffin. *Schizophrenia: the major issues:* 107–26. Oxford, U.K.: Heinemann.

McLachlan, R. S., and W. T. Blume. (1979). Isolated fear in complex partial status epilepticus. *Annals of Neurology* 8: 639–41.

McManamy, M. C., and P. G. Schube. (1936). Caffeine intoxication. *New England Journal of Medicine* 215: 616–20.

Meador-Woodruff, and L. Grunhaus. (1986). Profound behavioral toxicity due to tricyclic antidepressants. *The Journal of Nervous and Mental Disease* 174: 628–30.

Meddis, R., A. Pearson, and G. Langford. (1973). An extreme case of healthy insomnia. *Electroencephalography and Clinical Neurophysiology* 35: 213–14.

Mendelson, W. B. (1987). *Human Sleep: Research and Clinical Care.* New York: Plenum.

Miller, E. (1984). *Recovery and Management of Neuropsychological Impairments.* New York: Wiley.

Miller, H. (1969). Problems of medicolegal practice. In A. E. Walker, W. F. Caviness, and M. Critchley, eds. *The Late Effects of Head Injury:* chap. 42. Springfield, Ill.: Thomas.

Morris, J. B., and A. T. Beck. (1974). The efficacy of antidepressant drugs: A review of research. *Archives of General Psychiatry* 30: 667–74.

Murphy, E. A. (1972). The normal, and the perils of the sylleptic argument. *Perspectives in Biology* 75: 566.

Naylor, C. H. (1976). Discussion on section C: Psychological aspects. In S. Campbell, ed. *The Management of the Menopause and Post-menopausal Years:* 169–72. Baltimore: University Park.

Nelson, J. C., and D. S. Charney. (1980). Primary affective disorder criteria and the endogenous-reactive distinction. *Archives of General Psychiatry* 37: 787–93.

Owen, J. (1958). *Temptation and Sin.* Evansville, Ind.: Sovereign Grace Book Club.

Patton, R. B., and J. A. Sheppard. (1956). Intracranial tumors found at autopsy in mental patients. *American Journal of Psychiatry* 113: 319–24.

Payer, Lynn. (1988). *Medicine and Culture.* New York: Holt.

Penfield, W. (1975). *The Mystery of the Mind.* Princeton, N.J.: Princeton University.

Pettinati, H. M., and K. M. Bonner. (1984). Cognitive functioning in depressed geriatric patients with a history of ECT. *American Journal of Psychiatry* 141: 49–52.

Petursson, H., and M. Lader. (1984). *Dependence on Tranquilizers.* Oxford: Oxford University.

Pfeiffer, C. C., et al. (1970). *The Schizophrenias: Yours and Mine.* New York: Jove.

Phillips, J. B. (1985). *The Price of Success.* Wheaton, Ill.: Harold Shaw.

Pitt, B. (1968). Atypical depression following childbirth. *British Journal of Psychiatry* 114: 1325–35.

Price, W. A., and D. Heil. (1988). Estrogen-induced panic attacks. *Psychosomatics* 29: 433–35.

Quoist, M. (1965). *The Christian Response.* Dublin: Gill & Macmillan.

Raymond, C. A. (1988). Studies question how much role menopause plays in some women's emotional distress. *Journal of the American Medical Association* 259: 3522–23.

Reda, M. A., et al. (1985). Thinking, depression, and antidepressants: Modified and unmodified depressive beliefs during treatment with amitriptyline. *Cognitive Theory and Research* 9: 135–43.

Relkin, R. (1966). Death following withdrawal of diazepam. *New York Journal of Medicine* 66: 1770–72.

Restak, R. (1983, October). "Is free will a fraud?" *Science Digest:* 50–53.

Robertson, E. G. (1954). Photogenic epilepsy: self-precipitated attacks. *Brain* 77: 232–51.

Rosenberg, C. E. (1962). *The Cholera Years.* Chicago: University of Chicago.

Ross, H. M. (1975). *Hypoglycemia.* N.p.: Academy of Orthomolecular Psychiatry.

Rubinow, D. R., C. Hoban, and G. Grover. (1988). PMS: Medical and psychiatric perspectives. In W. R. Keye, Jr., *The Premenstrual Syndrome:* 27–45. Philadelphia: Saunders.

Ryback, R., and R. Schwab. (1971). Manic response to levodopa therapy, report of a case. *New England Journal of Medicine* 285: 788–89.

Sacks, O. W. (1970). *Migraine: The Evolution of a Common Disorder.* London: Faber.

_____. (1985a). *The Man Who Mistook His Wife for a Hat.* New York: Harper & Row.

_____. (1985b). *Migraine: Understanding a Common Disorder.* Berkeley: University of California.

Scheinbaum, B. W. (1979). Psychiatric diagnostic error. *Schizophrenia Bulletin* 5: 560–64.

Schenkenberg, T. (1979). *Psychological issues confronting the patient with multiple sclerosis.* Unpublished manuscript.

Schlauch, R. (1979). Hypnopompic hallucinations and treatment with Imipramine. *American Journal of Psychiatry* 136: 219–20.

Schmeck, H. M. (1988, March 8). Region in brain is linked to obsessive disorder. *The New York Times:* C1, C11.

Scovern, A. W., and P. R. Kilmann. (1980). Status of electroconvulsive therapy: Review of the outcome literature. *Psychological Bulletin* 87: 260–303.

Segraves, R. T. (1988). Psychiatric drugs and inhibited female orgasm. *Journal of Sex and Marital Therapy* 14: 202–07.

Shontz, F. (1975). *The Psychological Aspects of Physical Illness and Disability.* New York: Macmillan.

Shulman, R. (1977). Psychogenic illness with physical manifestations and the other side of the coin. *Lancet* 1: 524–26.

Shultes, A. (1985, February 11). "I have difficulty speaking . . . please be patient." *Daily Intelligencer, Montgomery County Record.*

Shutts, D. (1982). *Lobotomy: Resort to the Knife.* New York: Van Nostrand, Reinhold.

324 Counselor's Guide to the Brain

Sills, J. A., A. J. Nunn, and R. J. Stankey. (1984). Visual hallucinations in children receiving decongestants. British Medical Journal 1: 1912–13.

Slagle, P. (1987). The Way Up from Down. New York: St. Martin's.

Slovenko, R. (1984). The meaning of mental illness in criminal responsibility. Journal of Legal Medicine 5: 1–61.

Smith, A. (1984). The Mind. New York: Viking.

Solyom, L., M. Turnbull, and M. Wilensky. (1987). A case of self-inflicted leucotomy, British Journal of Psychiatry 151: 855–57.

Speroff, L. (1988). PMS: Historical and social perspectives. In W. R. Keye, Jr., ed. The Premenstrual Syndrome: 2–14. Philadelphia: Saunders.

Stasiek, C., and M. Zetin. (1985). Organic manic disorders. Psychosomatics 26: 394–402.

Steege, J. F., A. L. Stout, and S. L. Rupp. (1988). PMS: Clinical features. In W. R. Keye, Jr., ed. The Premenstrual Syndrome: 113–27. Philadelphia: Saunders.

Stern, Y., and R. Mayeux. (1987). Intellectual impairment in Parkinson's disease. In M. Yahr and K. Bergmann, eds. Advances in Neurology, vol. 45: 405–8. New York: Raven.

Sternbach, R. A. (1986). Psychological management of the headache patient. In S. Diamond and D. J. Dalessio, The Practicing Physician's Approach to Headaches. Baltimore: Williams & Wilkins.

Sternberg. D. E. (1986). Testing for physical illness in psychiatric patients. Journal of Clinical Psychiatry 47 (supplement): 3–9.

Stewart, J. W., et al. (1983). Efficacy of desipramine in depressed outpatients. Archives of General Psychiatry 40: 202–07.

Stuss, D. T., and D. F. Benson. (1984). Neuropsychological studies of the frontal lobes. Psychological Bulletin 95: 3–28.

———. (1986). The Frontal Lobes. New York: Raven.

Surridge, D. (1969). An investigation into some psychiatric aspects of multiple sclerosis. British Journal of Psychiatry 115: 749–64.

Szasz, T. (1984). The Therapeutic State. New York: Prometheus.

———. (1987). Insanity: The Idea and Its Consequences. New York: Wiley.

Tattersall, R. B. (1981). Psychiatric aspects of diabetes—a physician's view. British Journal of Psychiatry 139: 485–93.

Torem, M., S. M. Saravay, and H. Steinberg. (1979). Psychiatric liaison: Benefits of an active approach. Psychosomatics 20: 598–611.

Torrey, E. F. (1988). Surviving Schizophrenia: A Family Manual, rev. ed. New York: Harper & Row.

Trimble, M. A. (1988). Biological Psychiatry. New York: Wiley.

Tucker, D. M., R. A. Novelly, and P. J. Walker. (1987). Hyperreligiosity in temporal lobe epilepsy: Redefining the relationship. Journal of Nervous and Mental Disease 175: 181–83.

Tucker, G. J., et al. (1986). Phenomoenology of temporal lobe dysfunction: A link to atypical psychosis—a series of cases. *Journal of Nervous and Mental Disease* 174: 348–56.

Tyler, D. B. (1955). Psychological changes during experimental sleep deprivation. *Diseases of the Nervous System* 16: 293–99.

Tyrer, P. J. (1982). *Drugs in Psychiatric Practice*. Cambridge, U.K.: Butterworths.

Van Keep, P. A., and J. M. Kellerhals. (1974). The impact of socio-cultural factors on symptom formation. *Psychotherapy and Psychosomatics* 23: 251–63.

Walker, M. D. (1975). *Malignant Brain Tumors—A Synopsis*. N.p.: American Cancer Society.

Warner, R. (1985). *Recovery from Schizophrenia*. London: Routledge & Kegan Paul.

Watson, J. P., et al. (1984). Psychiatric disorder in pregnancy and the first postnatal year. *British Journal of Psychiatry* 144: 453–62.

Waxman, S. G., and N. Geschwind. (1975). The interictal behavior syndrome of temporal lobe epilepsy. *Archives of General Psychiatry* 32: 1580–86.

Weiss, R. D., and S. M. Mirin. (1987). *Cocaine*. Washington, D.C.: American Psychiatric Press.

Wender, P., and D. Klein. (1981, February). The promise of biological psychiatry. *Psychology Today*: 25–28.

West, L. J. (1975). A clinical and theoretical overview of hallucinatory phenomena. In R. K. Siegel and L. J. West, eds. *Hallucinations: Behavior, Experience and Theory*: 287–311. New York: Wiley.

Whitlock, F. A. (1987). Adverse psychiatric reactions to some non-psychotropic drugs. In G. D. Burrows, T. R. Norman, and B. Davies, eds. *Drugs in Psychiatry*: vol. 4. Antimanics, anticonvulsants and other drugs in psychiatry: 415–432. Amsterdam: Elsevier.

WHO Expert Committee on Drug Dependence (1974). *Twentieth Report*. (WHO technical report series No. 551.) Geneva: WHO.

Williams, S. E., D. S. Bell, and R. S. Guy. (1974). Neurosurgical disease encountered in a psychiatric service. *Journal of Neurology, Neurosurgery, and Psychiatry* 37: 112–16.

Woody, G. E., C. P. O'Brien, and R. Greenstein. (1975). Misuse and abuse of diazepam: An increasingly common medical problem. *International Journal of Addictions* 10: 843–48.

Subject Index

Index of Drugs
and Medications

For categories of drugs, such as anticholinergics or street drugs, see other index. Also see appendix B, which is not included in this index.

335